Fair Trade

The fair trade movement has been one of the most enduring and successful civic initiatives to come out of the 1960s. In the first transnational history of the movement, Peter van Dam charts its ascendance and highlights how activists attempted to transform the global market in the aftermath of decolonization. Through original archival research into the trade of handicrafts, sugar, paper, coffee, and clothes, van Dam demonstrates how the everyday, material aspects of fair trade activism connected the international politics of decolonization with the daily realities of people across the globe. He explores the different scales at which activists operated and the instruments they employed in the pursuit of more equitable economic relations between the Global South and North. Through careful analysis of a now ubiquitous global movement, van Dam provides a vital new lens through which to view the history of humanitarianism in the age of postcolonial globalization.

Peter van Dam is Professor of Dutch History at the University of Amsterdam. He has published extensively on the history of fair trade activism, sustainable consumption, and the role of religion in civic engagement.

'Fair trade has been an amazingly resilient idea, and Peter van Dam brilliantly analyzes how that rallying cry has evolved since the 1950s. His history offers many provocative insights into the activism born of globalization.'

Adam Rome, University at Buffalo

'These days, "fair trade" evokes associations of product labels and certification schemes. In his book *Fair Trade: Humanitarianism in the Age of Postcolonial Globalization*, Peter van Dam offers a rich historical account of the transnational fair trade movement. He shows how certification was only one of many strategies discussed by activists to make global trade relations more just. The movement was much more diverse than present-day associations might suggest, and contestation about the goals and means of fair trade a constant in its history.'

Liesbeth van de Grift, Utrecht University

'This groundbreaking and elegantly written study on the fair trade movement is a real treat. By positioning his protagonists between local activism and the emergence of a global humanitarian "market place", Peter van Dam has written a book that will soon become a standard reference for historians in the field.'

Daniel Roger Maul, University of Oslo

'This exploration of how principled but practical people have evolved and negotiated Fair Trade principles and material practices is a timely reminder of the intricate connections between Fair Trade and social justice movements at multiple levels – indeed, its roots in transnational collaboration and advocacy for economic justice.'

Anne Tallontire, University of Leeds

'Peter van Dam's book is a must-read for anyone interested in global social movements, humanitarianism, and postcolonialism. The meticulously researched book shows that fair trade movements and decolonization have been siblings since the 1950s. In troubled times, Peter van Dam encourages us to think about the role of hope in local activism, about alternative economies in global capitalism, and about the attempts to diminish social inequalities. Although the movement failed to achieve the latter, the local lens provides us with historical examples of global relations, political struggles, and international solidarity that will be indispensable as the climate crisis progresses.'

Sandra Maß, Ruhr-Universität Bochum

Fair Trade
Humanitarianism in the Age of Postcolonial Globalization

Peter van Dam
University of Amsterdam

Shaftesbury Road, Cambridge CB2 8EA, United Kingdom

One Liberty Plaza, 20th Floor, New York, NY 10006, USA

477 Williamstown Road, Port Melbourne, VIC 3207, Australia

314–321, 3rd Floor, Plot 3, Splendor Forum, Jasola District Centre, New Delhi – 110025, India

103 Penang Road, #05–06/07, Visioncrest Commercial, Singapore 238467

Cambridge University Press is part of Cambridge University Press & Assessment, a department of the University of Cambridge.

We share the University's mission to contribute to society through the pursuit of education, learning and research at the highest international levels of excellence.

www.cambridge.org
Information on this title: www.cambridge.org/9781009586252

DOI: 10.1017/9781009586283

© Peter van Dam 2025

This publication is in copyright. Subject to statutory exception and to the provisions of relevant collective licensing agreements, no reproduction of any part may take place without the written permission of Cambridge University Press & Assessment.

When citing this work, please include a reference to the
DOI 10.1017/9781009586283

First published 2025

A catalogue record for this publication is available from the British Library

Library of Congress Cataloging-in-Publication Data
NAMES: Dam, Peter van, 1981– author.
TITLE: Fair trade : humanitarianism in the age of postcolonial globalization / Peter van Dam.
DESCRIPTION: Cambridge ; New York, NY : Cambridge University Press, 2025. | Includes bibliographical references and index. | Contents: Introduction: Shaping postcolonial globalization from below – Handicrafts : humanitarianism after empire – Sugar : goodbye to grand politics – Paper : the politics of everyday life – Coffee : turning towards the market – Clothes : activism in a network society – Conclusion. Humanitarianism in the era of postcolonial globalization.
IDENTIFIERS: LCCN 2024054970 | ISBN 9781009586252 (hardback) | ISBN 9781009586269 (paperback) | ISBN 9781009586283 (ebook)
SUBJECTS: LCSH: Anti-globalization movement – History. | International trade – Social aspects. | Postcolonialism – Economic aspects. | Humanitarianism – Economic aspects.
CLASSIFICATION: LCC HF1365 .D36 2025 | DDC 337–dc23/eng/20250228
LC record available at https://lccn.loc.gov/2024054970

ISBN 978-1-009-58625-2 Hardback
ISBN 978-1-009-58626-9 Paperback

Cambridge University Press & Assessment has no responsibility for the persistence or accuracy of URLs for external or third-party internet websites referred to in this publication and does not guarantee that any content on such websites is, or will remain, accurate or appropriate.

CONTENTS

List of Figures	*page* vi
List of Tables	viii
Acknowledgements	ix
List of Abbreviations	xii
Introduction: Shaping Postcolonial Globalization from Below	1
1 Handicrafts: Humanitarianism after Empire	19
2 Sugar: Goodbye to Grand Politics	43
3 Paper: The Politics of Everyday Life	69
4 Coffee: Turning towards the Market	105
5 Clothes: Activism in a Network Society	136
Conclusion: Humanitarianism in the Era of Postcolonial Globalization	177
Notes	194
Bibliography	231
Index	250

FIGURES

0.1 Women sewing in a garment factory in Dhaka, Bangladesh, March 2010 [*page* 2]
1.1 Edna Byler with needlework [25]
1.2 Paul Meijs presenting handicrafts and coffee imported by SOS [34]
1.3 A sample of the products advertised and distributed by SOS Wereldhandel in 1973 [37]
2.1 Cane Sugar Campaign members present a heart made out of cane sugar to the Dutch minister of Economic Affairs, Leo de Block, in The Hague on 3 December 1968 [44]
2.2 A sugar bag used in the cane sugar campaign [51]
2.3 Harvesting sugar cane [55]
2.4 Poster of the Cane Sugar Campaign in West Germany [61]
3.1 A letter from the international secretariat of development activists about the world shop as a model for action [76]
3.2 A world shop group from Doesburg in the Netherlands protests against the economic ties between Shell and the South African government with an improvised stand in 1979 [87]
3.3 Poster 'Portugal kills with NATO-weapons in Africa' [89]
3.4 Announcement for the International Workshop of Third World Producers [98]
4.1 Poster of the fictive coffee farmer Juan Valdez [111]
4.2 A package of Indio Coffee marketed in West Germany in the 1970s [113]

- 4.3 Representatives of coffee farmers from Peru, Mexico, and the Congo visit the new coffee depot at the Neuteboom roastery [116]
- 4.4 Three types of fair trade coffee on a poster advertising 'Zuivere koffie: een kwestie van smaak' [119]
- 4.5 Poster announcing the Max Havelaar certificate [125]
- 5.1 Clean Clothes Campaign in Sittard in April 1991 [142]
- 5.2 Poster advertising fair trade bananas issued for a Solidaridad campaign, c. 1996 [145]
- 5.3 New Koforidua, the first fair trade town in Africa [169]

TABLES

5.1 The repertoire of fair trade activism [*page* 157]
5.2 Total value of retail sales by FLO members, 2004–2009 [171]
5.3 Number of world shops in selected European countries, 1995–2007 [173]

ACKNOWLEDGEMENTS

It is a sobering task to confront the long succession of attempts to avert an unfolding global disaster, only to realize the issue remains as daunting as ever. Since the reordering of global relations after the Second World War, people across the world have persistently denounced global inequality, addressing politicians, businesses, and their fellow citizens. Proposed actions have ranged from new international trade agreements to 'true' pricing that would account for the payment of a living wage as well as environmental impact.

The history this book recounts is thus a sorrowful history. We have not been able to do justice to one another and to the planet we live on. Humanity's ability to create a just and sustainable world has proved to be very limited. In fact, relationships amongst people and to the planet have on the whole become less sustainable during the waves of global interconnection which have unfolded since 1945. On a planet which is heating up, these sustained inequities yield a frightening prospect. If we haven't been able to change the way we live to right these injustices, how will we be able to cope with the advance of climate change? This book presents a reckoning with the persistent injustices addressed by fair trade activists over the past seventy years. It is through the attempts of those who did try to change the world for the better that this reckoning comes into view.

But in writing the history of people who have taken action against injustice, a history of fair trade should offer more than an indictment of our current predicament. Despite the failure to achieve change on a grand scale, the humanitarian impulse to at least make a difference for *some* people in *some* places has driven people to engage in a wide range of activities to promote fair trade.

Their histories enhance our understanding of the changing material, political, economic, and social conditions that shape global connections. They also highlight the importance of specific practices like selling products, boycotting, and meeting like-minded individuals, activities that have enabled people to engage with fair trade over a long period of time.

The history of fair trade thus brings to the fore a distinct phase in the history of globalization, characterized in this book as 'postcolonial globalization'. During this period, many attempts to achieve a more sustainable world emphasized socio-economic inequality over environmental concerns. At the same time, the history of fair trade activism demonstrates how activities promoting fair trade were often mindful of the environment. Activists participated in rallies for environmental causes, sold recycled paper, and applied the notion of sustainable development to the work carried out in fields and orchards. Now, at a time when climate justice is a key issue and climate activists apparently have to prepare for long-term engagement, the history of fair trade is highly relevant. The constant manoeuvring between achieving small steps and effecting meaningful large-scale change remains similarly instructive.

Fair trade's history has occupied me for the last twelve years. In 2012, I had the good fortune to receive funding for this work by the Dutch Research Council (NWO). In the ensuing years, I was even more fortunate to work with colleagues across the globe and to meet people formerly and currently involved in the fair trade movement. They shared their knowledge, experiences, and sometimes even their archives with me. I continue to admire the capacity of many fair trade activists to engage in critical reflection and think about their engagement despite the exigencies of their pressing daily affairs. Contrary to the popular image, scholarship is very much the work of many hands: interlocutors, librarians and archivists, colleagues, reviewers and editors, family and friends, hosts, and babysitters. It would take a separate book to thank all the people that have accompanied me during this protracted voyage. I am immensely grateful to all of them.

Being this long in the making, this book is a composite of sorts. Many earlier publications are complemented with material I had previously not been able to discuss, along with new insights. The book draws its overarching structure from my 2018 book on the Dutch fair trade movement, *Wereldverbeteraars: een geschiedenis van fair trade* (Amsterdam University Press). The individual chapters combine material from that book with previously published articles and new material. Chapter 1 reworks sections of 'No Justice without Charity: Humanitarianism after Empire' from *The International History Review*.[1] Chapter 2 presents a revised version of 'Goodbye to Grand Politics: The Cane Sugar Campaign and the Limits of Transnational Activism, 1968–1974' from *Contemporary European History*.[2] Parts of Chapter 4 have previously been presented in the chapter 'Challenging Global Inequality in Streets and Supermarkets: Fair Trade Activism since the 1960s' from the edited volume *Histories of Global Inequality: New Perspectives*.[3] Where particular passages explicitly build on other relevant previous publications, these prior contributions are referenced. Compared to my earlier publications, I have devoted greater attention in this book to the transnational dynamics of the fair trade network, the materiality of activism, and the relation of these insights to the broader historiography.

As I was preparing to write this book, the COVID-19 pandemic exploded on the world. It highlighted the importance of understanding how the world had become globally interconnected in a highly unequal fashion. The pandemic proved challenging even in the privileged living conditions that my family and I enjoyed in Amsterdam. The delay of a book manuscript surely was the least of our worries. Nonetheless, finally seeing it realized provides an opportunity to look back on those years and to thank those who lived through those days with me – Beatrix above all.

ABBREVIATIONS

CCC	Clean Clothes Campaign
EEC	European Economic Community
EFTA	European Fair Trade Association
FLO	Fairtrade Labelling Organizations International
GEPA	Gesellschaft zur Förderung der Partnerschaft mit der Dritten Welt
IFAT	International Federation for Alternative Trade
MCC	Mennonite Central Committee
SERVV	Sales Exchange for Refugee Rehabilitation Vocations
SOS	Stichting Ontwikkelings-Samenwerking (Stichting Steun Ontwikkelings-Streken until 1972)
UCIRI	Unión de Comunidades Indígenas del Región del Istmo
UNCTAD	United Nations Conference on Trade and Development
WDM	World Development Movement
WFTO	World Fair Trade Organization
WTO	World Trade Organization

INTRODUCTION
Shaping Postcolonial Globalization from Below

As summer made a cautious appearance in the streets of Amsterdam, shoppers were invited into a new clothing store. It boldly advertised inexpensive clothes and alluring special offers. Picking items from the stacks, an eager customer wandered into the back of the store to try them on. Instead of finding a fitting room, she found herself in a cramped, hot, windowless chamber where women were sewing the kind of clothes she had just selected for herself. This was 'The Mad Rush', an initiative of the Clean Clothes Campaign in 2016 to draw attention to the abominable working conditions of women in the clothing industry.[1]

Such attempts to locally confront people with the injustices of global commodity chains have been a staple of a certain brand of activism which emerged during the 1950s. This 'fair trade' activism encompasses a range of civic initiatives which aimed to achieve more equitable economic relations between the South and the North. Since the 1950s, a global network of individuals, groups, and organizations has evolved around the issue of fair trade. They have publicized the need for a transformation of global trade and have put alternatives into practice.

The movement promoting fair trade has arguably been one of the most enduring movements to come out of the postwar years. Fifty years after the first campaigns were launched, more than two million farmers and workers in seventy different countries were growing and manufacturing fair trade-certified products, which had become available in 143 countries.[2] The network of fair trade activists had grown remarkably over these same years, with the World

Figure 0.1 Women sewing in a garment factory in Dhaka, Bangladesh, March 2010. Clean Clothes Campaign.

Fair Trade Organization connecting 359 trading organizations, 25 support organizations, and 26 fair trade networks across the globe.[3] Similarly, the Clean Clothes Campaign has established a global network of more than 230 organizations which work towards better working conditions for workers in the garment and sportswear industries.[4] The fair trade movement has been pivotal in the broad acceptance of 'corporate social responsibility'. It has also fuelled recent debates about legislation on the responsibility of companies to uphold workers' rights and to account for their own environmental impact in commodity chains.

The historical relevance of the fair trade movement, however, goes beyond its immediate and sustained impact. Charting the history of people working towards a more equitable world brings into view a social history of globalization after the Second World War. The process of global integration we have come to label 'globalization' has not unfolded self-evidently. The unprecedented wave of global integration which occurred after 1945 reinforced existing inequalities and created new imbalances as many countries gained their independence from the late 1940s through the 1970s. The emerging interconnected world and its discontents were not just a matter for politicians in meeting halls and managers in boardrooms. The daily lives of people across the globe were also significantly affected. Producing and consuming, trading and boycotting, negotiating and protesting, these individuals, too, helped shape this world. If we focus on humanitarian initiatives which challenged the prevailing shape of postcolonial globalization, we can recover the views held by people across the world concerning fair global relations and their efforts to promote these views, and we can grasp the networks they created and the limitations of their endeavours. Peering through the looking glass of fair trade activism, this book thus delineates an era of postcolonial globalization and charts how humanitarianism evolved during this period.

A Social History of Postcolonial Globalization

Historians currently espouse two versions of the history of globalization.[5] The first presents globalization as a novel phenomenon, which emerged during the twentieth century as the world became smaller due to new means of transportation and communication. This technological development was mirrored by the rise of global political institutions such as the United Nations and the development of a 'global consciousness' among people all over the world.[6] The second conception of globalization places the current global integration within a much longer history of global interaction and thinking about the world as a single unit. In this vein, historians point out how people in the nineteenth century understood their societies within a global framework or even trace the roots of 'global consciousness' all the way back to ancient civilizations.[7]

The history of the fair trade movement shifts the perspective on globalization from intellectual discourses and structures to the ways that ordinary people have attempted to change the global market. From this vantage, thinking globally (and acting accordingly) evolved out of missionary activities, humanitarian campaigns, and acts of international solidarity. But it is also evident that globalization has not proceeded continuously. Three important transformations stand out. The first is the impact of decolonization. The fair trade movement emerged during a period that saw the political decolonization of countries in the Global South challenging prevailing relations on global politics and the world market.[8] Traditional views on what was a just division of wealth and resources were critiqued by politicians and intellectuals from the South and their supporters in the North. Implicitly, and sometimes explicitly, fair trade activists called into question the persistence of colonial relations and mindsets.

The fair trade movement's history thus highlights how ideas about the world and about transnational relations entered a new era, the era of postcolonial globalization. Recent historical scholarship has drawn attention to the importance of decolonization on the way the world was ordered after the Second World War.[9] The alliance of so-called non-aligned countries and the constant back and forth amongst people in the Global South, the Soviet Union, the United States, and European countries were crucial to the way postwar international politics took shape.[10] Decolonization was also negotiated in societies in the Global South and North, where its consequences became visible through migration and new political projects such as African and European cooperation.[11] Decolonization, it turns out, affected people's everyday lives across the globe, prompting them to attempt to shape an emerging postcolonial world.

A second transformation characterizing postwar globalization was the increasing importance of long-distance economic relations. This development was not just reflected in the establishment of global economic institutions like the International Monetary Fund and the World Bank and the expansion of multinational corporations. It also changed how people across the world interacted. In the North, the notion that citizens held power *as consumers* became a commonly held belief. Through marketing, companies had asserted that the customer was king. Governments in the United States and Western Europe, for their part, came to regard 'buying power' to be an essential indicator of their performance.[12] Citizens themselves had learned to exert their power as consumers in numerous campaigns, which applied pressure to companies and governments by deliberately buying or neglecting to buy certain products – boycotting and buycotting became staples of civic activism.[13]

Since the 1950s, the promise of prosperity and the corresponding ability of individual consumers to make deliberate choices about what to buy became inseparable from the way people in the West regarded their 'consumer societies'. The emphasis in the North on consumers' power of choice collided with the process of decolonization. Although people everywhere could identify as consumers and organize accordingly, consumer activists in the South often had to advocate for access to consumption rather than focusing on matters of choice.[14] The history of the fair trade movement demonstrates that this tension was reinforced by the fact that the power to choose held by consumers in the North was often mirrored by the economic dependency of producers in the South.

Whereas decolonization and global economic integration were important preconditions for the emergence of the fair trade movement, a third striking transformation in the history of globalization is observable over the course of its history. The advent of digital communications, creating new opportunities for establishing transnational networks around issues of fair trade, significantly changed the dynamics within the movement. The advent of widespread internet use made it possible to involve actors from across the world in campaigns for fair trade. More people could establish direct lines of communications, and the potential visibility of local circumstances to people all over the world was heightened. The internet also provided novel ways to generate publicity, address relevant actors, and mobilize support. The efforts to create equal relations between North and South within the movement were fostered by these new opportunities. There was a particular emphasis on directly involving actors in the South in the planning and conducting of activist campaigns. At the same time, the structural inequalities created by the prevailing global division of resources and labour were not eliminated by the new structure of global communications.

These three phenomena – decolonization, global economic integration, and the advent of digital communications – have exerted a crucial impact on the shape of globalization since the 1950s. An investigation of this novel epoch in the history of globalization reveals the crucial role that middle-class groups and moderate approaches to achieving change have played in postwar history. Whilst the fair trade movement's primary base in the South was amongst marginalized producers, in the North it has predominantly been a middle-class phenomenon. Historians have traditionally paid scant attention to middle-class groups and their initiatives. These groups lack the romantic steadfastness and ideological purity of more radical activists. Compared to the grand gestures of revolutionary movements, their activities often come across as pedestrian. Even as historians shifted their view from high politics and intellectuals towards common people, the exceptional remained their primary concern. In assessing postwar transformations, it is student activism and the Beatles, rather than consumer associations and the blockbuster movie *The Sound of Music*, that have taken centre stage, even though the latter arguably impacted people's everyday lives in the 1960s just as much.[15] A broad range of moderate views and small gestures is largely missing from the study of postwar history, even though many of the most consequential changes can be traced back to them.

Approaching globalization from the perspective of social history entails a reappraisal of the locus of its politics. A history of the fair trade movement, as I will present in what follows, reinforces and refines the historiographical trend of looking beyond institutional politics to understand how people within a society debate one another and attempt to shape their world. In this history, civic initiatives emerge as crucial activities for defining and addressing societal issues. In recent years, historians have highlighted how decolonization spurred a new group of humanitarian organizations to come to the fore. Oxfam, War on Want, CARE, and Save the Children, as well as many smaller outlets, became important links between the Global North and South. Besides providing support to people in the South, these organizations and their officials also established themselves as experts on international cooperation and development in national and international politics alike.[16]

This book expands on this historiography by including the connections of everyday life with postcolonial globalization. It incorporates the small-scale actions of groups throughout the world in a history which ranges from international trade negotiations to Mexican coffee farmers reacting to the 1980s debt crisis. Alongside international and national development organizations, a host of local and often more haphazard initiatives addressed issues of justice and development. These latter efforts often wanted to raise awareness in their own communities. Sometimes they attempted to address institutional politics at national and international levels, too. These minute initiatives were crucial to the functioning of the field of civic initiatives around fair trade. Some of these endeavours turned out to be precursors of larger operations. Many were staged in partnership with transnational campaigns and challenged prevailing practices of humanitarian action. Moreover, the interconnections between themes like development and the environment are much more readily apparent on the level of local activism than on that of professional organizations focused on a specific policy area. The evolution of global relations since the 1950s can thus be seen to have produced new ideas and practices not just in the sphere of national and international civic organizations but also amongst people who felt urged to address the same issues in their own environment.

This broader history of civic initiative in the wake of decolonization is similarly instructive in light of the history of the global market. The history of markets has been a central theme in social history since the field's inception, with its traditional focus on economic relations, social inequality, and the history of the working class. The fair trade movement provides more recent examples of civic initiatives which aim to transform the market. Whilst thus continuing the tradition of taking inequality and social movements as points of departure, this book proposes to take a transnational perspective as its starting point in thinking about inequality and social movements and to acknowledge the agency of a wider range of social groups.

The history of the economy was closely related to social history as the latter emerged at the beginning of the twentieth century. Across the world, extensive reports on the living conditions of the poor urban working class and colonized peoples were influential in generating a more comprehensive perspective of societies and prompting state interventions. Detailed analysis of economic conditions was the foundation of the 'scientific' strand of socialism which had emerged during the second half of the nineteenth century. These approaches gave rise to a new generation of historians who aimed to write social history as a 'history of society' and spurred calls for the incorporation of insights from economics and other disciplines into historical research. The current of social history which was closely tied to workers' movements, also looked to economic history to understand its current position and to substantiate its claims. As social and economic historians developed an increasing appetite for quantitative methods during the 1960s and 1970s, many scholars turned to approaches which were better able to provide history with a human face.

The last twenty years have witnessed a renewed interest in the history of the market amongst historians. This rediscovery treated markets less as collections of abstract numbers possessing a fixed logic and more as constructions which, through adaptation and contestation, have evolved over time.[17] Just as economists discovered institutions and path dependency, historians now present differentiated views of markets as social spaces. In this vein, this book contends that markets are not amoral spaces governed by a fixed logic. Markets are constituted through social interactions marked by inherent moral assumptions. Rather than regarding the 'moralization of markets' as an intervention by an external moral framework into a morally empty sphere, the history of fair trade highlights how expectations structuring markets are constantly contested amongst producers, regulators, vendors, buyers, and civic organizations.

Conceptualizing the History of Fair Trade

Ever since the fair trade movement emerged during the 1950s, it has attracted scholarly attention. Its history has been part of the historiography of the Third World movement, consumer activism, and humanitarianism. Although each of these areas reflects an important aspect of fair trade, the partition has caused a fragmentation in research. Its fissures were cemented by a preference for individual initiatives which fit the mould of solidarity with the so-called Third World, activities aimed at mobilizing consumers, or campaigns directed at relief. A further cause of compartmentalization has been a focus on fair trade activism in individual national cases, despite the obvious importance of unequal relations between the Global North and South and the emergence of a network of activists throughout the world. Nonetheless, the abundance of work on fair trade initiatives by activists and scholars, as well as the perspectives provided as a result of the different conceptualizations, contributes invaluable insights into the transnational history of fair trade.[18]

This study conceptualizes the fair trade movement as a transnational humanitarian movement which has evolved, since its origin in the establishment of alternative trading organizations in the 1950s, in close relation to the decolonization of the Global South. Social-scientific scholarship had primarily understood fair trade as an attempt to introduce social justice into economic relations.[19] Recently, scholars in this field have presented it as a broader movement engaged in trade and certification as well as campaigning and advocacy.[20] The present approach to fair trade as a transnational humanitarian movement advocating socio-economic justice similarly integrates campaigning, trading, and advocacy, asking how citizens have mobilized to shape the global market. It connects the historiography on social movements, consumer activism, and humanitarianism. It draws on social movement research to consider (1) the goals which activists pursued, (2) the repertoire of action they employed, (3) the networks they developed to achieve their goals, and (4) the conditions which drove the evolution of activism.[21] The recent attention to the ways that social movements have shifted between local, national, and transnational scales is crucial to this history.[22] In turn, it demonstrates that we should discern these scales as nodes of government, arenas for actions connected to perceived audiences, and levels of organization and of spatial imagination. The history of the fair trade movement reinforces the observation that these scales are not mutually exclusive but rather coexist with shifting relative weight to one another.[23]

Three strands of scholarship have addressed the history of fair trade activism, each highlighting a distinct feature of the movement. A first wave of scholarship on fair trade connected it to the history of what became known as the Third World movement.[24] This body of work, intimately tied to social movement research, proposed regarding fair trade campaigns as part of a larger movement concerned with transnational solidarity rather than departing from specific organizations or individual campaigns.[25] Historical development and historiography went hand in hand: the fair trade movement indeed evolved alongside transnational solidarity initiatives aimed at individual countries such as Angola, South Africa, Chile, Cuba, and Nicaragua, all of which became prominent between the 1960s and 1980s. Campaigns focused on these countries provided concrete examples and related products which fair trade activism could build on. In the 1970s, an activist could engage in a boycott against products from colonized Angola, take part in a demonstration directed at the United Nations Conference for Trade and Development, and then attend a lecture on the role of women in development projects without a sense of having divided loyalties.

Approaching fair trade from the angle of Third World activism foregrounds crucial aspects of its history. First, this vantage acknowledges the postcolonial framework within which the movement has to be understood.[26] The recent insight that the Cold War divide between East and West was interlaced with relations between South and North is particularly fruitful for understanding the contestation of the global market since the 1950s.[27] This interconnection pertains not only to the roots in radical activism, which resulted from leftwing solidarity with the Global South, but also to the direct influence exerted by actors from the Global South in circulating ideas and initiating actions in the North.[28] Whereas fair trade has traditionally been supported by a coalition ranging from radical leftwing activists to politically moderate churchgoers, the former has faded into the background as the historiographical focus has shifted towards understanding fair trade predominantly as a certification initiative. Regarding fair trade as part of a broader Third World movement, on the contrary, emphasizes its radical elements, whilst also calling attention to the broader repertoire it has employed. Selling products from the Global South has been pivotal, but picketing, boycotts, rallies, education, and lobbying have been just as influential.

Echoing the claims to novelty voiced by activists, scholars of social movements such as the Third World movement have insisted on treating them as different from earlier social movements.[29] This notion of 'new social movements', however important to the self-fashioning of activists at the time such claims were made, risks neglecting the continuities in the people, practices, and ideas shaping them. The fair trade movement did not break off from the traditions of leftwing solidarity and missionary concern with people in the Global South. Similar caution is warranted when using the label 'Third World movement', because it readily dismisses differences between those campaigning for the Global South and those acting in solidarity with specific countries. Although these aims could overlap, they have not always simply coincided. Moreover, the continuity of fair trade activism from the 1980s to 1990s cautions against overestimating the importance of the notion of the Third World for this strand of activism, which persisted after notions of the Third World all but dissolved.[30]

The dissolution of an imagined Third World at the turn of the 1990s coincided with the emergence of campaigns which aimed to increase the sales of fair trade products, eventually resulting in the practice of certification. Certification reinvigorated the activities which fair trade proponents had adopted from consumer activism. This was mirrored in the scholarly approach to fair trade, which increasingly conceptualized it as a manifestation of consumer activism.[31] The lens of consumer activism has yielded valuable insights into prominent ideas and practices like emphasizing consumer choice, buying power, and the repertoire of boycotts and buycotts. It foregrounded moderate groups which had been less visible through the lens of Third World activism. Much of the ensuing debate about fair trade circled around the issue of mainstreaming. Had the attempts to sell more fair trade products and to harness the influence of citizens as consumers produced practices which had been co-opted by businesses with no real interest in promoting fair trade? Had these companies suggested to consumers that they did enough to foster a better world simply by buying fair trade products in a supermarket, thus mitigating the critical impetus of the earlier movement and reducing citizenship to a consumerist repertoire? These questions, to be sure, remain vital to the history and future of the fair trade movement.

In turn, this aspect of fair trade history is relevant to debates about the relations between activism and consumption. Competing views about the relation between citizenship and consumption were on display as advocates and critics argued whether fair trade products should be sold only in 'alternative' stores or also in supermarkets. Did activism need its own space, or should it infiltrate other places, too?[32] Similar issues were at stake in assessing the viability of boycotts and the relevance of market share in political negotiations. Could economic indicators be translated into political power? The relation between citizenship and consumption is constantly being negotiated, with civic organizations playing a pivotal role in these negotiations.[33] Rather than focusing only on the organizations explicitly claiming to represent consumers, analysis of these negotiations should include consideration of the wider host of initiatives concerned with what historian Lawrence Glickman has labelled 'consumer activism'.[34]

Presenting fair trade as a strand of consumer activism, however, tends to reduce it to the practice of buying and selling fair trade products. Yet doing so neglects the campaigning and lobbying efforts of organizations involved in selling products, as well as organizations which promote trade justice without being engaged in selling products. In recent histories of fair trade, for example, the launch of the certification initiative Max Havelaar in the Netherlands has eclipsed the founding of the Clean Clothes Campaign in the same year. The resulting narrative favours the organizations most prominently claiming the label 'fair trade'. Framing fair trade activism as a consumer-driven phenomenon follows the lead of fair trade marketing, which often employs a rhetoric that attributes decisive power to the consumer.[35] This bias reflects the importance of the consumer to the selling of fair trade products and calls on people to reflect on their moral responsibility when buying. In doing so, it conceals the mediating role of civic organizations in providing consumers with products, setting standards for what is considered 'fair', and strategically deciding how to balance selling, campaigning, and lobbying. A historical analysis of fair trade has much to gain from looking beyond this rhetoric and its underlying assumptions.

By reconceptualizing the fair trade movement as a transnational humanitarian movement, this book attempts to integrate insights from the earlier perspectives I have mentioned into a history of transnational solidarity. This strand of historiography has broadly concerned itself with attempts to help 'distant others'. Nongovernmental organizations (NGOs) channelling such attempts have been a major focus.[36] Humanitarianism provides a fresh perspective on the history of fair trade. It aligns with the available archival material, which is dominated by documentation from NGOs in Western Europe and the United States. Histories of humanitarianism have a strong tradition of reading this material against the grain to include perspectives from the Global South. Stressing the transnational nature of the endeavours of civic organizations, they do not shy away from pointing out the drawbacks of, and power imbalances implied in, humanitarian initiatives, however well intentioned.

Recently, histories of humanitarianism have also grappled with religion as a crucial element, acknowledging the fluid borders between religious and secular impulses in this field.[37] In the historical studies devoted to fair trade, religious influences have long been acknowledged – in particular, the crucial role of religious networks during the fair trade movement's early history in establishing contacts between producer groups and people who wanted to sell products on their behalf. Recent histories of humanitarianism, however, question how fair trade histories have equated religious influence with conservative views and charitable practices. An activist organization like the Dutch Sjaloom group, which initiated some of the most radical political interventions around issues of trade and development in the 1960s and 1970s, was rooted in the ecumenical movement, which aimed for a simultaneous renewal of church and society. It drew supporters from different denominations as well as people without any clear religious affiliation. Such hotchpotch alliances are much more typical of the evolution of fair trade activism than a division between moderate religious and radical secularist circles.

When these strands of historiography are brought together, pertinent questions arise. How are the histories of movements and distinct organizations connected? To what extent could actors from the Global South impact the trajectories of humanitarian initiatives? And how do we embed economic relations within these histories? In reaction to these questions, this book attempts to address three silences in the prevalent source material on the history of fair trade and on humanitarian initiatives more generally. Most strikingly, voices from the Global South are crucial to this history. As the following chapters will show, producer groups as well as prominent political and scholarly spokespersons from the South have been important drivers for the evolution of the fair trade movement. Fair trade scholarship on more recent developments has been able to draw on fieldwork to incorporate producers more systematically. As far as the present analysis goes, their perspective has to be inferred from source material privileging the perspective of actors from the North.

Another significant dimension often overlooked is the importance of the specific materiality of the products involved in fair trade, perhaps most obvious in the means of communication amongst fair trade activists. The archival material for the 1950s up through the 1990s is dominated by handwritten and typed letters, flyers, and brochures. For national interactions, activists often mention phone calls as another medium. In international correspondence, faxes gradually turn up as a means to communicate quickly over long distances. Over the course of the 1990s, the materials from which historians construct their accounts changed notably. Printed emails start to dominate the files in the archives, and more and more material has been stored on CD-ROMs and external hard drives. But exchanges also took place outside these means of communication. As the following chapters highlight, the exchange of products itself was crucial to establishing a sense of connection between people in different parts of the world. Fair trade activism is hardly imaginable without this material grounding, even though ensuing activist efforts have often gone beyond or even criticized a focus on buying and selling. Moreover, the kinds of products being exchanged mattered greatly. Rather than mere passive conductors of human activity, the products which fair trade activists handled had their own part in shaping the history of the movement.[38]

An approach centred on commodities and their symbolic meanings for those involved is particularly suited to the history of this movement, as activists often focused on specific commodities and ascribed eye-catching meanings to them.[39] Early fair trade initiatives revolved around products like handicrafts and coffee for good reasons: these products were relatively easy to transport over long distances on a small scale without affecting their quality. Their chains of production and distribution were relatively clear-cut, too, which made it easier to present them to the public as symbols of global trade relations. That products such as coffee, tea, bananas, and cocoa could not be grown in the North produced a different dynamic of contention than handicrafts or clothing, because the latter were not limited to the South and could therefore also readily play a part in contesting the working conditions of people in the North.

Finally, this book attempts to decentre the leaders who draw most attention in histories of activism. Instead, it stresses the importance of networks of organizations as distinct structures of cooperation and emphasizes the participation of 'ordinary' people in their activities. Many histories exploring the prominence of

NGOs since 1945 have focused on large organizations and their most prominent spokespersons. This emphasis has highlighted the role of civic organizations in shaping postcolonial globalization, the visions they have articulated, and the practices such organizations pioneered. Organizations and individuals with a longstanding commitment to fair trade have taken centre stage in the movement's history. Those who remained involved continued to recount their experiences as part of fair trade history. People who have disengaged tend to disappear from accounts of the movement's history, whilst defunct organizations have, more often than not, left hardly any documentation. It is thus particularly important to consider the less visible actors and the discontinuities in the fair trade movement's history.[40] Increasingly, historiography is turning towards the specific practices of humanitarian initiatives, particularly in situations when humanitarians wanted to intervene to make a difference. Building on this trend, this book shifts the focus towards smaller organizations and groups and people who did not claim a place in the spotlight for themselves. It thus highlights how the shape of postcolonial globalization was negotiated between many local situations in the Global North and South – in boardrooms, local gatherings, and everyday encounters.

Outline

This book's composition reflects the importance of the materiality of specific products to civic action and foregrounds networks of actors rather than individual leaders. The rise of the fair trade movement from the 1950s onwards was closely linked to the renegotiation of commodity chains in the course of decolonization around products such as handicrafts, cane sugar, coffee, tea, cocoa, bananas, and textiles. Activists reacted to the imbalances and the possibilities of long-distance trade, which became politicized in the wake of decolonization. They provided information about the lives of marginalized producers and a sense of connection to them. In this way, these items countered the lack of knowledge about the circumstances of production and consumption due to the distance between production and consumption in global trade. Exchanging commodities produced new knowledge about and alternative channels for global trade.

The handicrafts imported by alternative trading organizations discussed in the first chapter were produced by women and men in precarious situations which were initially often a consequence of the Second World War. Soon refugees from other violent conflicts, including Chinese and Palestinians, also found their way into these networks. In other instances, products were procured by people with ties to missionary networks embedded in colonial relations. As civic groups in several countries started to sell these products as an act of solidarity with their makers, a 'global' outlook was fostered amongst producers and potential buyers. The networks thus established would shape many future interactions amongst fair trade activists.

In 1968, calls to transform the structure of trade between the South and the North became particularly attached to cane sugar, the focus of Chapter 2. Activists in the Netherlands took their cue from the analysis of economists from the South and the international discussions which took place within the framework of the United Nations Conference on Trade and Development. As people across Western Europe became involved in the 'Cane Sugar Campaign', the growing body of knowledge about the production and trade of cane sugar complicated attempts to publicize global trade imbalances through a concrete example. Since the launch of the Cane Sugar Campaign in 1968, activists have continuously publicized and practised fair trade at the same time. Cane sugar was an apt example of how the structure of international trade was stacked against producers in the South because European regulation rendered European beet sugar more affordable than cane sugar though the latter was actually cheaper on the world market.

As the Cane Sugar Campaign was followed by new attempts to raise awareness about global trade inequalities – the topic of Chapter 3 – paper arguably became the most important commodity circulating amongst those involved in fair trade activism. Paper is distinct from the products centred in the other chapters, as it was usually not produced in the Global South and did not carry the symbolic weight of the other products in connecting producers and consumers. Its exceptional status here points up the fact that fair trade activism in the 1970s and 1980s did not revolve primarily around the selling of products from the South. Paper is uniquely suited to the transfer of knowledge and to calls to action in the shape of booklets, flyers, stencils, and posters, all staples of the many local gatherings of fair trade activists which emerged during the 1970s. Paper also accommodated the exchange of knowledge between producers in the South and their supporters in the North, which fair trade activists championed.

Coffee, the focal point of the fourth chapter, marks a change in the balance between raising awareness and selling products, a shift which took shape during the 1980s. Whereas paper was associated with an approach which emphasized raising awareness and discussion, activism surrounding coffee focused on selling products as a means to fuse immediate impact with more effective long-term advocacy. Coffee producers were struggling to survive in the wake of the debt crisis of the early 1980s, compelling those involved in procuring fair trade coffee to make turnover a priority. In 1988, the Max Havelaar campaign introduced fair trade certification as a new instrument for activism. This venture was part of a broader range of attempts to conduct fair trade activism more professionally, whether in traditional settings such as world shops or in cooperation with new associates such as supermarkets.

The selling of coffee was closely related to a postcolonial perspective – the limits of which came into view during the 1990s. Initiatives like the Clean Clothes Campaign challenged the complex and stretched commodity chains of textiles, which are at the heart of Chapter 5. Textiles resisted being framed as an issue only of skewed relations between the South and North, as their chain of production and distribution, and the accompanying forms of malpractice extended across different parts of the globe. The possibilities of communication offered by the internet and the widening range of fair trade products prompted an evolution in the direction of a less hierarchical global network of actors. The growth and professionalization of the fair trade network gave rise to new debates about representation, which played out very differently now that global networks of digital communication and a more robust set of organizations were in play. The gradual dissolution of the era of postcolonial globalization was mirrored by the ascendance of the notion of sustainability. Emerging in the 1980s, the idea of 'sustainable development' had reframed the relation between equity and the economy by relating social, economic, and environmental concerns to one another and by applying this same logic of interconnectedness to any situation.

The focus here on these five products – handicrafts, cane sugar, paper, coffee, and textiles – is by no means comprehensive. Other analyses of fair trade activism have rightly discussed other crucial products, including bananas, cocoa, tea, and honey, all of which were important to the evolution of fair trade activism in different regions. Products such as wine, canned tuna, toilet paper, footballs, and, more recently, water bottles and computer software have also figured in this history. The products considered in this study have thus been selected to highlight important features of the movement at different moments in its history and are meant to be means to help us rethink activism.

The fair trade movement is remarkable for its longevity, its broad repertoire of action, and the diverse coalition it has mustered. Nonetheless, its economic impact remains slight when compared to the overall volume of global trade, and there are many reasons to be wary of the solutions to global inequality the movement has put forth over the years. These reservations aside, the fair trade movement has brought knowledge about the fraught nature of many global commodity chains into circulation. It has presented people with options for civic activism which can address and publicize these issues. It has contributed to the almost universal acceptance of 'corporate social responsibility'. Surveying the current state of the fair trade movement, the concluding chapter revisits these questions of impact and historical relevance. At a time when sustainability and the legacy of colonialism are firmly on the agenda in many parts of the world, this history of people attempting to shape the era of postcolonial globalization is more topical than ever.

1 HANDICRAFTS
Humanitarianism after Empire

Where to begin a history of fair trade? With Aristotle's thoughts on fair prices? Or in the thirteenth century, when the cleric Conrad of Marburg, as confessor to Elizabeth of Thuringia, instructed her to consume only that which had not been acquired unjustly from her subjects? The British antislavery activists' boycott of the 'blood-stained sugar' extracted from the plantations of slaveholders in the late eighteenth century?[1] Or the Consumers White Label, introduced in the United States in 1898 to be bestowed on textiles produced in factories that respected the guidelines set by labour legislation?[2]

Questions about fair exchange, though a constant concern in the history of human relations, took a distinct turn after the Second World War. The attempted and ultimately successful decolonization of much of the Global South shook up prevailing assumptions about the proper economic relations between people in different parts of the world. In the effort to leave behind colonial economic relations, questions arose: What should be produced, and by whom? What should be exchanged, and with whom? How should markets be ordered in a postcolonial world? Should there be some kind of compensation for the legacy of colonialism, and should individual participants be guaranteed a fair chance to thrive? Or should things continue, business as usual?

These questions came to the fore at a time when connections between different parts of the world were being re-established after the war's disruption and a new postwar order was under construction. An as-yet-unparalleled availability of transportation and communication technologies were connecting the world, even though different regions experienced this new reality at diverging speeds and under unequal terms. At the same time, the expansion of welfare states fuelled new ideas about what constituted decent living conditions. The unprecedented increase in spending power amongst consumers in the North rested on global interconnection and a new understanding of human welfare. It also presented these consumers with new opportunities to express preferences and to feel a sense of connection related to their purchases.[3] These developments produced a new strain of activism contesting the morality of global trade. Within this context, existing networks of transnational solidarity were reconfigured, and the fair trade movement emerged.

The fair trade movement evolved as a network of people and organizations working to improve the position of people in the Global South within the system of global trade relations. Those involved have been preoccupied with producing, buying and selling, campaigning, and – beginning later on – certification.[4] Although it is helpful to subdivide the movement based on such activities, many organizations cannot be so neatly categorized: individually, fair trade supporters were often active in more than one organization at the same time, participating in campaigns whilst selling fair trade products, for example. This is also true of many organizations at large: producers have often instigated and contributed to fair trade campaigns, whilst fair trade shops have long been pivotal in planning campaigns whilst also selling products.

When people in the Global North think about fair trade nowadays, fair trade certification is usually at the top of their minds, and rightly so: fair trade certification is the largest part of the movement in economic terms, and consumers come across fair trade-certified products in many stores. Before fair trade certification took off in the 1990s, fair trade campaigns initiated by local activist groups and their federations, as well as national campaigning organizations such as Oxfam, Brot für die Welt, and Erklärung von Bern, dominated the image people held of fair trade activism. The activities of the alternative trading organizations, which established relations with producers, imported fair trade products, and channelled them to various outlets, have attracted far less public attention.

The organizations importing fair trade products have assumed an awkward position in the history of fair trade activism.

Often springing from denominational religious networks, they had forged close relations with traditional humanitarian organizations and thus their intentions were regarded with suspicion: Were they continuing a tradition of charity and colonial paternalism? As businesses, it was hard to reconcile them with the image of a social movement to which fair trade activists often aspired. Were the trading organizations committed to change, or were they primarily concerned with their own economic survival? The products they provided were constantly scrutinized: Could they function as symbols of unfair trading practices? Were their producers really benefitting from the terms of trade? And were these producers viable groups to support? Histories of the fair trade movement have also often neglected these alternative trading organizations because their members were less articulate than many activists about their ideals and policies, working in the background rather than taking to the streets themselves.

It is fitting to begin a history of fair trade activism with the marginalized people who, from the 1950s onwards, demanded more equitable global relations and who produced the products that allies in North America and Western Europe started selling. Groups of women and men set up workshops and engaged in handicraft activities. They lived all across the world, embodying a web of stories that included those of refugees in Singapore and West Germany, woodcrafters in Haiti, and seamstresses in Palestine. Representatives of such groups were in touch with their contacts elsewhere to explore whether their products could be sold in far-flung places on their behalf. They also sought to draw attention to their dire situations. The people hit hardest by global inequality have been the driving force behind this strand of humanitarian action, both through their own initiatives and because their plight has served as the raison d'être for various campaigns. Yet the paucity of source material makes it all but impossible to provide accounts of such groups. Their highly diverse backgrounds also make it hard to do them justice via generalizations. Moreover, we should be wary of any account presenting fair trade activism as simply the passing on of demands and goods from marginalized producers to sympathetic consumers in other parts of the world. The opinions and preferences of these producers held sway over the movement's activities almost as a matter of course. Without their consent, campaigning on their behalf would seem pointless. Nonetheless, they often lacked the means to ensure that their voices would be heard within the movement. Divergent positions and views made translating their situations into campaigns a matter of mediation. Ultimately the fair trade movement was constituted via the interactions amongst producers, representatives, trade organizations, and activists in Western Europe and North America.

As one of the focal points in these sorts of interaction, the alternative trading organizations thus present a suitable starting point for a history of fair trade. Serving since the 1950s as a kind of backbone for the movement, they were, historically, the first organizations to emerge in what would become an ever-broadening field of fair trade organizations. From the 1950s onwards, they were often the first point of contact for producers from the South looking for allies in the North. During the 1960s, alternative trading organizations offered products from the Global South to groups of fair trade activists, who then in their first campaigns were able to present tangible links between the South and the North. Before the onset of widespread long-distance air travel and pervasive internet and cellular communication, the personnel of these trading organizations provided direct lines of contact between people in South and North, at that time relatively rare. Moreover, they possessed close connections to older religious and secular networks of transnational solidarity, which can enable us to better understand how the fair trade movement built on earlier networks and ideas. In other words, alternative trading organizations provided an infrastructure and a network for the fair trade movement. The products they distributed were a tangible means of connecting producers, activists, and buyers. Their often practical approach provides an important perspective on the broad appeal of fair trade activism for moderate as well as more politically outspoken groups across the globe.

Early fair trade initiatives revolved largely around handicraft products such as needlework, weavings, and woodcarvings. Small organizations could transport these objects easily over large distances, as they were not perishable and in these early years were produced in relatively small numbers. The items conveyed a sense of a personal connection because the efforts of those who made them could immediately be observed in the form of an object. They appeared in Western Europe and the United States at a time when the artisanal skill required to make such products was no longer much in evidence, having being displaced by machine production or, at any rate, occurring only in workshops that were not part of most people's everyday lives. These objects thus could sometimes be romanticized, as were those people in other parts of the world who had 'still' mastered these crafts and were able to produce more 'authentic' goods.

The handicrafts imported and sold by the fair trade movement's forerunners provided evidence of a small-scale, personal, and practical approach – for the producers as much as those selling their products. Pioneers such as Edna Byler and Paul Meijs, around which this early history revolves, drew on a web of personal relations. They appreciated the needlework and woodcarvings they were offering for sale because these items said something about the people who made them and showed these makers' physical investment in improving their lives. The handicrafts sold by alternative trading organizations such as Self-Help Crafts, Oxfam, and SOS draw attention to the fluent transition from a notion of self-improvement on a small scale to visions of wide-ranging modernization during the 1950s and 1960s.

Setting Up Shop

The first alternative trading organizations were established during the 1950s and 1960s. They emerged out of networks of transnational solidarity often underpinned by religious communities. Religious networks not only provided the fair trade pioneers with inspiration but also linked them to producers and potential buyers, venues, and facilities. Although they publicized the idea that people in distress needed 'trade, not aid', these organizations positioned their activities somewhere between asking people to buy products and soliciting donations to others in ostensible need. As historians of religion and empire have pointed out, those carrying out missionary work followed a tradition of distancing themselves from the political project of empire and concerning themselves with improving the lives of those they engaged with.[5] As with this sort of missionary work, the early years of the alternative trading organizations highlight how their representatives assumed that their work was contributing to a long-term transformation in the communities where these products were made, of which self-reliance was the ultimate goal.

This attitude is especially apparent in the history of the North American alternative trading organization now known as Ten Thousand Villages. Its activities can be traced back to the efforts of Edna Ruth Byler, a woman linked to the Mennonite Central Committee (MCC), a relief organization founded by Mennonites in 1920 to aid their co-religionists in Ukraine. The MCC later expanded its activities to support Mennonites and others across the world. Byler had worked for the MCC at its headquarters in Akron, Pennsylvania, during the Second World War, as the committee had taken up the responsibility of deploying the many conscientious objectors from their religious community.[6]

After the war, Byler accompanied her husband in his capacity of Overseas Director to locations where the MCC was doing its work. During a visit to Puerto Rico, she met a group of women who asked her to sell their needlework on their behalf in the United States. Soon groups from Hong Kong, South Korea, Taiwan, India, Jordan, Greece, and West Germany also sent handicrafts which could be sold locally and in the United States and Canada. Byler would sell these items during visits to local Mennonite communities and meetings with women's groups across North America. Eventually she established a gift shop in her hometown of Akron, where these articles could be bought regularly.[7] In these Mennonite circles, trading products on behalf of others was related to a tradition of 'relief sales', where people would buy products made by people in distress (or which others had made on their behalf) in order to raise money for them. Handicrafts were especially suitable commodities because they could be connected to a North American Mennonite culture which valued artisanship, frugality, and self-reliance.

Byler's work on behalf of handicraft producers availed itself of the MCC network in locating producers and buyers. The organization officially became part of the MCC only in 1962. After Byler's husband passed away, she became a project manager for the organization and soon went to the Canadian province of Manitoba to visit a host of groups related to the MCC's work. Anne Giesbrecht, one of the organizers of the trip, remarked in a letter to William T. Snyer at the MCC headquarters that Byler's

Figure 1.1 Edna Byler with needlework. Mennonite Central Committee: Ten Thousand Villages/Selfhelp Crafts.

visit had been very well received, particularly amongst women in the missionary societies of the vast province's various churches. Her talks had been an opportunity to present a tangible aspect of the MCC's international activities. One woman's reaction underscores how, to those involved, these activities were not solely about practical ways to help one another: 'in our everyday chores around the house (…) we would be reminded to pray for the women who are struggling to make a living, we could pray that someone might lead them to the Lord'. Those present had also appreciated the meetings as an opportunity to find common ground between different but like-minded churches.[8] The shaping of transnational networks of assistance, then, was crucially informed by the personal involvement of people within the MCC's network, who could convey their experiences to others. In his response to Giesbrecht's letter Snyder, indeed, wrote that he expected the MCC to play a more prominent role amongst Manitoban religious communities now that someone actively involved in the MCC's work was planning to settle there.[9]

During the 1950s and 1960, the Cold War produced in the collective mind a psychological division of East and West, supplemented and sometimes challenged by a division between South and

North.[10] Remarkably, these global imaginaries had little impact on the way Byler and her companions took up their work. They made no clear distinction separating producing from consuming countries. Handicrafts could be sold locally as well as in North America, whilst Byler would also sell toys made by a group in Appalachia, a region known for its poverty.[11] There was also no clear-cut division between charity and a focus on structural transformation. In 1954, Byler stopped ordering products from Puerto Rico because she deemed that improved standards of living there would enable seamstresses to make a better living by other means. Similarly, when the programme officially became part of the MCC's work, its guidelines stated that it aimed to provide 'meaningful employment' and that producers should receive fair remuneration; the programme itself should be self-supporting.[12]

Around the time Byler started selling items from groups with links to the MCC, another American Protestant group embarked on a similar initiative. The Sales Exchange for Refugee Rehabilitation Vocations (SERVV), with its main centre in New Windsor, Maryland, grew out of the network of the Church of the Brethren and its involvement with the activities that the interdenominational humanitarian organization Church World Service had deployed worldwide since 1946. The Sales Exchange for Refugee Rehabilitation Vocations aimed to enable refugees in particular to provide for themselves via the sale of their own handicrafts.[13] Notably, it was the voluntarist nature of the enterprise which initially strengthened the position of the producers. 'This is a church program, not a business', stated Ray Kyle, who coordinated the programme during the early 1960s. This meant that all profits from the sales were channelled back to the producers.[14]

The activities of SERVV during the 1950s and 1960s illustrate how the group of producers and the consumer base of such organizations would gradually expand beyond the initial focus on the organization's own denominational network. The operations of SERVV were primarily directed towards related denominational groups of producers, which it supported by selling their products through channels the religious community provided in North America. By establishing 'international gift shops', SERVV appealed to a public beyond its own religious community, although some products were earmarked to be used to strengthen the ties between denominational groups in different parts of the world.[15] Products could even be channelled to commercial partners, if they were interested.

The correspondence of SERVV is laced with examples of producer groups seeking out trading partners. After contact was established, the two parties would exchange samples and estimated sales figures. If both sides were satisfied with what they had been given, new trading partnerships would be established. The resourcefulness on display in this correspondence of producer representatives, tirelessly contacting people they managed to locate through their networks, is remarkable. The producers may all have been looking for people to buy their products, but there was no common pattern of interaction. Sometimes Ray Kyle would insist on professional standards or that North American consumer expectations be satisfied, or specify a minimal volume of production. In other exchanges, the producer groups were more professional and enterprising than SERVV, hoping to sell more and set up more regular exchanges than Kyle could manage.[16]

In Western Europe, Cold War imaginaries were more influential in the 1950s and 1960s but only in a roundabout way. Initiatives to promote products from marginalized producers were related to a discourse of development which thrived in an era of competing US and Soviet claims about the potential of their respective societal models to transform the world for the better. At once tying into this discourse and expressing mistrust of partisan claims, fair trade advocates often presented transnational solidarity as a morally superior alternative to the promotion of ideological and military conflict. The networks established by missionaries, political allies, and relief workers trumped ideological allegiances and often superseded denominational boundaries. For the North American organizations, the care they provided to refugees in Europe and Asia initially led to a humanitarian reaction which transcended regional and ideological boundaries. In the case of the Western European organizations, this impulse was amplified by the experience of hardship during the Second World War and its aftermath and of aid received through transnational channels. The emergence of the Cold War brought with it the fear of a new war resulting from the destabilizing effects of poverty and global inequality, which were also invoked as a justification to aid those in need.[17]

The growing ambitions of fair trade pioneers also drove efforts to abandon the distinction between supporting people from one's own network and working for the good of all humanity. The leadership of Oxfam and SOS in particular wanted to operate as professional organizations on a large scale. In the United Kingdom, members of Oxfam developed an approach similar to that of MCC and SERVV during the 1950s and 1960s. After the tireless Quaker campaigner Edith Pye visited Oxford to advocate for famine relief in war-torn Europe, a group of concerned citizens came together and, in October 1942, founded the Oxford Committee for Famine Relief (it adopted the shortened name 'Oxfam' in 1965). At the outset, the organization was firmly rooted in the religious networks of the Society of Friends, though when compared to Self-Help Crafts and SERVV it was less focused on a specific religious community, in part due to the Friends' more inclusive approach, directed towards relief work that placed no particular emphasis on its own constituency. The Committee's initial activities were part of broader campaigns involving coalitions of national and local groups. It would evolve, albeit in a hardly straightforward manner. Although a national Famine Relief Committee had been active in the United Kingdom since 1942, its activities were predominantly politically oriented by necessity, as there was scarcely any opportunities to provide concrete assistance to people in Europe. As a result, the group all but fell silent.[18]

A chance to spring into action came in 1943, when the Oxford Committee was asked if it could contribute to relief work in Greece. This opportunity coincided with the eccentric philanthropist Cecil Jackson-Cole taking a lead role within the organization. In March of that year, the committee officially registered as a charity and started fundraising on behalf of people in Greece. As continental Europe was liberated up through the European War's end in May 1945, relief work became part of an effort to ensure peace by securing people's basic needs and rebuilding the continent. The Oxford group extended its activities to the collection clothing on behalf of people in the Netherlands and supported relief and reconstruction efforts carried out by the Quakers and other groups.[19]

The 1948 Marshall Plan and the growing rift between Eastern and Western Europe made support for relief and reconstruction less urgent. Scaling back their activities, the Quakers and groups like them closed off opportunities to continue to contribute to European relief work. At this juncture the Oxford Committee might have been disbanded, but Jackson-Cole pursued instead a programme of expansion. Quite unusual for the time, he wanted the charity organization to adopt a businesslike approach, installing professional management and aiming to use part of its funds to expand the organization. In 1949, it formulated a new mission statement: 'The relief of suffering arising as a result of wars or of other causes in any part of the world'. Thus the door was opened to relations with the Global South. In 1951, the Oxford Committee raised funds on behalf of people struck by famine in the Indian state of Bihar. Once again, religious networks proved invaluable in establishing contacts for administering relief: the Committee cooperated with the wife of the bishop of Bhagalpur. At the same time, the Committee would continue to be active in Europe, too, responding to provide disaster relief after an earthquake in Greece in 1953, amongst other efforts.[20]

The organization's professional approach quickly became discernible in its day-to-day activities as well. The Committee turned to advertisements to draw attention to its fundraising. In 1947, it also opened up a permanent gift shop instead of being only intermittently present at its drop-off points and sales stalls.[21] Members of the campaign had sold items such as Christmas cards on behalf of relief and development programmes at temporary stands as well as stalls and shops since the late 1940s. During the early 1960s, they began selling items such as pincushions made by Chinese refugees living in Hong Kong. Contact with these producers – indicative of the international networks enabling such activities – had been established through Ludwig Stumpf, a German pastor whom the Lutheran World Federation Department of World Services posted in Hong Kong to assist these refugees. Oxford Committee staff had deemed such products suitable for sale through the organization's channels due to the direct relation to the kind of programmes it was engaged with 'overseas'. At the same time, these items were of good quality and were priced affordably, which made them preferable to things which volunteers could make at home or which could be bought from professional outfits in the United Kingdom.[22] During the 1960s, other suitable products from countries such as Mexico and Kenya were identified through the international network established by the organization.[23] Christmas cards, however, remained the best-selling item for the time being.[24]

The Oxfam Shops were a pivotal channel for the sale these items. Members of the Oxford initiative had opened a gift shop in the city in November 1947. At first, it served as a drop-off site for clothing and other items intended as donations to Oxfam's relief work, whilst some gifts were sold on the side. After two years, Joe Mitty was appointed as a full-time manager, turning the location into a lively gift shop which would trade anything from candles to false teeth and feather boas.[25] The gift shops would become a fixture for Oxfam's fundraising, whilst also providing the organization considerable local visibility. The expansion of such activities which bordered on commercial ventures in their practice of selling products raised concerns by the Charity Commission which monitored the work of recognized charitable organizations in the United Kingdom. It advised Oxfam to nominally separate charitable from commercial activities, leading to the establishment of Oxfam Trading as a separate organization which formalized and directed Oxfam's trading activities since 1964. In 1967, imports from the Global South were transferred to yet another separate organization, which was named 'Helping by Selling'.[26]

The expansion and professionalization of the gift shops' work became, accordingly, an organizational priority during the 1960s. In 1967, the committee advising on this process articulated the uneasy position of the gift shops within the organization's overall work:

> Oxfam exists to bring the most effective aid in its power to people who suffer from hunger or disaster. To do this it must raise money and advance public opinion to a deeper and more active support for such work. It is not an inherent part of Oxfam's job to run shops or trading operations unless these serve its two primary objectives – and serve both of them in some reasonable measure.[27]

The committee advised following the lead of four shops which by then had been established as 'principal shops'. Each was overseen by a professional manager and had been established on commercial leases. About a hundred more shops sprouted up during the 1950s and 1960s, run by local Oxfam groups throughout the United

Kingdom. Often temporary stations when they first appeared, such shops would become more permanent fixtures, allowing them, in the eyes of the advisory committee, to adopt a similar approach to that of the four 'principal stores'. Each region could designate a 'principal shop' with a full-time manager.[28] A subsequent advisory report, two years later, reaffirmed this approach and recommended that the shops develop a deliberate form of presentation to improve sales. It warned against a makeshift approach apparently observable at the time, which would make the shops look like 'jumble sales'.[29]

The work of Oxfam and the other groups discussed in this chapter are quite different from what we now understand as 'fair trade'. Oxfam's activities were rooted in a view which presented trading in labour-intensive goods from developing countries as an apt way to provide employment in these countries whilst generating profits for Oxfam to devote to its operations. Consistent with the popular slogan 'trade, not aid', they built on the idea that being able to trade would provide people in developing countries a natural path to development.[30] Oxfam, however, had to tread carefully to avoid difficulties with the Charity Commission, which advised that charitable and commercial activities be separated and warned Oxfam not to engage in political activities relating to legislation and regulation. The Commission was also suspicious of activities which could be deemed 'development aid' – as opposed to charitable work – outright.[31]

These Charity Commission concerns highlight how 'charity' bore a legal status which limited the range of activities Oxfam could engage in. References to charity link the initiatives of alternative trading organizations in the 1950s and 1960s to a longer history of religiously inspired humanitarianism. In practice, however, Oxfam stretched the notion of charity to support a transformative agenda when it asked people to buy particular items as a way of helping others and then used proceeds of the sales for development. The objectives of charity and structural reform thus became almost indistinguishable. The case of Oxfam in the 1960s shows how such blurring could emerge out of regulative frameworks and strategic considerations. The early years of alternative trading initiatives in France and the Netherlands underscore that a charitable approach, more often than not, entailed a transformative agenda.

In France, this expansion of charitable practices was embodied by the renowned Abbé Pierre. Born Henri Grouès, the abbé had steadily built a reputation as an uncompromising priest. During the German occupation of France, he was active in the French resistance, barely escaping deportation on several occasions. After the war, he moved to Paris, where he founded a small community called Emmaüs, a refuge run by a collective that pledged to work to support themselves and others. Soon the community was not just offering living accommodations to those in need but also building small shelters and semi-permanent homes. Some members began collecting rags and repurposing junk, which could be resold to support their community. The group became famous when Abbé Pierre called attention to the plight of the homeless during the severe winter of 1954 via a radio appeal, eliciting an unexpectedly generous response to his call for donations that were directed towards food and shelter. To make structural improvements that would benefit the homeless, he also asked the government to invest in housing, which eventually resulted in the government ordering the construction of 12,000 emergency housing units. The 1950s and 1960s saw the emergence and evolution of a network of Emmaüs groups throughout France and other parts of the world. Seventy groups from twenty countries would attend an inaugural world assembly in 1969.[32]

Significantly, Abbé Pierre stressed that only solidarity and self-reliance, rather than incidental acts of charity and dependency, could solve poverty. Although the Emmaüs groups were focused on change within their own environment, this philosophy of solidarity and self-reliance was also applied in transnational relations. In 1971, Abbé Pierre transmitted an appeal from Bangladeshi citizens to French communal governments, in which the former hoped to pair French and Bangladeshi municipalities as sister communities. At that time, the country in the Ganges delta was being hit hard by the effects of a civil war and by flooding. Mirroring the efforts of fair trade pioneers in the United States (Self-Help Crafts), Great Britain (Tearfund), and Switzerland ('Jute statt Plastik'), Abbé Pierre ventured that people in Bangladesh could be supported by selling in France what they had made in Bangladesh.[33] Following an example set in surrounding countries, the first French shop specializing in selling products from the South was set up in Paris in 1974 under the umbrella of the organization coordinating the twin-municipality initiative and the Emmaüs network. Many more shops would follow, eventually leading to the foundation of Magasins du Monde, the French branch of the international world shop federation (see Chapter 4).[34]

Although hardly noticed at that time, many of the shops which inspired the Magasins du Monde initiative had, in turn, their roots in a visit to the Emmaüs community in Paris. In fact, an encounter with Abbé Pierre's work would be an important spur to the creation of the alternative trading organization Steun Ontwikkelings Streken (SOS) in the Netherlands, which would in turn found similar outlets in West Germany, Belgium, Switzerland, and Austria. During her summer holidays, 23-year-old Enny Wolak had travelled to Paris to participate in the work of Abbé Pierre. A priest whom Wolak met whilst in Paris subsequently contacted her from his new post in Sicily about the dire lack of medicine and deficiencies in child nutrition. Wolak and her Catholic youth group decided to raise money for powdered milk in their Dutch hometown of Kerkrade. The success of their fundraising inspired a Catholic youth leader, Paul Meijs, to commit to his own efforts in this regard. SOS[35] hosted numerous campaigns to support projects in developing countries during the ensuing years. In 1962, for example, it raised money to fund a hospital and a school for domestic science in Malawi, projects which Catholic missionaries had brought to its attention.[36]

Like its North American and French counterparts, SOS thus developed out of a distinct religious community, gradually extending beyond this community in the course of its activities. Just as SOS initially relied on a worldwide network of Catholic missionaries for its foreign contacts, the network of Catholic churches and political and youth groups was crucial to its work. In the Netherlands, a network spanning churches, youth groups, and missionary societies was called upon to promote fundraising campaigns and to host lectures about SOS's work. SOS's expansion was possible only because of transnational cooperation, however. Looking for support for his initiative, Meijs had turned to the nearby West German city of Aachen, where he established a good relationship with the Catholic development agency Misereor. SOS had much to

Figure 1.2 Paul Meijs presenting handicrafts and coffee imported by SOS. Fair Trade Original.

benefit from the financial support offered by such a large organization, which could also provide contacts with many producer groups and access to West German networks. In return, Misereor regarded SOS's emphasis on self-reliance to be an attractive model for its development activities.[37]

The ambitions of Meijs and his fellow campaigners soon took them beyond Catholic communities. During the 1960s, they would distribute 100,000 leaflets and would cold-call numbers from local phonebooks in the course of their fundraising. In 1960, an attempt to enlist the support of the main Catholic political party, the Katholieke Volkspartij (Catholic People's Party), reinforced this trend in an unexpected way. Party representatives demanded that SOS refrain from issues related to missionary work, in order not to interfere with the work of other organizations in this field. Instead of complying, Paul Meijs redirected his efforts beyond the Catholic community. He also increasingly explored opportunities for transnational expansion. Beyond his contacts in West Germany, he also sought out possibilities in Belgium and eventually in Austria and Switzerland.[38]

Trade, Not Aid: Contesting Development

The campaigns initiated by SOS gravitated towards ideas about development which were common in Western Europe and North America during the 1960s. They entailed supporting 'developing countries' to build 'modern' economies after the Western example. By financing local initiatives with one-off grants and monitoring subsequent progress, social and economic projects would be guided towards self-sufficiency. Positioning SOS somewhere between the philosophies of Edna Byler and SERVV on the one hand and Oxfam on the other, Paul Meijs promoted the selling of products which helped producers in developing countries achieve economic independence, whilst SOS could invest its profits from these products into new projects.[39] Although SOS appealed to the charitable sentiments of potential supporters and buyers, it combined such appeals with the aim of transforming economic and social conditions in the Global South. This fluid relation of charity, self-help, and more encompassing visions of modernization offers us an important window onto the evolution of visions of colonial and postcolonial development, which were rooted not only in an interwar expert culture attempting to apply technological and scientific insights but were also related to activities and modes of thinking in the realm of transnational solidarity.

Handicrafts, more than any other product, embodied this way of thinking about solidarity. Meijs made an extensive explanation of this point in 1971 when he summarized SOS's 'development strategy'. The aim of SOS, he stated, was to provide 'concrete assistance'. Therefore, the items which SOS imported had to improve the lives of as many people as possible. Priority had to be given to those producers living under the direst circumstances. Partners had to be cooperatives redistributing their profits amongst their members, companies contributing to development assistance, or schools supporting these producers' activities by selling their items. They could also be individual missionaries or development workers.[40] Handicrafts were the most obvious sort of product to focus on, because producer groups could usually obtain their raw materials almost free of cost and because it was possible to begin producing and distributing products almost anywhere without serious financial or logistic hurdles. Meijs stressed that making handicrafts should not be regarded as an endpoint but rather as a first step towards creating an 'industrial climate'.[41]

On the buyers' side, handicrafts were equally to be preferred, Meijs argued. More than other sorts of items, handicrafts would incite their buyer's curiosity, transferring something of 'the culture, history and tradition of the countries of origin. When such a product is bought, one wants information about the country where it was made, about its inhabitants, their culture and customs'. As a result, information would not have to be imposed upon consumers – they would ask for it.[42] Notably, his views on this were slightly different from prevailing opinions within Self-Help, SERVV, and Oxfam. Meijs considered handicrafts to be products not available in Western Europe, a judgement that in part depended on the kind of handicrafts imported. SOS's catalogue revolved around slightly exotic woodwork items, whereas the needlework Edna Byler set out more closely resembled what the women she spoke to in the United States and Canada would produce themselves. Oxfam had opted to import handicrafts from Southern producers on a larger scale because the relation between quality and price was better than that of similar gifts then obtainable in the UK. Regardless of these differences, however, they all shared the appreciation for handicrafts as an expression of the producer's culture; selling such products was regarded as a unique opportunity to help people currently on the margins of the global marketplace.

Meijs's particular emphasis in 1971 on the use of handicrafts to transmit information about producers also points to how ideas of transnational solidarity had evolved during the 1960s. It was not only that the organizations discussed earlier had become more professional and had established networks that extended beyond a single religious denomination. They had also adopted and promoted the notion of development through support, an idea which had become widespread within the frameworks of colonial governance and of Europe's postwar reconstruction. Helping distant others was not just a matter of emergency relief or charity. In most instances, it also entailed a vision for a more encompassing transformation of the beneficiaries' situation. At the start of the 1960s, this vision of assistance and development had predominantly been applied to relations between the South and the North, as the United Nations declared the start of the Development Decade

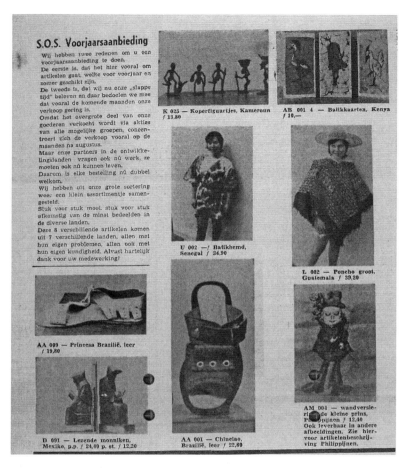

Figure 1.3 A sample of the products advertised and distributed by SOS Wereldhandel in 1973. *Wereldhandel* 1:1 (1973): 4.

under the influence of states across the world attaining political independence. Efforts in the realm of development were promoted in Northern countries by civic groups, which regarded development as an important way to practise solidarity, secure peaceful international relations, and sometimes even foster more profitable trading relations. As the global community stumbled into a postcolonial era, promoting development became a crucial theme in the North and the South alike. Within new campaigns to create a postcolonial world, the activities of alternative trading organizations would be catapulted into a new, and sometimes uncomfortable, context. The intent and practices of alternative trading organizations such as SOS, Selfhelp Crafts, SERVV, Oxfam, and their successors came to be increasingly contentious during the second half of the 1960s, when they became part of a broader fair trade movement. Many new groups and younger activists questioned these organizations' relation to earlier humanitarian initiatives and their commitment to structural improvements – as opposed to sporadic incidental relief efforts. The attacks particularly focused on the idea that alternative trading organizations were rooted in a tradition of charity. Ignoring or downplaying the expanded interpretation of the goals and methods associated with this tradition, many fair trade activists stated that they had moved on from the kind of charitable tradition they disapprovingly supposed alternative trading organizations were upholding. Instead, they anchored their work in a notion of justice, leaving religious and colonial restraints behind and focusing on the structural reforms to which the disadvantaged had a right. In their foundational texts, activists repeatedly distanced themselves from the motive of charity. In the United Kingdom, the informal network of development activists known as the Haslemere Group stated in their 1968 declaration that

> We do not align ourselves with the Third World out of charity. We do so because we are concerned with the health of our own society, because we recognise that it, too, is damaged by an exploitative system. (…) We recognise the value and humanity of the work done by the overseas aid charities and the genuine motivation of many of those who contribute to them, but we refuse to accept this salving of consciences.[43]

Similarly, in the booklet *Je geld of je leven* ('Your money or your life'), the Dutch activist Piet Reckman, from the ecumenical activist group Sjaloom, wrote:

> The UNCTAD-conference in New Delhi signals the end of an era, to which we cannot return. It is the era of the quiet conscience, bought with a few silverlings. Of development aid, which covered up the true issues: a more just distribution of the earthly goods and opportunities.[44]

Statements such as the Haslemere declaration and *Je geld of je leven* broke with a humanitarian tradition which had valued charity. They were important touchstones for initiatives promoting equality in global trade and solidarity with the so-called Third World which emerged during the late 1960s. The Sjaloom group would help to launch the so-called Cane Sugar Campaign in the autumn of 1968 as a reaction to the disappointing results of the second United Nations Conference on Trade and Development in New Delhi (see Chapter 2).

Activists within this network often consciously resisted framing their activities in terms of charitable initiatives, presenting them instead as efforts based on the principles of equality and justice. This emphasis signalled a focus on achieving structural change (rather than merely providing relief) and striving for postcolonial relations between South and North to be based on equality. Additionally, their orientation entailed an inclusive view of those potentially involved, surpassing denominational divides and bridging the gap between secular and religious circles. Consequently, these activists related their work to the sociopolitical analysis and ideological viewpoints of interlocutors in the Global South rather than to distinct groups of producers.

The dismissive view of charity resulted in an ambivalent view of 'old' humanitarianism, which had purportedly not worked towards structural transformation or had even hampered such change by alleviating problems in the short run. Not only was this view articulated by fair trade activists in the late 1960s, but it has also come through in historical accounts. Maggie Black's groundbreaking account of Oxfam describes how, during the 1960s, the organization moved on from relief work and adopted an agenda of international reform, setting out to apply the famous ideas of the economist William Beveridge for a national welfare state – 'freedom from want, from disease, from ignorance, from squalor, and from idleness' – to the whole world.[45] Such aims can also be discerned in the histories of other Western European groups. The activist and journalist Hans Beerends has observed how a 'structural' approach to the predicament of the Global South emerged amongst Dutch Third World activists during the 1960s. At the same time, he noted the considerable variety within this group, which attracted an array of people, ranging from moderate reformers to radical anticapitalists.[46] However, acknowledgement of this diversity often takes a backseat to a more schematic view. In his collaboration with the journalist Marc Broere, for instance, Beerends wrote that 'the rise of the Third World movement in the fifties and sixties was in fact a protest against the (…) illusion that the problem of poverty could be solved by gathering many generous gifts'.[47] Similarly, the German social scientist Claudia Olejniczak has argued that the West German Third World movement had no direct predecessors but was rooted in the international solidarity of left-wing internationalists, omitting any relation it might have had to charitable organizations.[48]

At the end of the 1960s, many activists felt it important to break with a past tradition of charitable work. Doing so allowed them to present their own agenda and mark a new beginning. The shift towards a framework of justice also signalled the emergence of a new discourse revolving around shared human rights rather than moral obligations.[49] Recent historiography on humanitarianism has similarly foregrounded the commitment to human rights and social justice evident since the late 1960s.[50] The narrative of a breakthrough of human rights as the dominant frame of reference for civic activism aligns closely with contemporary activists' proclaimed shift from charity to justice. But the ongoing historicization of human rights has called this periodization into question, with scholars pointing out the historically influential presence of human rights ideas before the 1970s and the continued contestation of its dominance up through the present.[51]

Telling the history of the alternative trading organizations in the 1950s and 1960s enables us to re-evaluate the relation between charity and justice before and after the 1960s. Because scholars of the history of humanitarianism have recently reconsidered the relation between solidarity and humanitarian aid, the permutations of the notion of charity merit special attention.[52] The distress of others has traditionally prompted communities to feel compelled at such moments to reaffirm their sense of righteousness by demonstrating their solidarity through moral and material support. In this sense, charity has usually been connected to notions of justice, in both an immanent and a transcendent sense. Expressing solidarity through actions ranging from prayer and fundraising to actually lending a hand, concerned people had both the plight of others and their own moral standing in mind, demonstrating their good intentions to higher powers and their fellow citizens.

Despite the growing importance of universal human rights and justice during the 1960s, calls to promote the cause of the Global South continued to be underpinned by appeals to the sense of righteousness and moral prestige of communities and 'civilized nations' in the North.[53] At the same time, the history of alternative trading organizations indicates the gradual expansion of the ideas and practices related to charity. The sale of products made by people who were once the recipients of charity shifted the view of them: once regarded as helpless on their own behalf, they now could be seen as individuals who, when given a fair opportunity, could fend for themselves. The sense of a moral obligation to help was thus supplemented by the idea that assistance should result in a structurally altered situation, in which currently disadvantaged people would be self-reliant rather than dependent on the help of others.

The re-evaluation of the shift from charity to justice is part of a more wide-ranging reappraisal of the relation between 'old' and 'new' social movements.[54] Postwar activism has often been divided into histories of social movements like trade unions and co-operatives on one side and 'new' social movements – groups promoting environmental causes, human rights, and fair trade and solidarity with the so-called Third World – on the other. In the case of the Third World movement, its purported radical altruism was put forth as a significant difference from earlier initiatives. Olejniczak has argued that, instead of promoting their own interests, this movement was driven by moral indignation.[55] Similarly, the sociologist Luuk Wijmans opined that the Third World movement was a unique case amongst social movements because it promoted human rights globally, even in the absence of a direct relation to the interests of its members.[56] The historian Konrad Kuhn has made a similar point about the movement in Switzerland, noting that 'the Swiss Third World movement (…) was about enforcing global justice, for which it campaigned without direct community relations'.[57] The history of the alternative trading organizations, however, demonstrates that the borders between older and newer initiatives were fluid: taking up an older tradition of charitable action, these organizations reconceptualized and expanded it, cooperating with traditional institutions such as churches and political parties as well as new campaigns. New initiatives and ideas did not emerge as an alternative to their predecessors but rather were incorporated into the creation of a new amalgam. The decolonization many people in the South attempted during the 1950s and 1960s thus impacted how transnational solidarity was envisioned and practised. Their trading partners and the changing rhetoric of international relations pressured alternative trading organizations to relate their work to ideals of equality and independence. Pioneers such as Edna Byler and Paul Meijs adapted conventional practices like selling products on behalf of others to this new situation, looking to help producers attain economic self-reliance after initial contributions of support and stressing how their handicrafts embodied their artisanal skill and their humanity. This approach was not without its pitfalls, as it tended to reinforce the idea, modelled on an idealized version of Western progress, that there was a universal road to becoming a 'modern' society. Paradoxically, it could also bolster the romanticization of a postcolonial 'other' who possessed the knowledge and willingness to practise crafts which had receded from the everyday lives of those who bought their products in Western Europe and the United States. In the new, postcolonial world, the imagined division between South and North grew more influential and their respective properties were reimagined. People in the South were primarily envisioned as producers of raw materials and traditional handicrafts in need of (temporary) support. Those in the North were predominantly conceived as consumers in a position to support distant others, even as they were in danger of losing their own craft traditions to progress.

2 SUGAR
Goodbye to Grand Politics

On 3 December 1968, a rather shabby-looking man with a long white beard approached the Netherlands' minister of economic affairs at the Binnenhof – the heart of Dutch political affairs in The Hague – wearing a mitre and a robe. In plain sight, he handed a parcel to the minister. It contained a heart made of cane sugar, accompanied by the words 'Put a heart into the world economy'.[1] This playful hint at the traditional celebration of Saint Nicholas in the Netherlands was part of a national demonstration mounted during the Cane Sugar Campaign – a campaign launched by Dutch solidarity activists in the autumn 1968 to support demands from the Global South for global trade reform. The campaign's stated goal was to render visible the 'structure of world trade disadvantageous to developing countries' through the use of sugar as a telling example.[2]

As the cane sugar activists announced their campaign to citizens across Western Europe, people throughout the world acknowledged its objectives and actions. With European economic policies as a common target, the leaders of the campaign successfully forged a Europe-wide network of likeminded groups. By 1971, however, it was clear that Europe was dividing as much as it was uniting them. National perspectives on the European project were divergent, and activists struggled to find ways to impact European politics. 'The illusion that the European Economic Community contributes anything to unifying Europe, let alone the world, is already very old and very worn down', an anonymous activist observed in 1971.[3] Cane sugar would be the commodity which embodied the criticism and the hope for change, as well as eventual disillusion.

Figure 2.1 Cane Sugar Campaign members present a heart made out of cane sugar to the Dutch minister of Economic Affairs, Leo de Block, in The Hague on 3 December 1968. National Archives, The Hague, Collection Anefo/Ron Kroon.

The history of the Cane Sugar Campaign from 1968 to 1974 demonstrates how decolonization and Europeanization became intertwined in the daily lives of Western Europeans. People in the South and the North did not undergo these processes passively but positioned themselves to shape them. Within the framework of a social history of globalization, the campaign brings to the fore different approaches to impacting globalization. Whereas alternative trading organizations practised fair trade primarily in the form of buying and selling products so as to exert immediate impact, the Cane Sugar Campaign revolved around impacting international political and economic governance. Buying and selling, if practised at all by these activists, were aimed at raising awareness about political issues rather than providing immediate support to producers. Yet the desire to act on behalf of marginalized producers enabled the cooperation of fair trade advocates whose emphases varied. European economic and political integration provided them, moreover, with a common perspective in thinking about their position in the world. This proved an important catalyst for their establishment of a European network and corresponding campaigns, even though their actions would have little impact on institutional politics. The demise of this campaign sheds new light on a trajectory which became apparent during the second half of the 1960s, an arc that can also be observed amongst other 'new social movements'. Fair trade activists' optimistic outlook on global and European politics as a focal point for swift and drastic transformation – a view of 'grand politics' – gave way to a more incremental view of change, which focused first and foremost on local activism. Hopes for a postcolonial world in which the Global South would not just be politically but also economically autonomous knit global and European politics together during the 1960s. Rather than representing distinct levels of thought and action, now global, European, national, and local frames of reference had become intertwined, realigning themselves according to presumed opportunities and experiences. The demise of 'grand politics', then, did not imply reduced ambitions to shape postcolonial globalization. Rather, it entailed a shift of the primary locus of change away from international politics and towards the immediate environment.

Europe has not figured prominently in the histories of the social activism of the 1960s and 1970s. The growing body of scholarship on European integration has also remained relatively silent on the relation to globalization, particularly as it presented itself to Europeans.[4] The historiography of social movements such as the fair trade movement has traditionally emphasized local and national manifestations. Increased attention to transnational history has also brought the global dimension considerable notice in recent years.[5] However, European integration had made Europe a relevant frame of reference for civil society actors by the 1960s, as is clearly visible in the history of trade unions, in which European cooperation became an important dimension.[6] Scholarship on the history of the consumer movement has also illustrated Europe's importance for relatively new forms of social action.[7] As the sociologists Douglas Imig and Sidney Tarrow have claimed, European integration redirects the expectations and actions of social movements towards European-level governance.[8] The history of fair trade highlights that 'Europe' indeed mattered to European citizens during the 1960s and 1970s, and it was closely related to the way they positioned themselves as global citizens. Europe served as a carrier for hopes of sweeping global transformations, and it was also a political target for joint campaigns and a relevant space in which to establish a network. This chapter highlights how, from the perspective of civic activists and their allies, neither globalization nor European integration developed in a straightforward fashion. This is evident from the cane sugar activists' presentation of the entanglement between Europe and global trade, as well as the limited extent to which Europe could unite them despite this common framework and their difficulties in impacting European politics. The shifting relation of global, European, and local perspectives becomes particularly apparent when we survey the eventual demise of the Cane Sugar Campaign around 1974. The Europe-wide network of likeminded groups nonetheless survived the demise of 'grand politics'. It continued to provide a means for fair trade activists to connect with one another even as they prioritized incremental and local change, enabling a continuous exchange of ideas and repertoires and preparing the ground for the establishment of transnational fair trade organizations during the 1980s and 1990s.

The impulse to strive for a systemic reform of global economic structures came from what was by the 1960s being called the 'Third World'. Through this dialogue on the political economy of trade, the range of interlocutors within fair trade activism expanded from marginalized producers to politicians and intellectuals representing a more generalized vision of global inequality. Taking up traditions of anticolonial struggle and Pan-Africanism, leaders of countries from Asia, Africa, and Latin America such as Indonesia's Sukarno, India's Nehru, Egypt's Nasser, and Ghana's Nkrumah discussed their position in a world order now dominated by the Cold War.[9] Instead of a divide between East and West, these countries proposed to view global relations in terms of a divide between North and South.[10] Assuming their economic dependence on industrialized nations to be one of the crucial factors hindering their development, these countries channelled their collective political weight into international politics. As a result of decolonization in the 1950s and 1960s, the number of states willing to associate with this movement increased rapidly. During the 1960s, they could muster a majority of votes at the United Nations.[11] This majority ensured the adoption of a UN resolution to set up the United

Nations Conference on Trade and Development (UNCTAD) for 1964, with the insistence in a following resolution that this conference take steps in the direction of self-sustaining growth for developing countries.[12]

Neither the 1964 and 1968 UNCTAD conferences nor the more limited attempts to negotiate single commodities brought about manifest improvements for developing countries. Competing national interests as well as regional agreements hampered the negotiations.[13] In particular, the Common Agricultural Policy, a cornerstone of the European Economic Community (EEC), contributed to the stalling of the UNCTAD negotiations during the spring of 1968. It encouraged sugar production within the EEC and fixed its price. It inserted an additional level of negotiation, binding the European participants at the UNCTAD conferences and regulating the relations of EEC countries with their respective former colonies separately from their relations to other sugar-producing countries.

The failure to achieve change at these international conferences led European observers to conclude that change would have to be initiated elsewhere. Encouraged by conversations with delegates from the Global South, correspondents engaged with issues of global development pointed out Europe's crucial role. In this vein, the Dutch journalist Dick Scherpenzeel speculated that European politicians could become more forthcoming if the general public in their countries were made aware of the issues.[14] He had become a vocal critic of Western development policies due to his conversations with representatives from African, Asian, and South American countries during international conferences. Scherpenzeel's reports fed into the activism being pursued in countries like the Netherlands. 'The political unwillingness of the rich countries has been exposed', concluded the energetic and articulate activist Piet Reckman after the disappointing second UNCTAD conference in 1968. 'Isolated actions to achieve a little increase in the budget for development aid are no longer meaningful', the representative of the ecumenical group Sjaloom continued. In past years, the group had initiated several campaigns to promote global equality, and the course of the UNCTAD conference reinforced this commitment. 'After New Delhi, we have to find a completely new strategy. They in the South. We in the North'.[15]

Attempts to transform the structures of global trade in favour of developing countries thus resonated with activists in

Europe, where since the 1950s a host of groups had been devoting their attention to issues such as emergency relief, the problems of development, transnational solidarity, and notions of global citizenship. The Third World's appeal for radical European groups has drawn the most attention from historians.[16] However, the coalition which emerged around the issue of fair trade at the end of the 1960s is just as remarkable for the broad range of groups it managed to integrate. Its supporters could be found amongst secular and Christian groups, radicals and moderates, young and old. Youth groups, student organizations, church groups, and political parties found common ground. Despite many differences in views and styles of engagement, they could collaborate because of a shared concern over global tensions stemming from inequality and their common frustration over the unsatisfying results of intergovernmental negotiations.

Regarding the politics of global trade, which cane sugar came to symbolize, fair trade activism reacted more explicitly than heretofore to the emergence of a postcolonial world, as representatives of the Global South, European politicians, and fair trade activists alike attempted to shape this new era.[17] People in Western Europe came to grasp the intricate connections between the global and the European spheres. Not only was the EEC a crucial player in global trade. The existence of transnational governing institutions at the United Nations and on the European level also led fair trade activists to believe that swift, far-reaching changes to the system of global trade were within reach during the second half of the 1960s.

The new strategy proposed by the Sjaloom group aimed to change public opinion by targeting not just politicians and administrators but individual consumers as well. 'It's about sugar and cacao. Including therefore any consumer of these commodities of world trade'. If regular consumers could demand to buy the products which were being kept out of the European markets due to import tariffs and subsidies for European products, they would be able to make a difference. 'At least by taking at face value what we have always been told: "The customer is king"', Reckman exhorted, invoking a well-known mantra of postwar consumer society. 'Well then, the customer king from now on demands cane sugar from his grocer'.[18]

Rallying around Cane Sugar

A group of Amsterdam students, who had become concerned about global inequality through lectures and international student exchanges, ambitiously took up these ideas. Cane sugar presented itself as an ideal product to rally around. This type of sugar was extracted from two-to-five-metre-high tropical plants that branched out in up to twenty stalks. Harvesting these stalks and crushing the cane to process it made for strenuous and dirty work. Producing sugar from sugarcane had been part of the colonial exploitation of people and land, compelling labourers to perform degrading work and using up large swathes of land.[19] These circumstances were little known to the group of young people who singled out cane sugar as the focal point of a campaign to protest the unfair structures of global trade in 1968. The advocates of the Cane Sugar Campaign urged their fellow citizens to put their power as consumers to work by demanding this kind of sugar. However, buying cane sugar was not the ultimate aim but rather served as a means to achieve a larger goal. The campaign's initiators regarded the buying of cane sugar to be primarily a symbolic political act made on the behalf of people in the Global South. The group's focus was not on the volume of sales but rather on drawing public attention to the systemic imbalances in the structures which continued to mark global trade after decolonization.

In sharp contrast to the dire conditions under which plantation workers had to harvest the cane, cane sugar was relatively easily extracted and transported. By the 1960s, it had long been a politicized product.[20] As far back as the late eighteenth century, it had been targeted as 'blood-stained sugar' by British antislavery activists because slave labour on cane sugar plantations was widespread.[21] Under the rule of Napoleon, producing beet sugar domestically, instead of importing cane sugar, had become a symbol of continental European autonomy. As an agricultural product, cane sugar was at the heart of the structural inequality in global trade which economists and politicians from the Global South had challenged since the 1950s. Whereas the prices of industrial commodities were steadily rising, the prices of raw materials such as cane sugar had lost ground in relative value. People in the South had to produce more in order to buy the same amount. Though nominally cheaper than beet sugar on the global market, cane sugar was more expensive for the average buyer as a result of European agricultural and economic policies. Because sugar was regarded as a basic household product, its price was of great interest to the public. Trade relations dating back to colonial times ensured that cane sugar would be available, through the intermediary of Dutch wholesalers, for shopkeepers (and now, for activists) to sell.[22]

The Amsterdam students' first attempts to sell cane sugar emboldened them to form a committee which planned a large-scale campaign for the autumn of 1968. After finding a wholesaler to provide them with the requisite amount of cane sugar, gathering support from prominent figures such as the outspoken and influential economists Jan Tinbergen and Gunnar Myrdal, and devising promotional material, the committee was ready for action by the end of the summer.[23] In the course of these preparations, the social base of the campaign was decidedly broadened. The students reached out to political organizations across the party landscape and contacted Catholic and Protestant churches, along with a host of other outlets. Their outreach also cut across age groups, involving a host of sympathetic people beyond their own age cohort.

The Cane Sugar Campaign marked a shift from fair trade as a mode of incremental transformation to an effort to reform the system of global trade. This emphasis on changing the structure of international trade was distinct from the earlier manifestations of the fair trade movement discussed in Chapter 1.[24] In this sense, the fair trade movement only really began around this time, as the unfairness of global trade relations became the issue around which the Cane Sugar Campaign rallied. The activists who drew attention to the unfair structures of trade gradually also influenced other groups and organizations around them, as already noted with regard to the alternative trading organizations.

On 30 September 1968 the Cane Sugar Campaign officially kicked off. Local action groups were provided with several ways to draw public attention to the issue of cane sugar and the inequalities of world trade. 'The aim is to bring about a change of mentality, which will force the government, facing a new attitude amongst its citizens, to choose the side of the poor countries in international negotiations', the campaign brochure stated.[25] Locally, the campaign groups reached out to churches, town councils, political

Figure 2.2 A sugar bag used in the cane sugar campaign. Private collection Peter van Dam.

parties, trade unions, and many other contacts to promote their campaign. Individual consumers were asked to demand cane sugar at grocery stores of their choosing. Cane sugar was also sold door-to-door by certain groups. Organizations and individuals alike were called upon to substitute cane sugar for beet sugar, thus directing attention to the global and European trade regulations which put producers from the South at a disadvantage.[26]

The particular position of Europe in a postcolonial world was a crucial issue right from the start of the campaign. In line with the aim above all to inform the public about the unfair structures of global trade, the campaign committee had created amply documented promotional material. The activists' background in a student movement which prized intellectual substantiation and their claim to expertise were unmistakable. The brochure informing the public about the issue took a clear aim at Europe: 'They receive 15 cents per kilo of sugar, we pay 60 cents per kilo of sugar on export subsidies', it stated. 'The EEC countries should admit the cane sugar producing countries to their markets', the brochure's authors continued.[27] Page after page of documentation brought up the role of the EEC. During the UNCTAD negotiations on sugar, EEC members had displayed a 'bewildering' attitude. They had demanded a special position for the EEC regarding production subsidies and import tariffs. Moreover, the subsidy policy and the protectionism pursued by the Community encouraged overproduction of European sugar producers, even as producers in developing countries were depending on their sugar exports for direly needed income. The EEC therefore acted in a way that was 'strongly inward-looking, selfishly and short-sightedly', the authors concluded. National governments, for their part, hid behind their EEC membership, pledging their sympathy to developing countries whilst blaming their lack of concessions on European commitments.[28]

The importance of European politics to the issue of global trade was reaffirmed when the considerable public acclaim bestowed on the Cane Sugar Campaign did not trigger a corresponding political response. During a radio debate about the campaign, the labour politician Henk Vredeling noted his approval of the attempts to raise awareness about the inequalities of world trade and to encourage citizens to act. As for the political consequences, however, he deemed the influence of Dutch officials to be very limited. Their earlier attempts to improve European agricultural policies had proved ineffective, Vredeling noted. He therefore took issue with the campaign being organized predominantly on the local and national level. A European issue had to be addressed on a European scale.[29] Even those less sympathetic to the campaign concurred. Dutch sugar producers countered with a brochure of which 50,000 were sold and another 120,000 distributed for free.[30] It regarded inequality in the global sugar trade to be a problem beyond the reach of Dutch consumers to solve. What was needed, according to the Dutch sugar industry, was a more effective system of global regulations.[31]

Realizing that national governments of European states were bound by common agreements regarding international trade, the Cane Sugar Campaign took particular aim at European economic policies. All the ingredients for a successful internationalization seemed to be in place: the sugar trade, a distinctly international phenomenon, was one of the few commodities at the end of the 1960s to be served by a functioning framework for international trade. That this commerce was regulated both at an international and a European level ensured a common framework for activists. Along with the efforts of international governing bodies such as UNCTAD, European integration thus fostered the hopes for 'grand politics' by providing activists with a target that promised far-reaching change in a relatively short amount of time. The Cane Sugar Campaign therefore focused on a European public, and its activities were accompanied by the attempt to establish a network which could support a Europe-wide campaign.

From early on in the campaign, the Dutch activists attempted to bring their concerns to other Western European countries. During the national demonstration held in December 1968 at the seat of the Dutch government in The Hague, protesters carried signs in English so as to reach an international audience (see figure 2.1). In January 1969, the campaign's secretariat drafted a letter in English summarizing its goals, its overall concept, and the practical opportunities to participate in the campaign. This first letter was sent to around 1,000 international contacts.[32] From then on, such letters were regularly updated and sent out across Europe. By the end of 1970, the activists proudly presented the results of their attempts to connect with interested parties abroad, noting ample attention to the campaign across Europe. Their key publication had sold 40,000 copies, and cane sugar consumption had doubled since 1968. On the less positive side of the ledger, the political pressure exerted by the campaign had only been 'moderately successful'. The Dutch Parliament, though expressing sympathy for its goals, had not taken any concrete actions. The European Parliament and the EEC Commission had considered the issue as well, but without tangible consequences. 'Changes in the EEC sugar policy are unthinkable unless there is political pressure in the other member countries as well', the campaigners wrote. By then, the coordinating committee estimated that around 2,000 international contacts had received information about the campaign.[33]

The attempts to expand the initiative across the Dutch border had some effect. In 1969, the World Council of Churches, in cooperation with the ecumenical Committee on Society, Development and Peace, recommended the initiative as an example of how churches could become involved in economic justice initiatives.[34] The Working Congress of Action Groups on International Development, convened in Egmond aan Zee at the beginning of April 1970, was a next attempted step towards internationalization. The conference was hosted by X min Y, a Dutch initiative for self-taxation on behalf of developing countries which had emerged from an earlier Sjaloom campaign. Its invitations had brought together some eighty activists from all over the world, most based in Western Europe, to gather at a holiday resort owned by the Dutch social democratic trade union federation. Participants travelled from Austria, Belgium, Denmark, England, France, West Germany, Italy, Peru, Sweden, Switzerland, and Yugoslavia with the aim of bringing about 'internationalized development action'.[35] This international gathering of activists was structured like international convenings such as the UNCTAD conferences: a general assembly meeting was to be followed by a breakout into smaller groups, which would discuss specific issues and report back to the general assembly. Amidst debates about several aspects of development action such as education and political pressure, liberation movements, and strategies for development, the viability of internationalizing the cane sugar campaign was discussed in a section on consumer action.[36]

Amongst the participants discussing development activism were delegates from both European and so-called developing

Figure 2.3 Harvesting sugar cane. The Leprosy Mission International. Wellcome Collection.

countries. At the time the Argentine union organizer Emilio Máspero, leader of the Christian-democratic Confederación latinoamerica de sindacalistos cristianos, drew most of the attention with his rousing speech about the legacy of colonialism and the evils of global capitalism. Yet the conversations during the working-group sessions may have been more eye-opening. Despite the attempts to gather extensive information about cane sugar, the campaign had mainly considered the system of global trade, to the relative neglect of the situation on the ground. Informed by participants who were knowledgeable about the situation in countries like Jamaica and Suriname, where cane sugar was grown, discussion about the campaign turned to the appalling conditions of workers on cane sugar plantations. Part of a 'slave culture', the work involved in the production of cane sugar 'degraded human beings and destroyed their dignity'. Adding insult to injury, production was mainly controlled by European firms. The campaign would thus have to include attempts to pressure these firms to improve working conditions in the sugar cane industry.[37]

Another issue the participants brought forward concerned the production of sugar in Europe: if it did not decrease, then

European consumption of beet sugar as an alternative to cane sugar would lead the European sugar surplus to be dumped on the international market, resulting in lower prices for cane sugar. The campaign would have to aim to reduce sugar production in Europe to achieve its aims. Finally, the report noted that the campaign could strengthen the economic ties between unequal partners. The dependency of the weaker partners in this relationship had been exposed during earlier economic crises, which had led to lesser demand for their products and services. In other words, development action should aim to increase the independence of developing countries, not their dependence on rich countries.[38] Environmental concerns were notably absent from these discussions. In the final report, 'nature' was used only to refer to character, and 'environment' only signalled sociopolitical contexts.

A European Campaign

Despite the criticism, the meeting ended with a discussion of the concrete possibilities for the campaign's internationalization. The participants agreed to exchange information relevant to the Cane Sugar Campaign. They decided to pursue actions that would pressure EEC members to sign the International Sugar Agreement, which had not previously been pursued due to the incongruity between the aims of the international deliberations and the EEC's policy on sugar production. The applications of four new members to the EEC were deemed an issue deserving collective action in order to prevent these countries from gaining admission 'at the expense of underdeveloped countries'. In conclusion, the participants agreed on the need to find an institution capable of coordinating international activities and on the desirability of sugar as a first focus of collective consumer actions.[39]

During the conference, a plan was launched to create an international secretariat, with the Third World Centre of the World Student Christian Federation in Geneva proposed as its location. Eventually, however, representatives of X min Y tasked themselves with hosting the international correspondence.[40] In the months following the meeting, they pushed for the rapid establishment of an international sugar campaign, in light of impending negotiations about British accession to the EEC.[41] International coordination proved almost impossible. The pace of the negotiations could hardly be reconciled with the practical challenges of coordinating a host of activist groups scattered throughout Europe. The first step towards a collective campaign was to be an open letter by the supporting groups to representatives of the ten governments involved in the negotiations, the EEC Council of Ministers, and the European Commission. The letter urged the negotiating parties to consider the interests of the Global South in their decisions. It was eventually presented on 21 July 1970, with signatories from all countries involved except Norway and Luxembourg. The transnational coalition, however, had not managed to initiate many local and national events in support of their aims.[42]

The ambition to organize a second wave of Europe-wide activities in the autumn of 1970 also proved too ambitious. Instead, Dutch representatives of the Cane Sugar Campaign and British members of the World Development Movement (WDM) met for a bilateral consultation on the Cane Sugar Campaign.[43] WDM had been founded in 1970, as certain members of Oxfam's staff had become vocal about the priority being given to educating the British public and targeting government policies instead of overseas 'development' activities. Rather than redirecting Oxfam's outlook and reconsidering its legal status as a charitable organization, WDM was established as an independent outlet which would focus on educating the public about global inequality's causes and possible solutions and on lobbying for policy changes.[44] Picking up on the Cane Sugar Campaign and reacting to the EEC membership negotiations, WDM planned its Europe '73 campaign in hopes that the trade terms for developing countries would be made a priority. Additionally, the European member states should be pushed to provide more development aid.[45]

The run-up to the campaign demonstrated the tensions that emerged amongst people promoting transnational solidarity due to this overtly political approach. Volunteers for Oxfam were invited to participate in local meetings to help plan and promote the campaign, which would revolve around a weeklong series of local and national events to be held around the beginning of December 1973.[46] Margaret Sargent, a volunteer who had attended one such meeting in Kensington with her husband, wrote to Oxfam to express her bewilderment. Although she thought herself 'politically very naïve', she recognized the importance of the topic but had felt overwhelmed by the approach presented by WDM's representatives. She seconded a remark made by another Oxfam volunteer present at the meeting, who had asked the hosts: 'Are you expecting us to dabble in the very complex matters of overseas trade and international agreements, which experts take years to study?'[47] Responding to her letter, an Oxfam official replied that Oxfam staff often observed that their overseas efforts were negated by political and economic structures. Volunteers could indeed not be expected to become experts in these complicated issues, but if WDM provided concise information, then Oxfam volunteers could become involved in the campaign. By attempting 'to persuade all those who influence European affairs to think more for the poor and less of themselves', this sort of participation and advocacy would tie right in with Oxfam's current work.[48]

Members of the WDM presented Prime Minister Edward Heath with a heart of cane sugar in November, echoing what their Dutch counterparts had done two years earlier in The Hague. The WDM called particular attention to the fate of sugar producers within the British Commonwealth. Due to the UK's planned accession to the EEC, cane sugar imports to England from Commonwealth countries such as Barbados, Jamaica, Fiji, and Mauritius were under threat, as they could soon be substituted by the sugar surplus produced within the EEC.[49] At the same time, local groups distributed leaflets and more than 200,000 packets of cane sugar amongst the public; they also held sugar-tasting competitions and addressed their members of parliament on the subject.[50]

The protest warning of the effects of EEC admission for sugar cane farmers demonstrates how the opposition to the UK joining the EEC forged an unstable amalgam of – amongst others – conservative nationalists, Commonwealth business interests, trade unionists concerned about job security for British sugar-industry workers, and Third-World activists pragmatically trying to salvage the privileges of former British colonies.[51] This coalition was especially uneasy for the latter group of activists, who found themselves cooperating with business representatives they would usually oppose. According to Clifford Longley of *The Times* (London), the WDM was quietly supported by the Commonwealth Sugar

Exporters' bureau and its powerful director, John Southgate.[52] Paradoxically, Third-World activists found themselves siding with the sugar industry, hoping that a system of preferences based on colonial ties would be sustained.

Europe divided activists as much as it united them. European political and economic integration provided them with a common cause, but the relevant timetables and political priorities diverged considerably depending on the country. The difference between the initial approach followed by the Dutch Cane Sugar Campaign and how its later British counterpart proceeded was striking to the members of the transnational coalition which had been forged in Egmond aan Zee. Whereas the Dutch campaign had aimed to change trading policies, the British version attempted to retain the favourable conditions under which former British colonies exported sugar to Great Britain.[53] Nevertheless, the pioneers of the transnational cane sugar coalition urged likeminded activists to support the British campaign. They could lend it additional weight by sending and publishing letters to stakeholders, demanding an explanation for the lack of a response to the previous open letter and reiterating their request to consider the interests of the South during the negotiations.[54]

Not much pressure was needed to persuade the British government to place special emphasis on the future of the Commonwealth sugar production within the EEC. Alongside New Zealand dairy products, sugar was a crucial issue for government negotiators.[55] To the dismay of many cane sugar activists outside Great Britain, the Commonwealth countries accepted the results of these negotiations, which included a substantial commitment by the British government to import cane sugar in the years following its admission to the EEC.[56] Europe remained a prime target of the protest activities mounted by the WDM. A nationwide advertisement in 1972 called on the public to 'Help turn Europe inside out', because – amongst other things – developing countries were denied free entry to the European market for cane sugar. Europe's trade policies were 'keeping them poor', and the British government, for its part, was neglecting the interests of poorer Commonwealth members.[57]

The coalition containing those critical of British EEC membership and the WDM could therefore persist after the period of negotiations had passed. The issue of cane sugar remained valuable to the movement both as a concrete bond between their campaign and sugar-industry workers and as a highly visible example of the inequality of international trade. Moreover, it was relatively easy to find support on this issue, because the interests of British workers were at least rhetorically united with those in developing countries; a foreign 'Europe' could be presented as the main problem. In 1973, in the wake of the UK joining the EEC at the beginning of the year, members of the movement joined workers from the cane sugar refining company Tate & Lyle in a protest march of about 2,000 people over the imminent fate of cane sugar in Britain. Whilst the workers were primarily concerned with their job security in an industrial sector which had come under increased pressure due to Common Market regulations, WDM activists stressed the needs of workers in developing countries, who also depended on British sugar cane imports. The protesters united behind slogans like 'keep the cane' and 'beat the beet'.[58]

The developments in Great Britain demonstrate how Europe at once aligned and divided transnational activism. The battle against the EEC united those focused on the potential loss of jobs in Britain with those concerned by the developing countries' trading position with Europe. At the same time, the relations of British activists with development advocates in other European countries were hindered by the EEC issue because the British activists claimed a special position for developing countries from the Commonwealth. Spokespeople from other countries deemed such privilege a neo-colonial arrangement. The distinct timetable of the British negotiations also impeded the coordination of a collective European cane sugar campaign, which had been planned for 1971.

As the initiative in Britain proceeded, so did preparations elsewhere. The international secretariat reported inaugural local actions in Belgium and the translation of the booklet on cane sugar into German in November 1970. Activists in Italy, France, and Denmark had also been in contact about setting up a campaign.[59] The West German campaign was planned by Aktion Selbstbesteuerung.[60] Elaborating on their plans, one of the organization's members, Werner Gebert, recalled how Dutch activists had presented their initiative at the international congress and proposed that it be transformed into an international campaign in order to

Figure 2.4 Poster of the Cane Sugar Campaign in West Germany. Private collection Paul van Tongeren.

effectively challenge the EEC's sugar policy. Even though British fellow-activists had had to start their campaign earlier, the international campaign remained desirable, according to Gebert, precisely because the sugar trade concerned all EEC member states.

Moreover, the focus on sugar would raise the general public's awareness of international inequality and help those affected by it to better understand its nature.[61]

As with the British campaign, West German activists adopted the ideas, repertoire, and even the literature which had initially been developed in the Netherlands. These similarities amongst the campaigns in several European countries and the transnational network sustaining them suggest that their endeavours should be regarded as an overarching transnational campaign. The members of the West German preparatory group planned to sell or hand out bags of cane sugar, accompanied by informative flyers, eye-catching posters, and possibly street theatre and audio messages. However, the packaging for and means of distributing a sufficient amount of cane sugar to support such an undertaking were not available in early 1971. Here ambitions hardly matched the means to realize them. Attempts to bring large organizations in as participants had failed. Gebert stated that he expected that churches, trade unions, and large charities would be interested in participating, based on their declared aims and philosophy.[62] The optimism surrounding the launch of a cane sugar campaign in West Germany was shared by fellow-activists in the Netherlands, who – alluding to the German word for cane (*Rohr*) – expected the *Ruhrgebiet* (the Ruhr) to be transformed into a *Rohrgebiet*.[63]

Drawing interest from several sides, the West German cane sugar campaign was nevertheless crowded out by other initiatives and lacked the support of resourceful organizations. Members of the Aktion 3. Welt Handel, who coordinated many initiatives to promote fair trade with the aid of the main churches, signalled that they had no capacity to participate.[64] Amongst the leadership of the Protestant churches, the question whether such local initiatives should be supported to promote development was decided only in 1973.[65] Many likeminded activists were sympathetic to the initiative, but their sympathies did not translate into tangible financial or personnel support.[66] Still, the campaign mustered around 10,000 signatures on a petition addressed to the Federal Ministry of Economic Cooperation.[67]

Considering these difficulties, it must have been quite a surprise to hear the cane sugar campaign suddenly mentioned in the Bundestag. On 16 June 1972 the West German minister of economic cooperation, Erhard Eppler, had to answer questions about the campaign. Gerd Ritgen, a Christian Democrat expert on agricultural policy, demanded to know whether Eppler's department had subsidized Aktion Selbstbesteuerung to help set up a cane sugar campaign. Eppler – renowned for his Third-Worldist sympathies – replied that funds had been provided to Aktion Selbstbesteuerung but not for this particular campaign. Ritgen pressed Eppler: Did the Minister regard sugar to be a product exemplifying the need for change in relations vis-à-vis developing countries? His answer was telling for the fate of the campaign. Although cane sugar could indeed be easily produced in developing countries, Eppler noted, the EEC had already decided not to allocate any further agricultural plots for beet sugar in its territory, so that developing countries might cover possible rises in demand for sugar. Moreover, although the sugar industries in developing and developed countries had fiercely competed with each other during the 1960s, the global sugar market had been marked by scarcity, and accordingly, sugar prices had risen considerably in recent years.[68] Even though the campaign had not effected significant change in European sugar policies, sugar was thus no longer a suitable rallying point. A combination of the complexities of the global sugar trade, the technocratic and distant nature of European economic policies, and cane sugar's loss of symbolic value had deflated the campaign.

European politics lost its appeal for activists as the Cane Sugar Campaign waned. Cane sugar itself was at least partly to blame: the circumstances which had made it an exemplary illustration of the imbalances of global trade had gradually evaporated around the turn of the decade. The exhaustive attention brought to cane sugar had unearthed tensions and complications amongst supporters of the campaign. Conversations with activists with first-hand knowledge about the plantations had highlighted their appalling working conditions. Profits from selling cane sugar were pocketed by companies – many of which were regarded critically by activists. In particular, much of the cane sugar sold in the Netherlands turned out to have been imported from Suriname, then part of the Dutch Commonwealth. There was all the more reason to be critical about the sugar's origin, because the sugarcane plantation was owned by a Dutch company, which thus benefitted from the campaign more than Surinamese workers did.[69] A group of agricultural students from the Dutch city of Wageningen which was particularly active in this debate, pointed out that selling cane sugar from developing countries would only make farmers in those countries more dependent on the West, whilst also pitting Dutch activists against farmers in their own country, though these farmers were also victims of a capitalist mode of production.[70] The environmental impact of cane sugar production was once again neglected despite the agricultural expertise these students brought to bear on the matter.

During the 1970s, moreover, the changing status of cane sugar on the global market caused its illustrative potential to be diminished. Potential sugar shortages became a vivid prospect for governments and companies. As a result, concerns about the impact of the preferential treatment of former British colonies were swept away. The EEC continued to buy large quantities of cane sugar from developing countries after the United Kingdom's entry in 1973 and the renegotiations with the associated developing countries in 1974. Moreover, skyrocketing sugar prices made consumers in EEC countries the beneficiaries of the existing sugar regulations. In 1968, consumers could be roused by the notion that they were paying prices well above those elsewhere on the world market. Now the contrary was true: sugar prices within the EEC had been markedly lower since the early 1970s, and the sugar shortages being felt in other parts of the world were also kept at bay.[71]

Sugar also came to hold a relatively unusual position in global trade. One of the few products to be governed by effective international market regulations, it was also one of the few primary commodities to yield good returns on the world market during the 1970s. Sugar could thus not provide an illustration of one of the main problems of developing countries: they usually had to sell their primary commodities at steadily decreasing prices, whilst paying increasing prices for the industrial products they imported from richer countries.[72] As the developmental ideal of an international division of labour – which would have led to an increase of international interdependency to the benefit of all – was replaced by the ideal of autarchy and the accompanying diversification of national production branches, the focus on importing cane sugar from developing countries gradually lost its appeal.

Cane sugar's loss of persuasiveness in this regard partly resulted from the new knowledge about its production and from changes in the global market. It was also affected by a larger crisis in the approach to fair trade. There was little room to pressure European policies, which were technocratic and removed from the national political arenas in which the campaign primarily operated. The notion that cane sugar could be substituted for beet sugar to the benefit of all was no longer tenable. The activists had failed to influence European-level policy and were similarly unsuccessful in pressuring the negotiations at the third UNCTAD in 1972. The great expectations for a transnational solution to the problem of unequal global trade evaporated.

Searching for an alternative vantage point, some fair trade activists adopted a radical perspective, which broke with the notion of increasing mutual interdependence. Instead, people in the First and Third Worlds were regarded as united in their struggle against their mutual oppressors, namely capitalists. For instance, in 1975 a group of former Cane Sugar Campaigners in the Dutch city of Amstelveen came up with the *riet-biet-aktie*, or cane-beet campaign. They offered cane sugar and beet sugar for sale at a local shopping centre. Their layout was accompanied by noticeboards informing the shopping public about the pros and cons of buying cane sugar. In ensuing conversations with passersby, group members attempted to elucidate how farmers and other ordinary people in developing and developed countries alike were victims of the capitalist system.[73] Even though this view set aside local and translocal differences, its ideological radicalism and lack of nuance were rejected by many supporters of fair trade, a movement which in its origins had been overwhelmingly oriented towards reform.

Rather than clinging to sugar, most fair trade activists moved on. A broader outlook had characterized the movement even as it had prioritized the Cane Sugar Campaign. Several different issues and approaches had been presented at the congress in Egmond aan Zee. Consequently, the international secretariat of development activists established there mustered several other attempts at coordinated actions after the collective Cane Sugar Campaign failed. The European network continued to explore new ideas and repertoires of action, which often shifted the focus of social action towards the local level. In November 1971, one year and a half after the first meeting, ninety representatives of Third-World countries living in Europe, Western European action groups, and international organizations met to consult with one another in the Belgian town of Dworp.[74] They decided that the secretariat would not take a leading role in directing activities. Rather, it would serve as a channel to provide likeminded groups throughout Europe with information and contacts.[75] Two new attempts at coordinated international action did follow: led by the WDM, associated members tried to define a common approach for the third UNCTAD meeting in Santiago, Chile, in 1972. A year later, a delegation of development action groups met with representatives of the European Commission in Brussels to talk about the relation between an enlarged EEC and the Third World. Associated groups were asked to engage in accompanying actions to draw additional attention to the meeting.[76]

The meetings and communications facilitated by the international secretariat did not result in a new collective campaign; the diversity amongst the associated groups was too large.[77] They did play an important role in the dissemination of ideas and models for local and national actions. During the 1971 Dworp meeting, the U-Gruppen, from Aarhus, presented an overview of a campaign which had aimed at fostering awareness about the EEC's relationship to the Third World amongst the local population via leaflet distribution and conversations with residents.[78] Another model presented in Dworp was the Dutch 'world shop', which will take centre stage in Chapter 3.

Though prioritizing local action, the U-Gruppen and the world shops also served as springboards for campaigns on a larger scale. The circular letters issued by the international secretariat called attention to several such initiatives. Turning away from attempts at quick, large-scale change effected through international politics, these campaigns often targeted specific countries or companies or promoted specific products. For example, the circular called attention to boycotts of coffee from Angola and of Outspan oranges from South Africa.[79] Despite the focus on more moderate, short-term goals, the conclusion reached during the preceding international consultation in 1971 remained a guiding principle: 'Whatever is planned during this consultation, in the end it has to be directed towards the goal of changing the structures within the industrialized capitalist countries and the Third World'.[80]

The rise and demise of the Cane Sugar Campaign calls into question our understanding of the spatial dimensions of civic activism. As a postcolonial world emerged, Europe gained a new importance for fair trade activists engaged in the campaign. Common economic policies prompted activists to initiate a campaign which targeted European politics and to build a network of likeminded citizens within the countries involved. Even though European integration provided activists with a common frame of reference, it did not simply replace local and national concerns with a new, shared perspective. The stakes within the process of European integration for various local and national activist groups were different. Their views of Europe and the world continued to be enmeshed with local and national viewpoints. The rise of European and global frameworks of governance forced citizens to find new balances between local and translocal spaces.[81] Their actions rendered European and global institutions more visible in daily life, but the emphasis on these perspectives could wax and wane. Activities such as the Cane Sugar Campaign show how Europe and the world at once functioned as integrating and disintegrating frameworks amongst European citizens and changed civic activism in unexpected ways.

This transnational campaign points to a crucial learning effect amongst activists during the early 1970s. Social activism in the late 1960s was inspired by the possibility of a change in global politics seemingly initiated by the decolonized countries. Supporting this goal, activists deliberately took aim at European politics and global institutions such as UNCTAD. The initiators successfully built on a foundation of intergenerational collaboration, broad coalitions of groups concerned with global development, and, increasingly, on transnational exchanges. Evidently, a broad segment of the Western European public felt it important to establish fair conditions governing trade with the Third World. However, the Europeanization of fair trade activism proved much more difficult than expected. Although the campaign could be judged a success in terms of its diffusion, visibility, and support across Western Europe, no comprehensive campaign had materialized. Neither did the activists succeed in noticeably impacting European economic policies. In the end, attempts to launch a Europe-wide campaign faltered because European integration did not firmly align activists across Europe. Efforts to address global and European politics also failed to elicit a meaningful response.

During the 1970s, civic activism turned away from campaigns aimed directly at European and global regulation on the level of policy.[82] However, it did not completely shy away from larger policy questions in the political sphere. Instead, activists turned to foregrounding specific issues and achieving change incrementally. Campaigns directed at specific companies, causes, and producers such as the Dutch boycott campaign against Angolan coffee in the early 1970s, the international campaign against Nestlé from 1977 onwards, and the alternative trade supporting Nicaragua during the 1980s did produce tangible results.[83] Many activists decided to follow this course during the first half of the 1970s. Initially, the postcolonial politics of international trade and development had aligned these activists with the agenda set by global and European politics. Their eventual disillusion led to a disconnect between civic activism and the transnational political domain. As a New International Economic Order and a green revolution in agriculture were being discussed in the hallways of the United Nations' institutions and national agencies, development activists turned their attention to markedly different issues. By attempting to change the world one step at a time, they kept alive their hopes to achieve a large-scale transformation in the long run.

3 PAPER
The Politics of Everyday Life

> There is a good reason to believe that in talking seriously about the eradication of worldwide poverty and oppression we are thinking about the making of a new historical epoch.
>
> Revolutionary initiatives must spring from local organizations committed to 'serving the people'. A pro-development transformation in, say, Belgium or Canada, would give a tremendous surge of strength and hope to those in, say, Peru or the Philippines who ware engaged in the hard struggle to create a developing society.[1]

With this call to remake the world, the Sri Lankan activist Dick Hensman appealed to a group of 'development activists' who had gathered in the small Belgian town of Dworp, just south of Brussels, in November 1971. The contrast between Hensman's impassioned appeal and the high-minded intentions of his audience on the one hand, and the provincial setting of a small Belgian village on the other, could not have been starker. Yet this tension was fundamental to this moment in the history of fair trade activism: the hopes for a sudden and comprehensive transformation of the world, mediated through local action, were at a high point. Soon they would mutate into a less grand but all-the-more-sustainable perspective.

Looking back, the first signs of what was to come can be observed at the Dworp meeting. It had been planned by an international secretariat for likeminded activists, which had been established during the Cane Sugar Campaign. The convening's goal was to identify opportunities for collective action and to exchange information about campaigns and approaches amongst attendees.[2] Ian Haig of the World Development Movement spoke about the Commonwealth Sugar Campaign, whilst members of the Aarhus-based U-Gruppen discussed how they engaged people in conversations to foster awareness about the relation between the EEC and the Third World amongst the local population.[3]

The Dutch activist Paul van Tongeren, one of the originators of the Cane Sugar Campaign in 1968, presented the model of the 'world shop' to the gathering. This type of shop was meant to be a local platform for activities concerning development in both the South and the North which could integrate all kinds of awareness-raising campaigns via the sale of items from developing countries. This model would become a staple of fair trade activism throughout Western Europe over the course of the 1970s and 1980s. It enabled this sort of activism to be embedded in local contexts and aimed to translate concerns about global relations to practical actions. Most of these local shops' activities took place beyond the view of national and international politicians and media. It has also not been grasped in social scientific and historical scholarship, which has often portrayed the years from around 1972 onwards as a period of crisis after years of flourishing activism.

As the history of the world shops in the 1970s and 1980s demonstrates, however, the shift to local action and a politics of everyday life did not diminish the enthusiasm for activism or put an end to the politicization of humanitarianism so highly visible over the course of the Cane Sugar Campaign. Rather, international and national politics lost their attraction for many activists. One's direct environment then became a natural centre of gravity for their activities. In such a milieu, they could reach out to people and make them aware of global inequality and exploitation. In their own daily lives, they could start to make a difference, too. Many fair trade activists found it comforting to disengage from detrimental practices. Buying products which were fairly traded and adopting a lifestyle which took hunger and environmental concerns into account also helped to publicize these issues in local communities. Places like the world shop, as it had been presented to an international audience in Dworp, would become laboratories to experiment with such practices and fora to discuss how they related to the wider world.

An indispensable part of this development was paper – a pervasive product that was the material basis for leaflets, posters, letters, and not least of all, recycled toilet paper. Paper was the medium which brought a ragtag band of activists together in small towns like the Dutch seaside resort of Egmond aan Zee and Dworp in Belgium to discuss how they could bring about more equitable relations between the South and North. Some were employed by development organizations throughout Europe, but most of the participants were devoting their spare time to this brand of activism or were combining it with their studies. The information on the Cane Sugar Campaign and the invitation to a collective consultation had been printed on thousands of sheets of paper and distributed to contacts of individual supporters and organizations. More specifically, paper embodied what these activists were prioritizing: raising public awareness in the North. They printed information and exhortations on posters and flyers. They exchanged, discussed, and sold pocket paperbacks with information on the structures of global trade and the situation in various countries, along with calls to political action and instructions on how to translate concerns about global issues to acts taken in one's everyday life. The world shops became pivotal locations for such exchanges and were rapidly adopted as local meeting places for people interested in issues such as development, international solidarity, the environment, human rights, and peace.

As a commodity, paper is notably different from the products discussed in this book's other chapters. The paper circulating amongst activists and used for booklets sold in world shops was generally not produced in the Global South: it provided no tangible connection between producers and consumers the way that handicrafts or cane sugar did. Paper was, however, just as crucial as these other products to the history of fair trade activism. Indispensable to the exchange of information, it was – in the form of books, leaflets, and posters – arguably the most important item on offer in world shops during the 1970s and 1980s. In the form of letter paper, it remained essential for building a transnational coalition. Although paper by the 1970s was quite an old medium when compared to modes of communication such as radio, television, and the telephone, it was arguably more important to the evolution of fair trade activism in these years. Crucially, producers from the Global South would send letters to potential supporters to inform them about the conditions they were facing and, sometimes, about their products which activists could sell on their behalf. Posters served to draw attention to campaigns. Leaflets and books provided the impulse for people to come together locally. Just like jute bags and cane sugar, these items provided, for people meeting in world shops, the means to agree on common objectives and forge a shared identity.

The proliferation of world shops came at a time when the global order was in crisis. Postwar global economic and political relations had been rooted in the Bretton Woods system, which had provided a stable framework for international negotiations. By the beginning of the 1970s, it was falling apart. The first oil crisis of 1973 dealt another blow to the confidence in the stability of the international order felt by people buying petrol throughout the world.[4] The belief in progress, which had underpinned Europe's postwar reconstruction, was now wavering, left reeling by publications such as *The Limits to Growth* (1972), written by a group of experts calling themselves The Club of Rome. The report reaffirmed prevalent doubts about the evolution of consumer societies in the North. It departed from the eye-catching idea that a 'global system' of interdependent 'economic, political, natural, and social' components impacted the 'predicament of mankind' at large.[5] Arguing that a continuation of the current global socio-economic trends could not be sustained by the resources available to contemporary humankind, the book left many readers convinced that the accepted blueprints for a prosperous future had become obsolete.[6] Other publications, like the similarly widely read *Blueprint for Survival*, argued even more vehemently against the prevailing social order, which it claimed undermined the planet's social and environmental living conditions.[7] The perception of a crisis in the global order was reinforced by two international conferences in the same year. At both the third United Nations Conference on Trade and Development in Santiago de Chile and the United Nations Conference on the Human Environment in Stockholm, experts noted the extent to which the current global state of affairs was untenable when viewed from the perspective of social equality and environmental capacity.

Despite the sense of urgency, attempts to accelerating the development of the Global South over the course of the United

Nations' first Development Decade yielded disappointing results. The activists who had rallied around the cause of the Third World during the 1960s were particularly disappointed about the meagre results of the third United Nations Conference on Trade and Development in Santiago de Chile in 1972. Once again, despite meticulous preparations and manifold attempts at drawing public attention, the conference produced few tangible improvements for the Global South. Santiago as a meeting site had been particularly encouraging to activists, as it was home to the government of the democratic socialist Salvador Allende, which had come to power peacefully in 1970. A rightwing coup assisted by the United States' Central Intelligence Agency a year after the UNCTAD conference resulted in the death of Allende and the installation of Augusto Pinochet as the head of a military dictatorship. Amongst activists in the North, the events in Chile in the early 1970s were a severe shock to hopes that the global order could be changing through the levers of international politics.

These concerns and upheavals have rightly earned the period its reputation as a time of crisis. The demise of the postwar economic order limited the options available to national states and social movements to target the structures of global economic relations.[8] The years following the optimistic activism of the late 1960s have often been cast as a time of disintegration, in-fighting, and violent radicalization. Activists became increasingly disappointed with the latent reluctance of many contemporaries to engage with the topics they were trying to bring to people's attention. In a retrospective historical survey, the sociologists Jan Willem Duyvendak and Ruud Koopmans have suggested that a first wave of activism ebbed at this time, to be succeeded by a second wave during the 1980s.[9]

However, the 1970s crisis did not lead to defeatism amongst everyone who had been promoting global change since the 1960s. In the realm of global politics, the events spurred efforts to establish a new, more equitable global order. The newly won influence now exerted by the oil-producing countries was regarded as an opportunity to achieve a new international economic order.[10] Similarly, concerns over the 'limits to growth' sparked debates about realigning economic activities to account for environmental considerations on a policy level, whilst stimulating a host of local initiatives to come up with ways of living more sustainably.

Diffusing the World Shop Model

The idea of setting up world shops emerged spontaneously and evolved in an uneven fashion. The first of these shops opened in the town of Breukelen in 1969. After the socially and politically engaged Catholic teacher Joan Derks returned from Uganda, where he had taken part in development work, he began selling handicrafts imported by the alternative trading organization SOS. At first, he had asked a local bookshop to sell them on his behalf. On some days, he would also sell them from his own home to people passing by on their outings to the popular waters around his hometown. Soon, he formed a committee with a couple of likeminded peers to set up a *Wereldwinkel*. The local council offered them a property that they could temporarily use in the town centre. The shop officially opened on 22 August 1969. Paul Meijs, SOS's ambitious director, had travelled 200 kilometres to wish the initiative well as a speaker at the opening celebration.[11]

Outlets to sell goods in support of humanitarian initiatives were certainly not a new phenomenon when Derksen and his colleagues opened their shop in Breukelen. Members of Oxfam had operated several shops since the late 1940s. The Oxfam Shops expanded in scope as Oxfam grew into a formidable humanitarian organization during the 1960s. Similarly, since the 1960s, the sales of needlework and other handicraft products under the aegis of Self-Help Crafts and SERVV in the United States had partly been conducted in shops. Like the Oxfam shops, these stores had often combined the selling of used products, the proceeds of which were donated to these organizations' humanitarian projects, with sales of handicrafts on behalf of producers from the Global South. Beyond these examples of establishing shops, which were likely known to the Dutch activists, the hosting of markets and fairs to raise money for projects was a lively tradition within many religious communities.

The initiative in Breukelen was quickly imitated in several other places in the Netherlands. The initiators of the Cane Sugar Campaign became aware of it and recognized this model's potential to consolidate and expand their campaign. By that point, their campaign had mobilized a remarkable number of local groups in many parts of the Netherlands. They had eagerly brought the unfair structure of global trade to the attention of political parties, trade unions, churches, and peace groups, as well as those involved in humanitarian initiatives. By the early 1970s, these groups had largely exhausted the possibilities for action around the issue of sugar. Paul van Tongeren, the campaign's pivotal figure, proposed taking concerted action to introduce the world shop initiative. To that end, he invited the world shop groups from Breukelen, Rotterdam, Haarlem, and Amsterdam, along with Meijs and several other sympathizers, to a meeting on 12 November 1969. Meijs explained the work of SOS, relating how the foundation had expanded into an intermediary for importing products from developing countries, which were then sold in Western Europe on the behalf of their producers. The world shops in Breukelen and Haarlem had followed SOS's philosophy, selling products on behalf of people in less fortunate circumstances. Paul van Tongeren and other members of the Cane Sugar Campaign took a different angle. They stressed the need for a political perspective. Nonetheless, despite this difference the attendees recognized the opportunity for cooperation and decided that setting up 'third world shops' (*derde wereld winkels*) was a viable strategy. They parted after deciding to work towards the creation of an exhibition, a joint secretariat, a publicity campaign, and a strategy to bring schools into the fold.[12]

The model was immensely popular. Many local cane sugar groups set up a world shop. The world shops continued to promote fair trade and the focus on specific products which had been brought forward during the Cane Sugar Campaign. In many world shops, in fact, cane sugar was one of the products on offer.[13] Former cane sugar activists could draw upon better organization, new opportunities for action, and more optimal coordination of purchases and sales.[14] They acquired a broader outlook and often employed a more radical attitude than heretofore. In the Netherlands, ten world shops joined forces in 1970. The stated point of departure for this foundation was 'to expose and attack the economic and political structures in the rich countries that obstruct a fair division of tasks and income in the world as a whole'.[15] The import duties levied by the European Economic Community were not the only obstacle to the fair allocation they desired. Rich Western investors hindered the governments of countries in the South in making policy independently. Liberation movements lacked support from the North. Such obstacles would be made visible by selling telltale products from the countries concerned, accompanied by documentation, posters, and

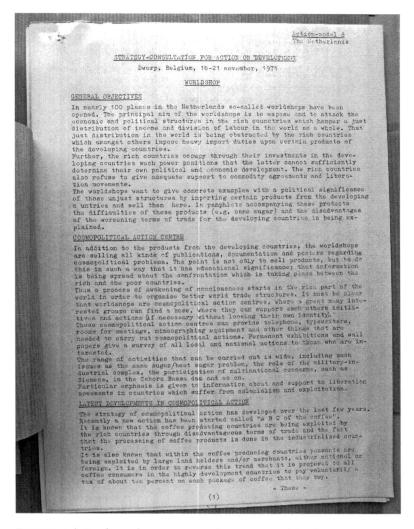

Figure 3.1 A letter from the international secretariat of development activists about the world shop as a model for action. Private archive Paul van Tongeren.

consumer guides. The founders of the world shop movement also mentioned the possibility of boycott actions and collection campaigns on behalf of liberation movements or countries in need of support. Increasing imports from developing countries was cited as 'an important secondary goal'.[16]

By 1972, the Dutch world shop's umbrella organization comprised 120 member groups.[17] Its quick expansion was facilitated by SOS's constructive support. To the world shop groups, SOS made the offer of taking up handicrafts on consignment, which allowed local groups to pursue activities with little initial funding. If the products obtained from SOS were not sold, they could simply be returned.[18] There was ample attention given to the initiative in newspapers and on radio and television.[19] In addition, it was backed by many sections of Dutch society. Despite internal divisions over the Cane Sugar Campaign and the world shops, the two largest Protestant denominations officially declared their appreciation for the shops' installation; in many instances, the shops could count on the cooperation of local church communities in finding facilities.[20]

The world shop model soon travelled across the Dutch border. Promoting it in meetings such as the one in Dworp and in international correspondence soon led to groups in other countries following suit. In 1972, the Dutch national secretariat reported that it received dozens of calls a week from the Netherlands, and from many other countries, requesting information.[21] As with the attempts to coordinate a Europe-wide cane sugar campaign, the model's proliferation could benefit from the active transnational relations of many humanitarian organizations, churches, and development agencies. The small-scale approach was an obvious advantage for the model. In contrast to ambitious campaigns, world shops needed little national and transnational coordination. The emphasis on hands-on local activism could easily build on existing activities. Many churches already sold products on behalf of producers in the South to support less fortunate people and missionary activities. Anyone considering starting a shop could also count on the network of organizations like SOS and Oxfam, along with the information provided by Dutch activists and the national umbrella federations soon established in other countries. Such social capital enabled a relatively easy start for local groups. They could follow a comprehensible set of suggestions and obtain a number of products straightaway.

The unexpectedly accommodating role of religious organizations was particularly pronounced in West Germany, both locally and nationally. Catholic and Protestant youth organizations, after initiating a host of campaigns to address the disadvantaged position of people in the South, went further and took up the idea of selling products from the South, an activity which would at once call attention to their situation and open markets for disadvantaged producers. In 1970, members of Catholic and Protestant youth and development organizations set up the Aktion Dritte-Welt-Handel to promote these practices, collaborating closely with SOS Wereldhandel from the Netherlands. Youth groups took to selling SOS's products at local markets and fairs as well as after church services. Such opportunities to act locally met with much enthusiasm: whereas 176 local campaigns took place in 1971, this number ballooned to around 500 in two years' time.[22] Shortly, local groups solidified occasional campaigns into more solid form by setting up Dritte-Welt-Läden, modelled on the Dutch example. Eleven of these groups decided to join a newly founded federation in 1974.[23]

In Switzerland, an inaugural world shop appeared in the town of Uster, the outgrowth of a local initiative to sell bananas and coffee at a regularly occurring street market in late 1973. The bananas were sold as part of a campaign launched by women in the town of Frauenfeld. They had handed out bananas for free, together with a newsletter which called for the introduction of an obligatory development premium for any banana sold in Switzerland. So-called Ujamaa coffee was imported from Tanzania. Selling this specific coffee signalled support for the political project of the popular Tanzanian president Julius Nyerere, whose government promoted a specific strand of Christian-inspired socialism. Importantly, this was soluble coffee processed in Tanzania itself. It therefore could be used to talk about the need to support self-reliance rather than reducing developing countries to mere exporters of raw materials.[24]

After offering these products at a market stall, the local volunteers had sought opportunities to explore the subject and to bring relevant issues to the attention of the local public. Following examples from England and the Netherlands, they set up a small shop to sell products from the Third World, accompanied by relevant information written on flyers, thus combining foodstuffs with paper to convey their message: 'The shop is explicitly aimed at providing information, that is, we are not interested in selling as much as possible', the founders wrote. The products they sold would ideally be of daily use rather than luxurious, because the group did not want to reinforce the trend of trade expansion. They had to be able to provide information about the need for global trade reform. In the short term, however, the shop was facing more mundane problems. Especially with Christmas around the corner, it was difficult to stock enough suitable products, whereas the hours of operation had to be restricted to Saturdays because of the voluntary nature of the work.[25]

Watching Dutch television on a dark winter Sunday in February 1974, viewers got a glimpse of the daily practice of world shop groups. A programme which presented innovative attempts to shape society turned their attention towards world shops. What they saw did not at all correspond to current expectations around fair trade and world shops. The broadcast showcased a lively hotchpotch: a group of teachers in a secondary school offered passersby all kinds of documentation on a loosely ordered set of tables. The world shop group was apparently engaged in activities which had little to do with local commerce. A world shop member from Eindhoven discussed the living conditions of guest workers in the Netherlands with a group of students in their classroom. One of the pupils reported that he found this topic much more engaging than issues about the Third World or the Dutch colony of Suriname. 'The Third World, that's something you hear everywhere nowadays'.[26]

World shops during the 1970s were not shops in the common sense. Rather, they related to the notion of a workshop, the 'shop' being a place to work together rather than predominantly devoted to commercial activity. A group of world-shop activists in Arnhem did run a store. The film crew was guided by a neat older lady, who showed the viewers the 'political corner' with books and leaflets on 'anarchism, Marxism, trade unions, imperialism, multinationals' and Third-World countries. These materials could be read in the store or taken home. Items ranging from braided reed and woodcarvings to earthenware were also in demand, she noted. An elderly gentleman involved in the shop's activities enthusiastically told the interviewer how important it was to work together in one place with people of different ages and with divergent political views. Neither did the customers comply with present-day expectations. A young couple with large 1970s glasses and matching clothes entered the store. The husband turned out to be a Protestant minister from a nearby congregation. His wife explained that they were not coming to the store to buy anything. The reason for their visit was to pick up posters for a campaign on behalf of Guatemala. In their conversation with the interviewer, they pointed out the importance of 'structural help', something that could be achieved, for example, by encouraging church members to buy coffee from Guatemala.[27]

The broadcast made clear that a world shop in 1974 was a place where a colourful assortment of younger and older people would meet to discuss a variety of pressing issues and to take part in a series of campaigns to address them. Selling products was only one way of drawing attention to unequal relations in the world. A world shop in 1974 sold many products which did not originate from the South, many of which were made from paper. Posters, flyers, and books documenting relevant issues and making calls to action were deemed equally or even more important than the items available for purchase. The commitment of these groups went beyond their efforts addressing the trading conditions for people in the South. Their members were also concerned with activities around peace, Apartheid, decolonization, the environment, nuclear energy, and international solidarity. Instead of being based solely on economic justice, their activities often rooted in a broader conception of human rights shared by people across the world. But whereas their outlook had broadened considerably since 1968, their immediate goals appeared to be more narrowly defined. Attempts to impact European and global politics had been replaced by attention to their own environment, support for individual countries and movements, and pressuring specific companies. These activists, though they had not given up their hopes of changing the world, now tended to focus on issues within their grasp.

The overriding goal of fair trade activism had been controversial ever since the start of the Cane Sugar Campaign: was the sugar being sold on behalf of its producers in the Third World or was it being sold to publicize the unjust structures of global trade? In practice, both goals could often coexist. As world shops began appearing, the tension was felt more acutely. Students involved with setting up world shops regarded them as 'action and information centres'. They could be used by activists as a base for meetings, actions, and storage. For these students, the shops were primarily meant to shake up public opinion. The products being sold there should come with information to provide buyers with insights into the unfair structures of global trade.[28] This was why the participants opted to name them 'world shops' instead of 'Third World shops' during a follow-up meeting, stressing that their activities concerned the whole world, including their own environment.[29]

For people focused on having consumers exert an immediate impact, however, the main goal was to achieve the highest turnover possible so that producers would reap the benefits of sales. In this vein, Meijs suggested that the world shop's national foundation be funded based on a percentage of the revenue flowing from sold products. He proposed offering a fixed price reduction to members of the foundation, who could then use the price difference as they saw fit.[30] The participants who regarded world shops as action centres rejected this proposal. It would cause an undesirable emphasis on selling, they argued. Members of the ecumenical activist group Sjaloom, who continued to support the pioneering fair trade activism that had been developed via the Cane Sugar Campaign, feared that this would also encourage world shop groups to choose a permanent location for their activities, instead of injecting their activism into as many different places as possible in everyday society. To emphasize selling would make fair trade activism insular, they warned.[31]

The world shops in Western Europe, then, were not simply adopting the model prevalent in the United States and United Kingdom or following the tradition of charitable selling. They did connect to the idea of selling products on behalf of others and to an approach which translated transnational solidarity to acts of daily life, like the buying of food and gifts. The most visible difference was that world shops did not sell second-hand items. Neither did they sell products on behalf of specific humanitarian organizations, as Oxfam Shops did at the time. Their perspective, not restricted to the Global South, was aimed at a global transformation, as the discussion about their designation as 'world shops' rather than 'Third World shops' had made clear.

To many members of world shop groups, signalling a break with the tradition of charity was significant. Instead of charity, they emphasized justice. Rather than a relationship of dependence, equality was to govern all exchanges. The break with charity was not always clear in practice, however. The practice of selling products had evolved out of charitable activities but had gradually been reconceptualized as a way to promote equitable economic relations. Many initiatives rooted in charitable traditions had undergone a similar evolution. The uneasy results were often evident. For instance, a group of young activists in Belgium had opened a world shop in Antwerp in April 1971. Though they had close connections to the network of Oxfam Shops which had been operating in Belgium since the 1960s, they felt that these shops – modelled after the English Oxfam Shops – were lacking in political orientation. Instead, they opted to follow the Dutch world shop model. Despite their combative stance, the founder of the Belgian Oxfam Shops, the eccentric baron Antoine Allard, had supported their attempts to find accommodations in Antwerp. By the end of 1971, there were eight world shops in Belgium. The Antwerp shop functioned as their de facto centre, coordinating communications and distribution.[32]

The tension between Oxfam's activities and those of these new world shops led to a remarkable incident at a conference in 1974. Because members of the world shop groups were now presenting themselves as a political campaigning organization rather than one rooted in the older humanitarian tradition, Allard disputed their right to represent Oxfam, especially because Oxfam had always refrained from overtly political activities.[33] The Antwerp group encountered similar problems when they founded an official umbrella organization in 1975. Several Belgian groups refused to become members, this time because they felt the name Oxfam signalled a conservative and hierarchical approach.[34] Despite these initial difficulties, Oxfam Wereldwinkels would go on to function successfully as an umbrella organization for world shops and as an alternative trading organization – a rare combination within the fair trade movement.

Local Hubs for Activism

World shops had to be more than just stores. Their founders envisioned them as action centres that spread information and hosted events. This mission was reflected in the practical instructions they provided to people planning to start their own shops. To comply with Dutch regulations, one of the group's members would need to have a trading license. If the group was able to secure accommodations, often provided by local governments or churches, a meeting room would have to be furnished, ideally with a phone and a mimeograph machine, amongst other things.[35] Once the group had joined the national collective, it would be provided with regular updates, training workshops, and opportunities to participate in joint procurement and to obtain documentation.[36]

These local hubs became pivotal in establishing a politics of everyday life, distancing fair trade activism from institutional politics on the national and international levels. Operating at such a remove allowed participants to adhere to their ideals in their own lives at least, which became all the more pressing since large-scale transformations could not be expected to happen quickly. At the same time, such initiatives continued to aim to raise awareness about global inequality, a crucial step in mobilizing a larger public in favour of change. Cookbooks sold in world shops strikingly illustrate how personal encounters were regarded as a steppingstone to solidarity. Being part of a wider world took on a more specific meaning for many of the Western Europeans who became involved with the fair trade movement. The idea of 'one world' implied that humans all lived together on the same planet and demanded a certain degree of mutual solidarity. Together, the people of the earth had only one planet to sustain them, with limited natural resources at their disposal. This world must be preserved through the efforts of all humanity. Attention to environmental issues thus became more widespread during the 1970s. Alongside 'one world to share', 'one world only' became another important catchphrase.[37] Nonetheless, many fair trade activists prioritized direct relations and economic justice over environmental concerns.

Cookbooks sold in world shops and used as manuals for group meetings during this period illustrate how limited resources and concern over the environment were present, even if issues of solidarity and economic justice remained the predominant concerns. The Sri Lankan Eileen Candappa and the Dutch priest Harry Haas pioneered the practice of cooking and eating together so that people in Europe would become acquainted with Asian countries through their cuisine. Their group cooking was as remarkable for its practical approach as it was for its demand that men and women share cooking duties – by no means a given at that time, even within groups of progressive activists. The experience of cooking Asian dishes, they noted, could be a springboard for conversations about people's place in the world. Cooking and eating would not change the world, they cautioned: 'We by no means believe that recipes and cooking demonstrations can change the world. But we also believe that it is hardly possible without establishing contacts between people, like we practice ourselves'.[38] A series of cookbooks that grew out of their culinary activities emphasized mutual understanding, with explanations of customs and common ingredients as well as notable differences from Western European culinary traditions.[39] Challenging these latter traditions, one volume discussed the prevalent 'meat cult'. Western European plates were dominated by meat, but their cooking was mostly artless. The demand for meat was satisfied at the expense of animals. Foodstuffs direly needed in less wealthy parts of the world were consumed profligately in the West. Instead, Candappa and Haas recommended an Asian approach, which put meat and vegetables on an equal footing. This approach would benefit others but also held the promise of being tastier and healthier for the eater.[40]

A 1978 booklet published under the auspices of Swiss world shops arrived at a similar conclusion, though it was based on a more explicitly economic and environmental analysis. The authors of *Bewusst kochen, herzhaft essen* (Cook with awareness, eat heartily) noted critically that the 'cattle of the rich' were fed with the 'food of the poor'. The industrialized treatment of livestock in particular used food suitable for human consumption. Adding injury to insult, this was 'a conscious strategy of large US cereal companies and the food industry'. To counteract that injustice, the booklet combined recipes for mostly vegetarian dishes with information explaining how the Western meat industry exploited natural resources and neglected the hunger of people in developing countries.[41]

The emphasis on a politics of everyday life centred on activities like cooking and shopping did not alter the constant necessity of navigating between confrontation and inclusion. The politicization of humanitarian action continued to be felt by fair trade activists and their contacts. World shop groups often took a more radical attitude than Haas and Candappa did in their welcoming cooking events. It was hard to reconcile calls for solidarity with leftist states such as Cuba, criticism of NATO, and condemnations of capitalism with the broad support their initiatives often evoked. The fate of the inaugural world shop is telling in this regard. After displaying a poster which accused Portugal of murdering people in Angola and Mozambique with NATO weapons, representatives of the world shop in Breukelen were summoned to the office of the mayor, who felt that the store was being instrumentalized for political propaganda. The town council, not prepared to support such activities, terminated the store's lease.[42] A request to put up a stall at the weekly local market would be granted only if the applicants restricted their activities to the sale of products. Providing information about political campaigns would not be permitted. Because the group failed to find new premises, the shop's inventory was moved to the attic of the local vicarage. In the years that followed, the world shop group fell dormant.[43]

The brittle basis of activism with a local emphasis became evident when thorny issues close to home were addressed. In 1973, the national federation of world shops in the Netherlands proposed a campaign advocating independence for the Dutch colony of Suriname. The time was right for such a campaign, as elections in Suriname and negotiations over its status in the Dutch Commonwealth were scheduled for the autumn. Attempts to cooperate with representatives from Suriname in the Netherlands failed due to divisions amongst them. A working group then gathered information and prepared a publicity campaign as well as a set of suggestions for local action. Local groups were asked to look into how they could campaign in their own environment.[44] There was little enthusiasm for the campaign amongst world shop groups, however. Only around thirty groups engaged in campaign activities during the summer of 1973, leading the national federation to issue a desperate warning: 'It is hard to convince people not to buy Outspan oranges [protesting Apartheid in South Africa, PvD], but it is even harder to involve them in changing the tide in favour of Suriname. (…) In Suriname, we are implicated instead of white South Africans or the Portuguese'.[45]

The Suriname campaign ended in disappointment. Only a handful of Dutch world shops participated. On top of the lacklustre involvement, participants noted a dearth of willingness to engage with the issue within their own communities. Churches, though they had been open to participation in many campaigns, appeared wary of this politically sensitive issue. Political parties and companies offered scarcely any cooperation, whereas the regional press also neglected local efforts on behalf of Suriname. The world shop groups themselves struggled with the campaign, too. Suriname had been a Dutch colony for centuries, yet their members were purportedly unfamiliar with the subject and found the campaign material too aggressive, which left them, they argued, little room to engage people in conservation.[46] However, the failure of the Suriname campaign was not viewed as a consequence of local activism's limits. Rather, it reinforced a trend towards reshaping the movement as a grassroots endeavour. The national federation should limit itself to supporting local groups with training, information, and the fostering of ties between local groups.[47] Pointing to Salvador Allende's successful popular movement, disgruntled local activists called for actions which were even more directly connected to everyday life.[48]

Such debates about the role of national federations raged in many Western European countries, as the emphasis within the movement decidedly shifted towards local campaigns which aimed to reach people in their everyday lives. Many world shop groups thus did not participate in these federations, which were removed from the practical activities of the local groups. Conflicts often erupted about their work's political objectives and its ideological framework, making national gatherings the sites of heated debate. Nonetheless, the national federations, along with the alternative trading organizations, did provide an important backbone: whereas local groups would often cease activity after a couple of years, new initiatives could turn to national federations and trading organizations for advice, materials, and goods to hit the ground running.

The flexible and varied array of world shops allowed them to function as local laboratories encompassing new forms and targets. These groups developed many impactful campaigns directed towards everyday life. With the shift away from the international politics of trade, the companies conducting this sort of trade were nonetheless caught in their sights. It turned out these firms were often more responsive to their actions, particularly if a larger group of citizens could be brought to pay attention. The first fair trade initiatives borrowed, from the arsenal of consumer activism, the buycott, invited people to buy cane sugar and products from outlets such as Oxfam, the Mennonite Central Committee (MCC), and

Figure 3.2 A world shop group from Doesburg in the Netherlands protests against the economic ties between Shell and the South African government with an improvised stand in 1979. International Institute of Social History.

SOS, whose sales were transacted on behalf of Southern producers. Targeting the trading policies of companies, the boycott also was a viable instrument for activists.

Local groups were pivotal in publicizing and implementing boycotts, as could be observed in one of the 1970s' most successful fair trade campaigns, focused on coffee from Angola, a Portuguese colony until 1975. The Netherlands was the second-largest importer of Angolan coffee, exceeded only by the United States. Angolan workers were forced to work the harvest whilst profits flowed into the coffers of colonizers. From the early 1960s onwards, the Angola-comité had publicized these circumstances through demonstrations and informational leaflets, as well as via its contacts with media outlets. In early 1972, the committee mounted an ambitious campaign to put a stop to the importing of Angolan coffee. Supported by local world shops, it distributed information about the provenance of this product, encouraging people to eschew any item which contained coffee from this country.[49]

Most supermarkets responded to the threat of turmoil in front of their stores by promising to discontinue selling coffee from

Angola. This pledge was abetted by the ample availability of affordable alternatives. Having achieved this first victory, the campaign directed its attention to the sizeable coffee roaster Douwe Egberts, which refused to make a similar commitment. Consequently, world shop groups took to the streets to ask shoppers not to buy Douwe Egberts coffee, installing themselves in front of supermarkets, putting up posters, distributing leaflets, speaking to local journalists, and selling Angola-free coffee door-to-door – laden with additional information, of course.[50] Once the trade unions chose to side with these activists, Douwe Egberts decided to cease its Angolan imports.[51]

The campaign wasn't over, though. The shareholders of one of the largest supermarket chains, Albert Heijn, were disgruntled about the company directors giving in to activists' demands. As a result, the company announced in the summer of 1973 that it would once more process Angolan coffee. The Angola-comité reacted by calling for a total boycott of the chain. Activists planted themselves in front of the stores to explain to shoppers why these customers' groceries were better bought elsewhere.[52] Thus members of the world shop group in the town of Stadskanaal loaded up a cargo bike with informational material, called the press and the store manager, and cycled to Albert Heijn's local store. After a policeman had directed them to place their bike at an appropriate distance from the entrance, they took up their posts some five metres away and began politely handing out leaflets to passersby. Reactions were mixed: some were in complete agreement with the activists, others enquired whether they did not have to go to work. The activists themselves estimated that their action had no impact on coffee sales. 'Nonetheless we have helped to raise awareness', ventured Henk Otter, well positioned to make the observation as an employee of Albert Heijn and a member of the world shop group.[53] Another activist-*cum*-employee from the town of Boskoop made the national newspapers when he announced his resignation, on principle, from his job at the supermarket there.[54]

Albert Heijn's management launched a counterattack. The company placed advertisements with the slogan 'In a free country: free choice for free people', framing its refusal to cease selling Angolan coffee as a principled struggle of the West against the communist East.[55] All the while, other companies were closely

Figure 3.3 Poster 'Portugal kills with NATO-weapons in Africa'. IISH International Institute of Social History.

monitoring the situation. A spokesman for the large coffee company Van Nelle commented: 'We are convinced that the majority of the public does not want boycotts, but as long as the public doesn't clearly state what it wants, we won't do anything'.[56] Albert Heijn finally buckled under the pressure of six weeks of campaigning. On Saturday, 13 October, employees handed out letters to the supermarket's customers that observed that the volume of sales of Angolan coffee did not warrant its removal from the shelves. Yet, the letter continued, management wanted to do justice to the concerns amongst its customers over the 'antagonisms' which had surfaced.[57]

The successful campaign against Angolan coffee in the Netherlands was celebrated by fair trade activists as a victory for consumers who had gained political awareness. The Angola-comité announced that consumers had proved that they did not just factor in price and quality when choosing products but also accounted for the political consequences of their buying choices.[58] World shop groups went on to cite the campaign as a classic example of what their activism could achieve.[59]

The boycott was well suited to target multinational companies, which came under scrutiny during the 1970s by activists and scholars alike.[60] Such companies benefitted from the absence of new political regulation of international markets whilst the international structures built up in the wake of the Second World War were disintegrating. Multinational companies could set workers in various countries against each other by favouring places with low wages and threatening to relocate production to other countries if workers voiced demands for better labour conditions. Companies, in some instances, played a dubious role in their dealings with leftwing governments, particularly in developing countries. These regimes were regarded as threats to their possessions in these countries and to their chances for profitable trading.[61] This adversarial attitude fed into the distrust of multinational companies amongst leftwing activists, a suspicion reinforced by the initial refusal of companies such as Albert Heijn and Douwe Egberts to refrain from supporting colonial regimes. In the years following the Angolan coffee boycott, new boycotts would be mounted with varying results, like the famous campaign against Outspan oranges from South Africa to protest Apartheid, the refusal to buy fruit from Chile so as to pressure Augusto Pinochet's rightwing regime, and the eschewal of Nestlé products to address its 'milking the Third World' by promoting formula for infants whilst disregarding the health risks involved.[62]

Politicizing Humanitarianism

The overt political edge of these humanitarian initiatives exerted a significant impact on the way alternative trading organizations regarded their work. In the case of the MCC's Self-Help Crafts, which had grown out of Edna Byler's initiative, debates ensued about the course of the programme. In 1977, Dorothy Friesen and Gene Stoltzfus, who were involved in MCC's activities in Indonesia, wrote a memorandum which proposed that social justice be taken as a guiding principle for Self-Help Crafts. If pursued uncritically, they feared, the programme could foster consumerism in the North and economic dependency amongst producers in the South. They also criticized the prominent role of MCC functionaries in producer groups and the gendered hierarchy of the projects, where women did most of the manual labour and men dominated management. 'The only justification for the self-help program is its potential use as a concrete consciousness-raising tool which directly connects the producer in the Third World with the consumer in North America', they concluded.[63]

The ensuing discussions showed that those involved in Self-Help Crafts had incorporated some of the ideas that critics had brought forward. The programme was deemed successful in demonstrating that people in the South were creative, skilled, and could provide for themselves.[64] In 1979, an internal organizational assessment showed that the people who sold Self-Help Craft's products also wanted to educate their customers about development work. Those involved in the programme had continued to promote 'self-reliance' but had expanded this notion beyond the traditional aim of providing producers in the South with a chance to earn a living, the study concluded.[65]

A similar debate about the justification of selling products on behalf of producers ensued between SOS and the Dutch world shops and became a source of internal discord in the alternative trading organization. The world shop movement had benefitted greatly from the support of SOS, which had offered favourable conditions for selling its products. However, the items SOS imported did not align all that well with the world shops' commitment to raising awareness.[66] To that end, raw commodities, with a colonial history stretching back centuries, such as coffee, cacao, and cane sugar, were best. But SOS primarily imported handicrafts. Ideologically, its emphasis was on 'trade, not aid' – the increasingly contentious idea that more just global relations could be achieved through trade being conducted on a more equal footing.

To clarify the terms of their mutual relationship, SOS and a group of Dutch world shop representatives drew up a list of criteria for products to be sold in world shops. The countries of origins had to be 'politically interesting' and the revenue coming from the sale of products had to benefit the people in these countries. The products themselves had to be accompanied by adequate information on a leaflet or the like so that local participants could use this material to address global economic relations from a wider perspective.[67] Despite these guidelines, the world shops soon clashed with SOS. In early 1971, the former contacted an expert to identify opportunities for importing suitable products on their own accord. When SOS's Paul Meijs found out about this, he felt betrayed. To his mind, his agency had gone out of its way to provide the shops with merchandise on very favourable conditions.[68] In a letter to all Dutch world shops, Meijs briskly announced that from April onwards, SOS would only supply items paid for in advance. He also threatened to terminate the policy of transferring 10 per cent of sales profits to the world shops' national federation.[69]

Sjaloom's Piet Reckman, still involved with the fate of the fair trade campaigns even as they established an independent profile, attempted to resolve the conflict. Reckman proposed setting up a cooperative in which world shops, SOS, and Sjaloom would together procure 'materials, products, publications, instruments of cosmopolitical importance' which could be of use to activists campaigning for peace and development.[70] But Paul Meijs rejected the plan, pointing to the international organization being set up by SOS and stating that this cooperative did not align with the aims of this international venture.[71] Remarkably, it turned out the world shops weren't all that interested in the initiative, either. Their representatives noted how their campaigns needed only a few items to attack the unfair structures of global trade. Given the small scale of their sales, they saw no need to set up a separate trading venture. As the Dutch world shops decided to transform the original national foundation into a federation with a more democratic structure, they accordingly established a commission to advise them on which items available through relevant outlets were suitable to their activities.[72]

SOS did take the world shops' criticism to heart. Paul Meijs published a new 'development strategy' on behalf of his agency in 1971, which had to serve as a blueprint for its international expansion. Meijs stated that the original aim of promoting development through equal trade was hindered by the self-interested policies of rich countries: 'We have to acknowledge that we have failed as Christians, both in our personal and in our joint actions. We live in a small world, in which distances have little meaning anymore. We cannot claim that the problems of others do not affect us. They are nearby and therefore also our problems'.[73] This meant that SOS would also have to contribute to efforts to change people's mentalities in the 'rich countries'. Its imports would have to balance the immediate social and economic interests of the people producing the goods with the aim of using their products to raise awareness about global inequality, particularly the Western impediments to equal trading relationships.[74]

Similarly, Oxfam's way of selling products came under scrutiny during the 1970s. In 1972, Roy Scott proposed a new approach that would address the structural confines determining how producers in the Third World made their living. Scott had managed Oxfam's programme Helping by Selling, which had boosted the sales of handicrafts from developing countries during the early 1970s. Working with producers, he felt that Oxfam should do more to provide people in the Global South with a firm economic footing.[75] In 1973, Scott and Paul Meijs jointly published a proposal for Bridge, a proposed European venture to be initiated by Oxfam and SOS. It built on the experiences of people like Scott and Meijs, who had concluded that the activities of Helping by Selling and SOS could improve the lives of people in the Global South only on a very limited scale. Beyond these ventures, whose primary value was as educational tools for the public in the North, producers in the South needed professional sales channels. Scott and Meijs observed how fair trade structurally relied on charity. Scott wrote:

> A producer does not want to have his product bought out of charity or because of its educational or political message. A basic human need is for people to know they are

playing a really valuable role in society – a producer needs to have his production bought simply because the products are good articles at attractive prices.[76]

Eventually, Bridge was founded as a trading venture which was nominally independent of Oxfam, even though Oxfam ensured it could control Bridge's activities. Roy Scott, disappointed by the organization's lack of political orientation and producer participation, left shortly after it was founded. However, Bridge did offer Oxfam a way of engaging more actively in work which went beyond the legal definition of charity, which hampered Oxfam's activities in this respect.[77]

SOS did not become officially involved with Bridge. After several years of rapid expansion, it was on the brink of collapse by the middle of the 1970s, a decade that saw the organization expand its activities throughout Western Europe. Meijs and his team had established subsidiaries in Belgium, West Germany, Austria, and Switzerland. As in the Netherlands, many of the groups in West Germany with a potential interest in cooperating with SOS, however, wanted to emphasize their political perspective rather than the immediate benefits of trade. To Meijs, there was no distinction between charity and transformation. The question, rather, was which brand of help would lead to what kind of transformation. In some cases, it was possible to sell products with a particular 'demonstrative value'. However, providing immediate support was a more pressing concern. Whilst improving the lives of producers was the immediate effect of SOS's activities, the ultimate goal was to enable producers to establish themselves in the mainstream market.[78]

The Limits of Transnational Cooperation

Despite the attempt to combine the political and pragmatic approaches, relations between activist groups across Western Europe and SOS became increasingly strained during the first half of the 1970s. Tensions partly arose around the question of products. Should activities revolve around products which could demonstrate the structural inequalities in global trade, such as coffee or cocoa, as many local activists demanded? Or should they focus on artisanal products, which could call attention to the 'culture, history and tradition of the countries of origin' of products, as Meijs would have it?[79] A second issue concerned the campaigns' focus. After the failure of the UNCTAD conferences, many activists had concluded that their main objective was to publicize issues of global inequality in the North in order to exert political pressure on those governments obstructing reforms. The alternative trading organizations prioritized direct trade that would improve the lives of producers. Finally, there was tension with regard to the movement's overall ends. Outfits such as SOS, Helping by Selling, SERVV, and Self-Help Crafts aimed to enable individual producers to become self-reliant economically. Many vocal activists had initially hoped to achieve a rapid, all-encompassing reform of global trade through the establishment, via political means, of a global framework. After their attempts failed in the years between 1968 and 1973, these activists shifted their attention to supporting producers connected to alternative economic modes, such as leftist states or cooperatively organized groups of producers.

The different angles on strategies, tactics, and goals could be reconciled in practice, because groups such as those associated with the world shops could easily combine more explicitly political campaigns with the selling of a range of products. SOS's downfall as a multinational venture, then, resulted mainly from the contentious relationship between the mother organization and its subsidiaries in different countries. Trouble started in West Germany when Paul Meijs accused the Gesellschaft für Partnerschaft mit der Dritten Welt (GFP) of being too preoccupied with its own affairs. This led to a break between the SOS and the GFP in 1974, after which the Gesellschaft zur Förderung der Partnerschaft mit der Dritten Welt (GEPA) was founded, led by former SOS employee Jan Hissel.[80] After similar struggles over autonomy, the alternative trading organizations in Austria and Switzerland continued independently of SOS as well.[81]

SOS's international ambitions had resulted in a Europe-wide network of alternative trading organizations which kept in close contact despite the organizational splits of the 1970s. SOS had also catalyzed the development of a network of relations between South and North. A series of international meetings had acquainted producers and members of alternative trading organizations with one another.[82] Even as these meetings helped participants understand what kinds of products were available and what kinds were in demand, they also served as platforms for debates about the goals of alternative trade. SOS managed to secure the support of the Dutch Ministry of Development Cooperation to host an international congress for those involved in alternative trade in 1976. The name of the congress, 'Alternative Trade Conference', made clear allusion to the UNCTAD conference hosted the same year, at which rich countries had once more neglected to respond to demands for concessions.[83] The former conference, held in the Dutch town of Noordwijkerhout, had been organized along similar lines, with an extensive preparatory meeting taking place in Frankfurt am Main a year before, where the main topics – 'practical business issues' and 'encouraging public awareness of the need for a more equitable distribution of wealth' – had been agreed on.[84] Like the UNCTAD conferences, it had plenary sessions alternating with a series of conversations on specific subjects. It was accompanied by an exhibition in Amsterdam with products from Tanzania, Thailand, India, Bangladesh, and Ecuador.[85]

The alternative trade conference was intended to demonstrate that it was possible to exceed the poor performance of the UNCTAD conferences in doing good. Representatives of twelve groups of producers and twenty-two alternative trading organizations from across the world discussed how they could improve cooperation. They also debated whether it was viable to sell products outside the network of alternative traders.[86] Paul Meijs deemed this a key question in the run-up to the meetings, particularly because he felt that any attempt to change the structure of global trade in the short term was 'lofty idealism' after four consecutive UNCTAD conferences had achieved very little. He pitted the conference in Noordwijkerhout against such high-minded international political gatherings as an example of a more pragmatic approach which would yield tangible results.[87] Through the close cooperation with a rapidly expanding number of world shops, Meijs expected a turnover of around 7 million guilders in 1976 (more than 8 million Euro at today's rate).[88] Over the course of the sessions, however, the producers' representatives and many Western European speakers found themselves in disagreement. Acknowledging their intention to develop their market access, they nonetheless published an official statement to underline that this was not their main goal:

> The efforts of groups like ours touch hardly the fringe of problems that lie at the foot of unequal exchange relations between the Third World and the first world. It is indeed encouraging for us to learn that more people in the first world are beginning to recognize the real nature of the problems involved and are increasingly coming out in solidarity with the cause of the Third World. It is our earnest hope that alternative marketing organizations will also increasingly pay attention to this aspect of the question in addition to direct relations with production groups in the third world countries.[89]

A similar workshop was held in Vienna a year later, bringing together a broad range of people from the field of 'alternative marketing' – from William P. Nyce on behalf of SERVV from the United States to Vincent Jaydee from the Bangladeshi Jute Works (a partner organization of both Bridge and the MCC) and Robert J. Webb from the Australian organization Trade Action.[90] Paul Meijs notably did not play the central role he had assumed the year before. For though a practical approach and the aim to make a large-scale difference could often be combined in the everyday activities pursued via world shops, these goals could also clash, especially if those involved felt either was being overemphasized. If anything, the shift towards an activism of everyday life was accompanied by a more outspoken political stance during the 1970s. Even within the ranks of SOS, this led to increasing tensions. By the end of the 1970s, the agency had parted ways with Meijs, its energetic but headstrong pioneer, and had abandoned its ambitions to become a European enterprise. A new generation of employees wanted to focus on products which could be sold in the Netherlands and would articulate a political impetus.

SOS's crises of the 1970s highlight how rapidly the idea of alternative trade had disseminated up until the point when those involved in different European countries were able to operate as individual organizations. The world shop groups which had appeared across Europe since the early 1970s were preoccupied with local action, and they set up national federations in most countries to exchange information, coordinate campaigns, and negotiate with alternative trading organizations. Nonetheless, they maintained a

Figure 3.4 Announcement for the International Workshop of Third World Producers. AMSAB-ISG, archive Oxfam-Wereldwinkels.

certain level of transnational collaboration, too, hosting regular international gatherings starting in 1976. The Dutch groups felt particularly responsible for these meetings, regarding themselves as the pioneers of this model for action. Their reports about the first international meetings in the Belgian village of Dongen in 1976, followed by successor meetings in Paris the following year, were less than enthusiastic, however. About forty-five representatives from France, Switzerland, Belgium, and the Netherlands had gathered in Paris. They certainly had a good time – the Algerian wine presented as an example of a 'political' product had been the subject of much careful interest. The overtures made by Dutch participants to convince the others that their activities should be politically oriented were less successful. Disparagingly, one Dutch observer noted that the Walloon and French participants in particular were 'less advanced in their political development'.[91] Strikingly, such evaluations of political awareness spoke of (under)development in terms which were just as problematically applied to countries in the 'Third World' as they were to people in the activists' immediate environment.

Despite such qualifications, the international meetings fostered awareness that their participants were part of a transnational movement. Such gatherings could also spur new forms of cooperation transnationally as well as closer to home, when groups from the same country became acquainted with one another.[92] Meanwhile, the Dutch world shops continued to promote an emphasis on political perspectives in fair trade activism through international gatherings. A group of representatives regarded the ten-year anniversary of the world shop in 1979 as an opportunity to strengthen transnational ties and promote a common approach. By then, they had gathered knowledge of groups in Belgium, France, Switzerland, West Germany, Great Britain, and Denmark. They had very little information on these latter three nations, however. 'The lack of a world shop federation in these (…) countries is the cause of our lack of information on these groups, and probably a reason for the lack of a real movement in these countries. That is why in many respects, the Dutch world shops are an example to them', wrote Wout Hagenaars, a man involved in the world shop in the Dutch town of Bergen op Zoom.[93] He could not have been more wrong. In fact, in West Germany and Great Britain, the fair trade movement had taken off early on.[94] The exchanges over launching cane sugar campaigns in these countries as well as U-Gruppen's approach in Aarhus were apparently unknown to a new group of world shop activists in the Netherlands.

This lack of knowledge about potential allies and common histories does not just reiterate how social movements often lack long-term memory. It also foregrounds the enormous changes which have affected transnational activism since the 1960s regarding the available means of communication. Indeed, paper-based media predominated during the 1970s and 1980s for these activists, who communicated primarily through handwritten and mimeographed letters. Locally and nationally, these missives could be supplemented with occasional phone calls and solidified through bulletins. Transnationally, more comprehensive communications were scarcely possible for local groups.

Physical gatherings played an important role in propelling the paper-based communications between activists. The hosts planning the tenth-anniversary celebration of the Dutch world shops hoped to establish common political positions in the course of the meeting. The prevalent focus on raising awareness locally, moreover, had caused no neglect of interest in international politics, as the place of world shops in European and international politics was an important topic on the agenda.[95] This combination of local activities and transnational politics was all the more palpable as world shop groups across Europe joined the campaigns of the rejuvenated peace movement during the early 1980s. During the sixth international meeting of the world shops near Strasbourg, the mood was notably resolute.

Although the hosts had tempered expectations, the world shops presented themselves as a vibrant group ready for coordinated action. Participants recognized that there were at least 700 world shops across Switzerland, West Germany, Austria, Belgium, France, Norway, Spain, Luxemburg, Great Britain, Denmark, Italy, and the Netherlands. West Germany, with more than 200 shops, appeared to be home to the largest number. After long hours of discussions, representatives from these countries decided to commit themselves to a common campaign on 'peace for development', aiming to highlight the consequences of a resurgent arms race for international trade relations and the position of the Global South.[96] Collaboration between world shops across Western Europe continued to develop haphazardly despite regular meetings and attempts to find common ground. A Belgian observer noted stark differences even within individual countries, where many local groups did not participate in national federations. Transnationally, a lack of funding, differing political priorities, and limited capacities were major factors.[97] The reliance on paper communications also highlights the difficulties in establishing regular exchanges across longer distances.

As the number of shops and their mutual acquaintance amongst their organizers grew, so did contact between fair trade advocates in the South and the North. Alternative trading organizations continued to act as important intermediaries, establishing relations between producers and outlets such as world shops. Producers from the Global South also continued to explore other channels, bypassing the alternative trading organizations. For example, the Sarvodaya Shramadana movement from Sri Lanka sought out potential buyers for its tea during the 1970s. In letters sent to potential allies, the movement presented itself as promoting the Buddhist principles of friendliness, compassion, shared happiness, and equanimity through the building of schools and hospitals as well as improvements made to the living conditions around tea plantations. Its tea eventually found its way to a world shop group at the Vrije Universiteit in Amsterdam, where it caused considerable turmoil. In 1974, the university world shop hosted an exhibition about the tea, sold it, and attempted to persuade the university's governors to buy it in large quantities.[98] The movement drew ample attention, and it was revealed that Sarvodaya Shramadana's tea revenue was a drop in the bucket when compared to the subsidies it received from European development agencies. Moreover, the movement apparently owned no tea plantations but rather bought its tea for export at regular Sri Lankan tea auctions.[99]

These revelations brought about a transnational dialogue about the situation in Sri Lanka, in which the movements chairman, Ariyaratne, participated through letters. Information from British fair trade activists also played a role, as the campaign outlet War on Want had been educating the British public about the 'cost of a cup of tea', informing people about the working conditions on Sri Lankan tea plantations.[100] The volunteers working at the university world shop concluded that selling large quantities of tea had no real impact on living conditions for tea plantation workers. Nor would Sarvodaya Shramadana make a significant amount of money via increased sales. This did not mean that selling it was pointless, however. Sales of tea were, according to Ariyaratne, primarily symbolic, a 'symbolic drop in the ocean of prevalent colonial channels of trade'. Selling Sarvodaya's tea could help identify this ongoing consequence of colonialism.[101]

Not just ideological principles, then, caused activists to regard products primarily as symbolic items. Particularly during their early years, world shops lacked the requisite reach to have a notable financial impact on producers' revenue. And though fair trade activists wanted to acknowledge the views and circumstances of marginalized groups, they had few opportunities for personal exchanges. In practice, most relations were established indirectly through import organizations and contacts at embassies.[102] With few direct links to producers, moreover, it was very hard to find plausible partners who could be supported through the selling of their wares. The situation gradually changed starting in the late 1970s, as a group of leftist states including Algeria and Nicaragua made their products available through alternative trading organizations.

The Stichting Ideële Import, a Dutch foundation, epitomized this development. Founded by activists who had been active in denouncing Portuguese colonialism, the organization established relations with Angola, Mozambique, Guinee Bissau, and the Cape Verdean Islands once they gained independence. Their foundation coordinated moving the belongings of people relocating to these countries, a task which soon expanded to include exporting items such as learning materials for development.[103] Mediating between local groups and development organizations, Stichting Ideële Import helped to develop a boat suited for Cape Verdean tuna fishers, designed by Dutch shipbuilders and subsidized by a West German development organization.[104] The tuna the fishers caught made its way back to the Netherlands, where it was sold in world shops. The states from which Stichting Ideële Import and its allies procured their products were not regarded suspiciously by world shop members, who were usually wary of conducting sales with any other goal than raising awareness. These products' provenance ensured that their sale fit the political engagement of the groups like a glove. Raising awareness and providing practical support could be seamlessly combined.

Many other world shop members – often less outspoken than those who fought the loud ideological battles – had been more pragmatic about selling from the outset. Moderate fair trade activists opted to promote the economic development of people in the South by selling items produced by cooperatives, which were the favoured partners of many alternative trading agencies because the cooperative tradition stood at some distance from capitalism. The South's economic development thus continued to dominate the agenda of the movement, but instead of promoting a reformed system of global trade, activists emphasized the empowerment of individual producers or progressive countries.

Despite temporarily stepping out of the limelight of national and international politics, fair trade activism thus persisted through the 1970s. Connected through written and mimeographed letters, bulletins, flyers, and posters, local groups adopted the world shop model across Europe. These functioned as local hubs, where common concerns, ranging from development and peace to ecology and gender equality, brought people together. Attention was drawn to these issues in small stores, at market stalls, or at tables installed in the backs of churches. Most of these shop groups' survival depended on the sale of at least some items, but otherwise they did not attempt to maximize their sales volume.[105] Their concerns were readily discernible by the products they sold: brochures on international economic relations, handicrafts by small cooperatives, wine from revolutionary Algeria, toilet paper rolls made from recycled paper. Even though these activists once more took aim at national and international policies and structures within the realm of politics, this did not entail a return to those campaigns for fair trade which had aimed for swift international reform. Many world shop groups participated in demonstrations for peace, but global economic justice for now was primarily to be attained through making a difference on a small scale, at the level of the individual and the small group.

This evolution sheds light on a development which likely goes beyond the fair trade movement. The years after 1973 were a period of crisis that lasted up through the onset of a second wave of activism in the 1980s. In the case of the fair trade movement, this period falls between the remarkable success of the Cane Sugar Campaign and the invigorating introduction of fair trade certification at the end of the 1980s. Scholarship on social activism has established that movements actually expand most during periods of less notable activity.[106] That paradox can be explained if we consider the new orientation adopted amongst activists. Local activism offered people across Europe the opportunities to connect large issues to their daily lives in personally meaningful ways, even if large-scale impact remained out of view for the time being. World shops and alternative trading organizations thus connected people in the North and the South, anchored the issue of fair trade in large and small towns, experimented with new repertoires of activism, and offered practical activities that allowed people to come together despite ideological differences. They found ways to target companies, governments, and their fellow citizens in their own communities. Instead of declining, fair trade activism gradually took root and transformed itself, and did so beyond the purview of national observers. Their actions would lay the foundation for the introduction of fair trade certification during the 1980s.

4 COFFEE
Turning towards the Market

Coffee has been a defining product of the fair trade movement since the late 1960s, when activists first recognized its potential as a means of addressing global inequality. Coffee, a well-known and popular beverage in many parts of the world, was regularly purchased. The need for woodcarvings and plaited baskets was limited, but demand for coffee would never wane. Like cane sugar, it was extraordinarily suited to expose the unjust structures of global trade relations. Over the course of colonial exploitation, coffee had become a product which Europeans associated with the exotic South. It was a commodity which could only be harvested and exported through hard labour, yet the meagre compensation received by workers was precarious income. Colonial rulers, later succeeded by multinational companies, made handsome profits from coffee, but coffee planters and pickers often made only a pittance.

The contrast between the harsh working conditions and the relative luxury of drinking a cup of coffee played into the hands of those who wanted to reform trade relations. Coffee was also a practical product. After being harvested and washed or dried, coffee beans were easy to transport without their quality being compromised. The possibility of combining coffee beans from a range of different producers during roasting and blending thus enabled fair trade initiatives to work with many small producers. Importers close to the consumer markets, because they could control the roasting and blending processes, could retain substantial control over the final product's quality.

Fair trade activists started selling coffee at the turn of the 1970s. It soon became the most popular product offered by alternative trading agencies and world shops. The introduction of fair trade-certified coffee in mainstream stores at the end of the 1980s brought about a remarkable expansion of the reach and trade volume achieved by the movement. The historiography of the fair trade movement therefore presents the late 1980s as a breakthrough, a transformation which made a marginal movement mainstream. Many accounts of activists who took part in this change regard it as a success story because the movement's visibility and economic scope expanded, and many more producers could be included in trading activities.[1] But numerous scholars, and not a few regretful activists, regard this era as a dangerous departure from the movement's initial ideals. According to this view, certification opened the door to co-optation by companies which did not share their ideals and an acceptance of the rules of the global market they had once set out to transform.[2]

These conflicting assessments about the history of fair trade are related to the broader evaluation of the global turn to the market during the 1980s. In international politics, development policies aimed at 'structural adjustment' prevailed. This orientation implied that countries encountering economic hardship had to adjust their policies to align themselves with international markets. Institutions such as the International Monetary Fund and the World Bank expected governments which failed to satisfy their debtors to reduce government spending, privatize state-owned enterprises, welcome international investment, and raise taxes. This new approach replaced the strategy previously propagated amongst 'developing' countries, which centred on substituting imports of processed goods with local production. This way, the international imbalance produced by the growing price gap between raw commodities and processed goods could be mitigated. The new demands no longer allowed for this approach. The population in the affected countries footed the bill for these adjustments as their real wages dropped significantly.[3]

In the history of Europe and North America, the turn towards the market has become known as the rise of neoliberalism. Advocates of market-centred policies experienced a remarkable ascendency from the 1970s onwards. To cope with the economic stagnation which then plagued many Western countries, conservative political leaders like Margaret Thatcher in Great Britain and Ronald Reagan in the United States deregulated markets and stabilized their nation's currencies. They championed so-called small government, which cut back public expenditure and gave priority to private investment. Similar to the structural adjustment policies demanded by the World Bank, governments across Western Europe attempted to promote market competition, curb wages, cut back on government expenditure, and privatize public services like railways and postal and financial services.[4] At the end of the 1980s and into the early 1990s, the proponents of these policies felt validated by the demise of communism in Eastern Europe and the ultimate collapse of the Soviet Union in 1991 – surely free markets had prevailed as the only viable underpinning for prosperous democratic societies.[5] The conclusion that policymakers saw no alternative to free markets after the end of the Cold War was bolstered by the course taken by the governments which followed in the wake of the more radical proponents of market orientation. Governments headed by the Democrat Bill Clinton in the US and social democrats like the German chancellor Gerhard Schröder, the British prime minister Tony Blair, and the Dutch prime minister Wim Kok did not reverse the turn to the market but rather seemed to advance it further.[6]

It is tempting to regard this era as a time when neoliberal economists, businessmen, and politicians transformed society to suit their agenda. This purported triumph of free markets during the 1980s and 1990s has coloured the assessments of the history of the fair trade movement in this era, too. Initiatives which were aimed at market actors or adopted market-based practices have been related to developments in the political realm.[7] Short of supposing some form of ignorance even amongst those fair trade activists who had been vocal critics of prevailing trade relations, how can we make sense of the turn to the market in this era? An analysis of the evolution of the fair trade movement during the 1980s and 1990s provides a better understanding of the turn to the market in this era. It can explain why and how people who were critical about what they called capitalism could come to regard market-oriented strategies as viable.

The early results of the global turn to the market may serve as a starting point to explore this question. The debt crisis which started in Latin America in 1982 would become an important rallying point for fair trade activism. At the time, world shop groups engaged with a wide range of topics in close collaboration with groups traditionally counted amongst other social movements such as the peace and ecological movements. World shop groups across Europe connected themselves to the revival of activism around these issues in particular. 'Disarmament for peace' had been the slogan anchoring a collective campaign mounted by European world shops in 1983.[8] Responding to a survey amongst world shops in the Netherlands that same year, almost two-thirds of the groups approached indicated that alongside 'Third World issues', they were also campaigning to address 'nuclear armament and peace'. Almost all the groups spent part of their time on activities devoted to changing their own environment, including ecological issues. Nonetheless, all deemed it essential to educate themselves and others about the situation in the so-called Third World. Every group which had campaigned in 1982 had engaged with that topic.[9] Fair trade activists thus also manifested distinct concerns and activities. As they started campaigning on behalf of Latin Americans heavily affected by the debt crisis, selling and educating once more went hand in hand. At the same time, fair trade activists explored new approaches due to their dissatisfaction over the preceding years' results and the realization that new circumstances called for new methods.

A first factor in fair trade activists turning to the market during the 1980s was the growing distance between social movements and institutional politics. The emergence of successful social movements around issues such as fair trade, the emancipation of women and of homosexual women and men, the environment, and peace had unintentionally undermined prospects for action in the sphere of parliamentary politics. These movements claimed to represent citizens just like political parties did. They questioned the idea that politics were made only in an institutional setting. Naturally, they collaborated with likeminded political parties, but they often pragmatically chose their partners according to who endorsed their aims. This was true not just of these new movements. Increasingly, 'old' social movements became flexible about their partnerships, too. Eschewing an ideal commonly held until the 1950s, social movements no longer aspired to constitute settled coalitions on the basis of shared collective convictions. Rather, they pursued inclusive partnerships wherever overlapping agendas allowed for them.[10]

Those active in the fair trade movement joined large-scale actions for peace and the environment aimed at national and international politics in the early 1980s. More often than not, these campaigns did not impact the policies they were targeting. This was particularly the case in the field of international economic relations. Activists advocating for a more equitable position for the Global South had come to expect very little from institutional politics. After experiencing the repeated failures of international meetings such as the United Nations Conference on Trade and Development (UNCTAD) conferences and the unresponsiveness characterizing European politics, activists had given up hopes of achieving change on behalf of the Global South directly through international political mechanisms. The network of organizations which had attempted to coordinate campaigns on an international level since the Cane Sugar Campaign continued to meet under the umbrella of the International Coalition for Development Action throughout the 1970s, but it served mainly as a network for exchanging information. The enthusiasm for large-scale campaigns directed at international organizations had all but evaporated.[11] The rise of rightwing governments during the second half of the 1970s in many Western European countries and the ongoing economic malaise produced a less welcoming climate for initiatives around development cooperation. In instances where activists had benefitted from government subsidies, as with the world shops in the Netherlands, this financial backing was becoming insecure.

A second reason to turn towards targeting the market directly was the success enjoyed by fair trade activists involved in such attempts over the years. Many of these efforts had revolved around coffee. Initial campaigns around this product had leveraged its symbolic potential. After the second UNCTAD in 1968, the Dutch activist Piet Reckman published an open letter to the fictitious Columbian coffee farmer Juan Valdez, a figure made popular by coffee commercials. Reckman wrote to him about the realities of poverty, unemployment, and high child mortality amongst Columbian coffee farmers and their families. Adding insult to injury, Reckman noted, the price for coffee beans had fallen significantly. Ten years ago, a Jeep had cost a coffee farmer fourteen sacks of coffee beans; now they had to sell at least forty.[12] Because UNCTAD had not addressed this strident inequality, Reckman believed that the only option left for people like Valdez was violent resistance.[13] Continuing the fictitious correspondence, after a couple of months, Valdez replied that he had indeed joined a band of guerrilla fighters. He asked people in the North who were sympathetic to their cause to find ways to resist the unjust global trade relations in their own countries. They could also send money to help the fight he and his comrades were waging. For instance, Dutch consumers could pay a voluntary 'guerrilla tax' on every coffee package they bought and send the money raised to support them.[14]

A campaign to sell coffee with an additional 'liberation tax' was actually launched by Dutch activists to support the Angolan resistance movement against their Portuguese colonizers and to provide funds for Latin American labour movements as well. These specific aims were accompanied by critiques of the structures of international trade and the legitimacy of capitalism.[15] The corresponding moneybox and poster disquietingly illustrated the tragic situation of coffee farmers: the coffee farmer was at once strangled by a fist called 'economic pressure' and force-fed with a spoon called 'development aid'. Frightened, the farmer echoes Jesus in the book of Matthew and reminds his tormentor of the latter's (Christian) duty and contradictory acts: 'Senor, does your left hand know what your right hand is doing?'[16] Such initiatives travelled quickly even in the early 1970s. Posters modelled on the Dutch campaign appeared in Switzerland in 1973 as part of a similar Café Solidaridad campaign.[17]

This campaign did intend to sell coffee, but not of the fair trade variety we know nowadays. The coffee sold was not bought directly from producers for a fair price. But in the next action in which world shops focused on coffee, the product's provenance did matter. The boycott of Angolan coffee launched in 1972 distinguished regular coffee from 'bad' coffee – coffee that benefitted colonial rulers and their associates at the expense of an oppressed population. After this boycott successfully drove all Dutch supermarkets to abstain from selling Angolan coffee (as detailed in Chapter 3), the world shop movement in particular sought out 'good' coffee. Tanzania turned out to be exactly the country they were looking for.[18]

Figure 4.1 Poster of the fictive coffee farmer Juan Valdez. Regionaal Historisch Centrum Zuid-Oost Utrecht, archive Sjaloom.

World shops and likeminded groups in countries like Switzerland, West Germany, and the Netherlands started selling tins of soluble coffee from Tanzania around 1975. They were imported by the Amsterdam coffee roaster Simon Lévelt. The Swiss coffee campaign quickly managed to sell 80,000 tins.[19] This soluble coffee was particularly attractive for activists, because coffee remained a product which could highlight the colonial legacy which continued to shape the structures of international trade to the detriment of countries in the South. Attempts to stabilize the international coffee market and to support diversification had generally stalled after good intentions were expressed.[20] Moreover, Tanzania symbolized a third way between communism and capitalism. Its first president, Julius Nyerere, fervently propagated a combination of African traditions and socialism as the notion of Ujamaa, from which the soluble 'Ujamaa-coffee' took its name. This philosophy called on local communities to develop autonomously by fairly dividing the income from agriculture amongst themselves and investing profits in common facilities.[21]

Some moderate fair trade groups had their doubts about Nyerere's socialism, leading West German fair trade pioneers to seek out other producers. The alternative trading organizations Gesellschaft zur Förderung der Partnerschaft mit der Dritten Welt (GEPA) and Stichting Ontwikkelings-Samenwerking (SOS) could turn to the network of the Catholic development organization Misereor in West Germany for help. They had identified the Guatemalan cooperative Fedecocagua as a source for coffee. Established with support from Misereor, it was led by Alfredo Hernández Contreras, who had studied in West Germany on a scholarship from the Christian-democratic Konrad Adenauer Foundation. In 1973, SOS imported its first shipment from Fedecocagua, which was sold under the label 'Indio-coffee' in West Germany and the Netherlands.[22]

Around 1980, a third variety was added after the Sandinista National Liberation Front took power in Nicaragua the year before. Their success made the country a focal point for solidarity activism in the North.[23] The Sandinistas nationalized agriculture, organized coffee farmers in cooperatives, and had the national umbrella organization Encafé coordinate the export of all coffee produced in the country. These measures made it relatively straightforward for any company to import coffee from Nicaragua. This coffee was uniquely suited for fair trade activism because the new government combined a socialist outlook with broad public appeal. SOS Wereldhandel, GEPA, and the Swiss OS3 all undertook to order portions of their

Figure 4.2 A package of Indio Coffee marketed in West Germany in the 1970s. GEPA – The Fair Trade Company/A. Welsing.

coffee imports from Encafé. In addition, the new Dutch alternative trading organization Stichting Ideële Import established itself as an important international mediator on behalf of Encafé based on previous connections to the radical left and anticolonial movements.[24] Nicaragua's wide appeal eventually declined as the Sandinistas radicalized in clashes with the so-called Contras, supported by the United States.[25] When the US government announced a boycott of Nicaraguan products in 1985, Stichting Ideële Import was one of the few alternative trading organizations to remain a staunch supporter. It managed to circumvent the boycott, providing American supporters with coffee from Nicaragua by roasting it in the Netherlands and then exporting it to the United States as a nominally Dutch product.[26]

Looking to Sell More

The appearance of coffee suppliers like Encafé fundamentally changed the relation between activists in the North and producers in the South. Until the end of the 1970s, there was scarcely any coffee which could be sold as a solidarity product. Under those circumstances, it had not been a fundamental issue if fair trade activists sold products as a symbolic means to spotlight and illustrate structural inequalities. World shops gave solidarity with the South a tangible presence throughout Europe, but their turnover was hardly significant in economic terms. Over the course of the 1980s, new producers could supply more coffee than world shops and alternative trading organizations were able to sell. Coffee producers from the South were sympathetic to their activities, but they also wanted to make a living from what they produced.

Selling coffee and targeting companies through boycotts had thus proved successful methods for fair trade activists to make a symbolic and material impact. These results reinforced a sense amongst activists that they should move on from well-meaning amateurism and an accompanying commitment to a distinctly alternative lifestyle, which became increasingly pronounced during the 1980s. For example, Belgian fair trade activists started to question the ideological jargon and the focus on intellectual issues even in official statements, an attitude evident in debates unfolding in response to a new position paper prepared by Oxfam Wereldwinkels during the early 1980s. Even though the Belgian movement adhered to the goal of achieving a socialist society, the members of the preparatory committee wanted to draw up a text which foregrounded the daily reality of those active in local campaigns.[27] Intellectualism and 'nineteenth-century' Marxist terminology had to be avoided, and practical experiences accentuated.[28] Similar conversations were common across the board amongst Western European groups at the local, national, and transnational levels.[29] For example, at the international conference of world shop groups in Cologne in 1987, Swiss world shop activists shared their experiences with setting up more market-oriented shops with salaried employees and discussed focusing on daily necessities. Their presentation led to a lively exchange amongst participants from across Europe, with subjects ranging from the practical advantages of having permanent staff to the ideological aims of the shops and the need to achieve sufficient turnover.[30]

A group of coffee farmers from the south of Mexico took the initiative to resolve the growing imbalance between supply and demand for fair trade coffee. In 1981, they had set out to find a new way to alleviate poverty in their region. Speaking to representatives of a Jesuit mission, they concluded that cooperation could improve their situation. If they built storage rooms for their coffee together and collectively sold their beans directly to coffee roasters, they would reduce their dependence on brokers and their harvest would yield more revenue. The same year, a first attempt indeed led to higher income, spurring a group of farmers to pursue a more permanent form of cooperation.[31] The cooperative Unión de Comunidades Indígenas del Región del Istmo (UCIRI), nowadays known as one of the world's most successful fair trade cooperatives, was born. The cooperative persisted despite violent opposition instigated by coffee brokers. In 1985 it was the first independent organization to obtain an export license from the Mexican government. Being allowed to sell their coffee directly to foreign companies, UCIRI set out to find suitable partners. European alternative trading organizations were delighted to be contacted by this new coffee supplier. It could offer an alternative to the coffee from the Fedecocagua cooperative, which had become controversial due to its murky relationship to Guatemala's authoritarian military regime, its lack of internal democracy, and the headstrong conduct of its leader.[32] UCIRI also provided a welcome alternative to the coffee from the socialist countries Tanzania and Nicaragua, neither of which was popular with the more moderate groups within the ranks of the fair trade outlets.[33]

Thanks to the contacts of the Dutch priest Frans van der Hoff, who had joined the UCIRI, the cooperative connected with several European importers. In 1985 Jan Hissel and Gerd Nicoleit travelled to Mexico on behalf of the West German alternative trading organization GEPA. They were accompanied by the Dutch coffee roaster Hans Lévelt and agricultural adviser Loek uit het Broek. The latter concluded that the farmers were producing their coffee in an ecologically responsible fashion. They had not taken up the use of pesticides, in part due to their high costs. The principles of organic farming also aligned closely with regional agricultural traditions. If they applied for their coffee to be sold as a certified organic product, they could significantly increase their revenue.[34] To Hans Lévelt – who had been advising fair trade activists off and on since the 1970s – certification was important because his company had specialized in supplying environment-friendly coffee. GEPA had also added ecological criteria to complement their social guidelines during the

Figure 4.3 Representatives of coffee farmers from Peru, Mexico, and the Congo visit the new coffee depot at the Neuteboom roastery. *Algemeen Dagblad*, 17 October 1992.

1980s. Jan Hissel pursued the issue for GEPA, leading to the German eco-label Naturland certifying UCIRI as an ecologically responsible producer in 1986.[35] The visit in 1985 did not result in any firm agreements at that time, but groundwork was laid for the trade relations that would flourish in the years to come. UCIRI first supplied coffee to GEPA in 1987, a year after it had begun supplying Simon Lévelt and the Dutch alternative trading organization SOS Wereldhandel.

Members of UCIRI soon concluded, however, that they could sell more coffee than these trade partners could handle. They therefore explored other channels. To UCIRI's members, the symbolic dimension of fair trade products did not automatically trump sales volume, dependent as they were on sales for their income. They urged their trade partners in the North to operate more professionally and find new sales opportunities. Some activists were reluctant to do so, insisting on the symbolic nature of their selling and finding commercial thinking distasteful. Because new approaches were explored, it was not surprising that a relative outsider would eventually take the lead: the Dutch ecumenical development organization Solidaridad, which had established close relations with many Latin American organizations, became UCIRI's primary partner.[36] This interdenominational organization began in 1966 as a yearly Catholic Advent campaign conducted on behalf first of Latin American churches and then, from 1969 onwards, of Protestant churches as well.[37] Since the middle of the 1970s, Solidaridad had also championed educating people in the Netherlands about the situation in Latin America. According to staff member Paul van der Harst, speaking in 1975, Solidaridad wanted to enable people in Latin America to transform their societies themselves.[38]

Just like the many world shop groups it cooperated with, Solidaridad had little appetite for setting up commercial ventures. In 1979 a couple of its staff members attempted to import tapestries from Chile as part of a campaign to draw attention to Latin American slums. World shops participating in the campaign could distribute educational material, but they could also sell tapestries made by women in Chilean slums.[39] Selling such items was not as straightforward as they had hoped, however. The first 400 tapestries, judged 'rebellious art' by Chilean customs officers, were confiscated. Paul van der Harst sent a slightly awkward letter to the prospective buyers: would they be willing to convert their payment to a donation in support of the women in Chile?[40]

A perceived lack of resonance and a gradual decline of donations from churchgoers made Solidaridad open to reconsidering its goals and tactics as the Latin American economic crisis set in.[41] Likewise, many fair trade organizations were confronted with less favourable governments reducing funding and decreased private donations due to the prolonged economic crisis and the dissolution of traditional religious and ideological communities. The evolution of an 'alternative milieu' in many European countries also increasingly stood in the way of appealing to a broader public. As this milieu became delineated through distinct activities, publications, and patterns of consumption, people not included within it felt less inclined to rally behind common goals.[42]

Solidaridad wanted to break the deadlock by promoting campaigns which offered people practical means of engagement, like writing letters or buying particular products. Such activities had worked for organizations such as Amnesty International and had been the most successful part of fair trade activism over the course of the 1970s. Moreover, Solidaridad's staff wanted to highlight how the Netherlands were implicated in the Latin American crisis. A 1984 initiative was thus directed towards the Dutch ministers of finance and development cooperation, amongst others. Participants would write letters encouraging them to stand up for the concerns of people in Latin America during the International Monetary Fund's annual meeting.[43] Companies also came into view. A 1985 campaign called attention to Dutch banks which had a stake in the debt crisis. The interest their customers received came at the expense of people in Latin America, their campaign argued.[44] These customers were asked to donate a portion of the interest they received to an 'interest solidarity fund' for Latin America. In addition, they were encouraged to write letters to the board of their banks demanding a policy change.[45]

This new strategy was a clear rejection of attempts to withdraw into an alternative milieu. This approach gradually evolved over a series of campaigns involving Solidaridad during the early 1980s. Addressing the role of banks in the Latin American debt crisis, for example, Solidaridad staff members opposed supporters who wanted to advise people to transfer their accounts to smaller, socially responsible banks. The campaign team at Solidaridad replied that it was not enough to be active within the margins of the banking system. Notable improvement could be achieved only if activists succeeded in getting large banks to change their ways. Alternative banks were important 'signs of hope', but the existence of an alternative did not absolve citizens of their duty to engage with the mainstream system.[46] Solidaridad's staff therefore proposed a two-pronged approach. Alternative organizations should show that there were feasible options for operating more sustainably, and customers, for their part, had to pressure regular companies into acting more responsibly.

Coffee companies were the central focus of this new approach from 1986 onwards. The ambitious organizer Nico Roozen had joined Solidaridad in 1984 and became a driving force there. According to the Solidaridad campaign team, the coffee trade could demonstrate that hunger was the result not of scarcity but rather of injustice. Everywhere in the Global South, poor coffee farmers depended on large companies which made profits reselling their beans. First, the campaign attempted to increase sales through existing channels. In 1986 a campaign around the slogan 'pure coffee, a matter of taste' highlighted the existence of fair trade coffee – Indio by SOS, Stichting Ideële Import's solidarity coffee, and Café Organico, offered by Simon Lèvelt. In collaboration with local groups, Solidaridad aimed to sell coffee in world shops, churches, and mainstream stores. Bulk consumers such as hospitals, offices, and schools were also approached. A coalition of national

Figure 4.4 Three types of fair trade coffee on a poster advertising 'Zuivere koffie: een kwestie van smaak'. International Institute of Social History.

organizations in the realm of fair trade hosted an initiative to persuade local councils to switch to fair trade coffee.[47] The 'pure coffee' campaign gained considerable support: many churches joined, and it was supported by the trade union federations and the largest Dutch consumer association.[48]

Paralleling these attempts to sell more fair trade coffee, Solidaridad's staff members were part of an interdenominational committee which contacted coffee roasters. Together, they asked them to buy coffee which was produced in an ecologically responsible fashion and for which farmers and workers would be fairly compensated.[49] The coffee roasters' representatives, however, opined that they *were* trading fairly as long as they were acting according to what 'the market' dictated. They took offence to the suggestion that their coffee was not 'pure', as Solidaridad's campaign was suggesting. If they paid producers according to market rates, there were no grounds for reproach. Buying selectively from cooperatives or leftist states, or artificially raising prices, would be engaging in politics rather than trade, the secretary of the coffee roasters' federation ventured to say.[50] Solidaridad and its partners, for their part, held that 'the market' did not dictate prices independently. Anyone engaged in the coffee trade was morally obliged to take broader factors into account: the work that farmers invested into growing coffee, how much money they needed to survive, and the environmental impact. The 'free market' was in fact a fiction. Individual coffee farmers usually had no choice but to sell to middlemen. Moreover, coffee was often traded under the conditions of trade agreements, even after the collapse in 1983 of the International Coffee Agreement regulating the global coffee trade.[51]

Despite the divide between their respective views, Solidaridad continued conversations with the coffee roasters in the hope of transforming the market. Roozen put forth a proposal to import 230,400 bales of coffee from small farmers 'under conditions favourable to the producers', starting with 10 per cent of the target volume and subsequently increasing the amount from year to year.[52] Although sceptical of the roasters' willingness to cooperate, Roozen hoped that societal mobilization would eventually make them go along with the proposal.[53] A visit from four UCIRI members in 1987 was one means to increase the pressure. They visited local churches to speak about their organization and the 'story behind coffee'. Next to such 'groundwork', they also spoke with the leadership of the trade union for the food sector, the minister of development cooperation, and directors of large Dutch coffee roasters.[54]

The members of the Mexican delegation had their own agenda. They wanted to draw attention to their organic coffee and to see for themselves how they could sell more of their product. According to Frans van der Hoff's recollections, they had considered different scenarios. Establishing their own import business in Europe proved too costly. Talks with the roasters made it clear that these firms were not likely to commit to buying around 10 per cent of their coffee from small farmers.[55] UCIRI's members thus opined that fair trade coffee had to become available in places where people bought their daily groceries.[56] Solidaridad staff had studied the possibility of marketing their own brand of coffee in supermarkets and grocery stores.[57] The Dutch market share of 0.2 per cent could easily be exceeded if customers would not have to go far afield to buy fair trade coffee. Based on market research, Solidaridad expected to be able to obtain a market share of up to 2 per cent. Several small roasters had already indicated they could process the corresponding two million kilos of coffee beans – one million from cooperatives, one million from Nicaragua. The greatest difficulty would be funding the project. One objective was to offer producers financial security through advance payment. This meant that before a single kilo of coffee was sold, substantial funds were needed to secure contracts with producers.[58]

This new approach had now become viable because fair trade coffee producers offered more coffee than could be sold on the existing alternative circuit.[59] A coffee brand available in mainstream stores would help producers sell more coffee and would pressure companies to behave more responsibly. Although the approach was strategically viable, funding and movement support for the project were uncertain. The world shop groups were particularly critical, as it was hard to predict the consequences of introducing fair trade coffee in supermarkets: Would world shops – which depended on selling coffee to a large extent – survive the introduction of the fair trade brand?[60] Was it really viable to collaborate with capitalist retail chains? And how could education about global inequality continue if fair trade products were sold outside of spaces dedicated to it?[61]

The Solidaridad working group pressed on, reassuring alternative trading organizations and world shops that they would also benefit from the endeavour. Getting supermarkets and other regular stores to sell fair trade products would be the crowning achievement of their efforts to make fair trade a common norm.

By August 1987, enough donors had been secured to move ahead. Solidaridad ventured to establish the Max Havelaar Foundation, which was officially founded on 20 May 1988. The choice of Max Havelaar as a name was remarkable, as it referred to the eponymous protagonist of a famous Dutch anticolonial novel published in 1860. The initiators claimed continuity between nineteenth-century resistance to Dutch colonial rule and their own attempts in the service of justice in the postcolonial world of the 1980s. Once again, fair trade activists positioned their struggle against global inequality as a way to overcome a colonial past which had not ended even as most countries in the South had achieved political independence.

The Max Havelaar Foundation was made up of a remarkable mix of coffee producers, alternative trading organizations, Solidaridad representatives, ecclesiastical organizations, coffee roasters, and consumer organizations.[62] Three-quarters of its funds were provided by religious organizations. Religious networks continued to possess the capacity to launch such civic initiatives in the 1980s. Solidaridad's familiarity with these networks as an interdenominational organization turned out to be an essential asset for the enterprise, as was the support of many church members.[63]

Stumbling Across Certification

The foundation established, but there was nonetheless the open question of how Max Havelaar coffee would end up on supermarket shelves. The original plan called for the foundation to introduce its own brand, independently managing coffee purchases, contracting with roasters, and hiring a professional partner firm to handle marketing.[64] In discussing the plan with potential commercial partners, however, the option of some form of fair trade certification had been developed. Certification could be applied to any product any company wanted to sell, as long as it satisfied a set of criteria determined by the Max Havelaar Foundation. Representatives of the sizeable Ahold retail chain had even agreed that their company could introduce its own Max Havelaar-certified coffee before the end of the year if the foundation opted to take this approach.[65] Certification had been developed to provide consumers with quality control over certain aspects of products not observable with their own eyes. Usually, businesses themselves vouched for the quality of products. A certificate, on the other hand, was granted by a third party, affirming to any buyer that the product in question met the criteria stipulated for the certificate. These guidelines mostly pertained to qualities which were difficult for an individual consumer to verify, such as the safety of engineered products or the organic methods used to grow certain crops.[66]

In discussions with Solidaridad's staff, the Ahold representatives had pushed for the development of a certificate instead of a distinct brand, because the former option would allow the retail chain to conduct its own business with coffee farmers deemed eligible under the rules of the certification programme. The company had positive experiences with certificates for organic food and meat. For fair trade, however, there were potential drawbacks. Certification would grant the initiators less of a say about the profile of the products marketed under its banner. Through competitive pricing, large-scale roasters would be able to oust smaller participants such as alternative trading organizations. Ironically, they would be able to absorb potential losses because of their profit margins on non-certified coffee. The advantages outweighed these reservations, however. The participating companies would conduct their business on their own accord. The foundation would not be required to raise large sums of money to pre-finance coffee purchases. Experienced companies could also react to growing demand much more effectively than the foundation could. The large roasters, moreover, would react much less aggressively to the initiative if it were introduced by other roasters instead of an outside entity.[67] The approach also aligned with Solidaridad's strategy to target regular market actors. If companies themselves engaged with the requirements of fair trade certification, fair trade could become part of corporate practice.[68]

Overall, the certificate had practical as well as strategic advantages. The introduction of fair trade coffee in supermarkets would be more manageable and comprehensive. The promise of a quick increase in turnover would benefit coffee producers in the short term. The participation of large companies in the field of coffee marketing advanced Solidaridad's goal of drawing mainstream companies into the practice of fair trade. In addition, Solidaridad's staff and many others involved had become acquainted with this approach in the parallel world of ecological activism. Certificates were a proven instrument in this domain and had helped to provide a much larger group of consumers with organic food.[69]

As the introduction of fair trade-certified coffee in supermarkets drew near, the large coffee roasting companies tried to undercut the initiative. First, they announced an independent plan to buy a portion of their coffee beans directly from small farmers.[70] Then, they successfully pressured Ahold into withdrawing from the Max Havelaar initiative. All of a sudden, the fate of the entire venture became uncertain. Only the willingness of Jan Fokkinga, from the Almelo coffee roaster Neuteboom, to stay on board ensured that the launch would take place in November 1988 as planned.[71] Other small roasters then signalled that they, too, were ready to participate. Several supermarket chains were also open to selling the coffee. Shortly before launch, Ahold returned to the fold and asked to re-join the initiative.[72] On 15 November 1988, coffee packages with a blue Max Havelaar stamp made their debut in supermarkets throughout the Netherlands.[73] Because many supermarkets had decided to participate only at the last minute, many potential buyers were disappointed when enquiring after the fair trade coffee they had seen advertised on television and in the papers.[74]

The introduction of Max Havelaar coffee was met positively, highlighting the significant demand for such an initiative and its importance to small farmers, who could now sell their coffee for a fair price.[75] Solidaridad, for their part, were quite content: they claimed that the 'power of the consumer' had prevailed. Shop owners had chosen to participate due to the pressure exerted by the public and the press. The considerable publicity around the introduction – supported by Prince Claus von Amsberg, the husband of Beatrix, the reigning queen – meant that 65 per cent of the public was aware of Max Havelaar coffee. Its market share had quickly risen to 3 per cent. That percentage was much higher than what alternative trade had previously achieved, although Solidaridad's staff felt that it would have to be even higher for large roasters to take them seriously.[76]

Certification was introduced with the intention of transforming international trade. The market was not fair or unfair in principle, and it could be used to advance justice – first and foremost by paying producers a fair price, but also by using market share as a lever. If consumers bought fair trade coffee, organizations

Figure 4.5 Poster announcing the Max Havelaar certificate. International Institute of Social History.

such as Solidaridad could use that fact in urging companies and politicians to act on behalf of a fairer market. This pragmatism was not an alternative to idealism but rather a strategy to bring their ideals into reach.[77] A matter that participants debated was whether their ideals entailed working towards some free-market alternative or towards a free market based on justice. In practice, however, the difference was hardly noticeable. After the Sandinistas lost the 1990 elections in Nicaragua, hardly any coffee production remained that directly supported anticapitalistic groups.

The relations between organizations within the fair trade movement shifted as a result of the introduction of fair trade certification. Local groups like those involved in world shops receded in importance because the products they sold could be obtained elsewhere. The national and international organizations which determined the policies around these products became more significant. Alternative trading organizations such as SOS Wereldhandel, GEPA, and Ten Thousand Villages were no longer central to the movement because others were now importing fair trade items. Until that time, they had vouched for fair trade with their names and reputations. In the eyes of consumers, this role had now been taken up by certificates. This development was all the more awkward because some partner organizations did not yet qualify for certification. Certification of many fair trade products, moreover, was not yet possible. Although the Dutch alternative trading organizations had supported the establishment of Max Havelaar, they soon sought an alternative which would burden them with fewer restrictions and provide them greater influence. This caused tension between them and the leadership of Max Havelaar as the latter tried to expand the use of the certificate to other European countries and to introduce new fair trade-certified products like bananas, cocoa, and jeans.

Attempts to broaden the certification initiative were first aimed at Belgium, Switzerland, and France, where sister organizations were soon established with the aim of selling Max Havelaar-certified coffee through regular trade channels. The rapid proliferation of certification was enabled by the manifold transnational relations within the fair trade movement, which had been cultivated ever since the Cane Sugar Campaign at the end of the 1960s. The first steps towards the certificate itself had emerged from the interactions of Frans van der Hoff, the Dutch roaster Hans Lévelt, Jan Hissel and Gerd Nicoleit of the German alternative trading organization GEPA, and Solidaridad's Nico Roozen. The introduction of the Max Havelaar certificate in Belgium and Switzerland was likewise facilitated through the networking amongst fair trade advocates sustained during the 1970s and 1980s.[78]

Transnational collaboration also won the movement a symbolic victory at the level of European politics. In 1991, the Dutch Social Democrat Maartje van Putten and the Belgian Christian Democrat Leo Tindemans sponsored a successful European Parliament resolution stipulating the use of fair trade coffee in parliament. In addition, the resolution called on the European Commission to do the same and to contribute to the international promotion of this initiative.[79] The new zest which certified coffee provided to fair trade activism was thus translated into attempts to influence institutional politics. The alternative trading organizations and world shops, for example, set up a joint advocacy office in Brussels.[80] A comparison of these activities to the Cane Sugar Campaign of twenty years earlier is instructive: certified coffee did enable activists to exert an impact on European politics. This time around, the activists did not ask for far-reaching policy changes, however. Rather, they focused on small, feasible steps.

The Scramble to Control Certification

Efforts to gain greater control over the distribution and labelling of fair trade products by the alternative trading organizations would instrumentalize their pre-established transnational networks. Over the course of the 1980s, European alternative trading organizations had developed closer partnerships with one another. Their employees had already been familiar with their counterparts because their respective businesses had originated as subsidiaries of SOS. After the demise of Paul Meijs's dream of a multinational version of SOS, relations between the West German, Swiss, and Austrian agencies and their former mother company in the Netherlands had not always been smooth, but their respective representatives did engage with each other when necessary. They all benefitted from the sharing of contacts and information. They would set up joint shipments and visit producers on behalf of another importer in certain cases.[81] Those involved found it important, moreover, to make arrangements which prevented sister organizations from venturing into each other's markets.[82]

The alternative trading organizations cooperated on the basis of shared interests, but they also shared a specific way of practicing fair trade which revolved around direct relations with producers in the South, fostering economic independence in a long-term relationship, and maintaining buyers' trust. How could they convey their shared version of fair trade with a broader public? In 1986, representatives of organizations from Norway, France, Switzerland, West Germany, Austria, Belgium, and the Netherlands discussed the introduction of a 'family symbol' which would signal to consumers that a particular product came from one of the European alternative trading organizations. It was not meant as a joint certificate with a set of common criteria for producers and importers. Rather, it was intended to be a kind of brand, one which would enhance the distinct profile of products from likeminded organizations.[83] As with many other instances of attempted cooperation, the idea of a family symbol was not realized. Nine alternative trading agencies did eventually set up the European Fair Trade Association (EFTA) in 1987. This federation sought to provide its members with common international representation and to streamline their collective efforts.[84] Because a new phase in European integration had been signalled at the turn of the 1980s, the participants wanted to strengthen their foothold in European politics through more robust partnership. They had little available funds for concerted activities, but they hoped to be able to more persuasively apply for European funding with joint bids.[85]

The Max Havelaar initiative yielded in its wake a broader field of organizations involving themselves with fair trade, which in turn put pressure on the position of the alternative trading organizations. They had taken part in the efforts to set up fair trade certification but did not control the new certification organizations and their policies for certification. In addition, they now had to compete with mainstream companies selling fair trade-certified products. Representatives of Max Havelaar had even intimated that the alternative trading organizations had had their day. Their efforts had cleared the field for the introduction of fair trade certification. Now that this had been achieved, they were no longer needed. How could they contend with the size and the professionalism of mainstream companies?[86]

Against that background, the EFTA's members considered establishing their own certification initiative after the introduction of Max Havelaar in the Netherlands, Belgium, and France.[87] Perhaps they had initially missed their opportunity, but they hoped to regain their preeminent role through their own certification initiative. Two options were on the table: either their own brand for products imported by EFTA members without external control or a new certification organization which would grant alternative trading organizations more of a say. The first option was attractive because the agencies would not have to adhere to rules stipulated by others and could market all their products under the same brand. But the participants did not want to substitute their respective corporate designs for a common one. This approach also left no room for participation by outside firms and would thus have little impact on the market.[88] They therefore opted for the second concept.

In Germany, like-minded organizations such as GEPA, denominational development organizations, and the social-democratic Friedrich Ebert Foundation had closely monitored the developments in the Netherlands. They had set up the Arbeitsgemeinschaft Kleinbauernkaffee to achieve similar results. In collaboration with members of the German Arbeitsgemeinschaft Kleinbauernkaffee, the EFTA elaborated plans for an alternative to Max Havelaar. The agencies felt they possessed crucial advantages. The EFTA members had considerably more experience in alternative trade. They knew how to market a range of products and had already built up a presence in many European countries. Moreover, the alternative trading organizations had developed their own markets and could muster the necessary funds for the operation.[89]

The international federation which emerged from these plans was called Transfair International. As it was being launched in 1992, members of the EFTA were already sensing the prospect of a weighty problem looming on the horizon. The alternative trading organizations, though ideologically committed to fair trade, also had a financial interest in certification, posing a threat to the certificate's independence and hence to its credibility. How could consumers trust a certificate if those responsible for issuing it would also be applying for it? Practical problems also emerged. In contrast to the Max Havelaar model, with its independent national certification organizations, Transfair aimed to develop a single international body. In Germany and Italy, the participants in the initiative were nonetheless setting up independent entities. In addition, these were exclusively focused on coffee. That way, the Transfair certificate would not obtain the desired international appeal and an association with a wide assortment of fair trade products.[90]

Soon the EFTA lost control over this organization, too. The number of votes granted to alternative trading organizations in the commissions of Transfair was limited due to concerns over their conflict of interest. As the secretariat of the organization gained traction, the alternative trading organizations lost their hold on its daily affairs.[91] For example, Transfair now entered into a partnership with large plantations to procure fair trade-certified tea. GEPA had cultivated relations with the same plantations, but other agencies felt uncomfortable about the arrangement. Marc Bontemps of the Belgian Oxfam-Wereldwinkels noted that the partnership counteracted the fair trade movement's philosophy, which was geared towards supporting small farmers. He concluded that it had become impossible for the EFTA's members to influence Transfair's decisions.[92] The alternative trading organizations therefore decided to give up on attempts to control certification and opted instead to use their own federation to secure for themselves an independent position. They did so by improving cooperation efforts and by devising advocacy initiatives at the European level.[93] The idea of a common brand was also abandoned. Agencies such as SOS instead chose to strengthen their own brand, applying marketing strategies to enhance their products' visibility and distinct profiles.[94]

Max Havelaar and Transfair thus competed with each other on the European market from 1992 onwards. The British market, meanwhile, had been claimed by the Fairtrade Foundation, which had introduced the 'FAIRTRADE mark' in 1994 after laborious preparations. Shortly after the introduction of Max Havelaar, a coalition consisting of the Catholic Fund for Overseas Development, Christian Aid, New Consumer, Oxfam, Traidcraft Exchange, and the World Development Movement – later joined by the Women's Institute – had explored ways to set up a similar initiative. The founders sought to move ahead only after they had found a company willing to introduce a certified product on the British market. The fair trade coffee brand Cafédirect, backed by Oxfam, Traidcraft, Equal Exchange, and Twin Trading, appeared to be a natural ally but was reluctant to commit to the initiative because the cost of certification meant higher prices. The company behind

Typhoo, a nationally renowned tea brand, signalled interest by way of its Technical and Quality Director Philip Mumby, but its board eventually reneged for similar reasons.

Finally, the chocolate company Green & Black's ventured to introduce one of their chocolate bars as a fair trade-certified product. The bar went on sale on 7 March 1994, but the company was reluctant to have more of their products certified, partly because of conflicts between different fair trade certification organizations within Europe.[95] Fairtrade chocolate in Great Britain would eventually be marketed by the new company Divine Chocolate. Divine's approach was notable, as it came close to Max Havelaar's original plan of setting up a distinct brand to market only fair trade products. Divine, however, also took the additional step of including the Kuapa Kokoo cooperative from West Africa as an owner.[96]

From the beginning, representatives found themselves discussing practical and more formal forms of collaboration. On a practical level, they shared their producer indexes, which meant that coffee from the same producers could be sold as Max Havelaar coffee in the Netherlands and France and as Transfair coffee in Germany or Italy. They also agreed that their activities would not overlap in particular countries: each would have its own country as a territory. A fierce battle erupted over Luxembourg, where a partnership with the Belgian Max Havelaar initiative had been active, only to be joined in 1993 by a Transfair subsidiary. Although the matter did not concern a particularly large market, Max Havelaar's representatives felt hoodwinked, laying bare the sensitivities at play between the two initiatives. Max Havelaar's representatives appealed to respect the gentlemen's agreement without having any effect. Discussing the matter internally, Bert Beekman, the director of Max Havelaar in the Netherlands, mentioned that coffee farmers in Mexico had even expressed worries about the discord amongst their supporters in Europe during a recent visit.[97]

Because collaboration with the same producers and a similar ideological commitment continued to ensure common ground, the staff at both organizations went on to pursue a formal partnership despite the tensions between them. In 1994 representatives of the Max Havelaar organizations, EFTA, and Transfair met in Brussels to discuss possibilities. By and large they agreed about the aims of their work. First and foremost, they wanted to support producers in structurally improving their position. Second, they wanted to persuade companies to adopt fairer conduct in the mainstream market.[98] Realization of these objectives in practice prompted a more contentious discussion. The discord pertained to the relations within a common organization: Would it be a loose federation of autonomous national organizations, as Max Havelaar's representatives advocated, or was it preferable to form a strong international umbrella organization with national sections?[99] The practice of fair trade was not straightforward, either. This caused additional friction amongst the participants. Should all the ingredients of a chocolate bar satisfy fair trade criteria, for example, or did it suffice if the cocoa was 'fair'? Was fair trade certification meant exclusively to support small farmers, or could plantations also participate in the initiative? Wasn't the fair trade premium facilitating the producers' development projects making fair trade products too expensive?[100]

In the end, the common aims and practical advantages of collaboration proved decisive. After several years of successful partnership, the representatives of Max Havelaar and Transfair decided to establish Fairtrade Labelling Organizations International (FLO) in 1997. The existing European labelling organizations were integrated into this new umbrella organization, as would TransFair USA, which was founded with Ford Foundation support in 1998 after protracted negotiations amongst several groups of fair trade activists. Any matter pertaining to producers was to be transferred to the international office in Bonn, Germany. FLO subsequently developed common visual material and established an internationally recognized standard for fair trade certification, which could be monitored by independent auditors.[101]

When the Dutch Max Havelaar Foundation celebrated its tenth birthday in 1998, the fair trade movement looked back on a decade of turbulent transformation. Fair trade certification had reinforced the gradual shift towards an approach which first and foremost provided producers with access to markets. In the span of ten years, fair trade certification had been introduced not just in one country but internationally. Fair trade-certified coffee now graced the shelves of stores well beyond the milieu of world shops and alternative trading organizations. The sales figures indicated that there were many people in new places who were sympathetic to the call for fair trade but had remained aloof until recently.[102] Products sold through mainstream retail channels enabled a striking expansion of fair trade sales. The fair trade premium generated additional funds aimed at local development for producers and set fair trade products apart. Fair trade activists thus doubled down on ways to reduce inequality between what had become known as the Global South and North by supporting producers directly. The structural causes of global inequality, though they continued to be addressed, received less of an emphasis as a result.[103]

The introduction of fair trade certification allowed the movement to exert an impact in the short run and substantially lowered the threshold for the public to participate in fair trade initiatives. Certification enabled the movement to improve the situation of the producers who cooperated with fair trade arrangements, even though their number remained modest and the scale of the impact varied from case to case.[104] It also significantly enhanced the movement's visibility.[105] The figures stating the turnover of fair trade products provided welcome 'hard' measures of the importance of fair trade. They could be used to persuade companies to participate in fair trade endeavours and convince politicians to enable them. They could also be referenced in relation to the general public to indicate the vigour and attractiveness of the movement. At the same time, this focus on economic success threatened to overshadow the publicity tactics of fair trade activism, such as boycotting and demonstrating. The movement was thus vulnerable to the objection that it overvalued immediate economic contributions and reductively regarded citizens as mere consumers who could contribute to fair economic relations simply by buying the right products. In addition, examples showing the practical limitations of certification initiatives became a serious threat for a movement which presented economic impact as the prime measure of its viability.[106]

Looking back during the anniversary festivities, the board of Max Havelaar in the Netherlands did articulate some cautious reservations. Would producers be represented adequately in the new international organization? Should the movement continue to focus on partnerships with small farmers? In the Netherlands, too, not all was peace and joy. A world shop member had complained to Max Havelaar's board about leaving the world shops out of the anniversary book.[107] Did this complaint hint at a larger pattern? World shops and alternative trading organizations continued their activities – many even flourished. These two pillars of the fair trade movement had been mainstays since before the introduction of fair trade certification. But they had certainly lost some degree of relevance. In the eyes of many consumers, fair trade had become synonymous with fair trade-certified products. The sales volume achieved under the banner of fair trade certification was much higher, too. The former flagships of the fair trade movement now had to compete with mainstream companies, which did not solely depend on revenue from sales of fair trade products.

Fair trade certification had emerged seeking to transform the market, but the market also changed the movement. The very success of the fair trade certificate caused a waning of enthusiasm for the initial form of social criticism embodied in organizations like Max Havelaar. Reviewing organizational strategy in 1998, its board crossed out the passage which presented Max Havelaar as an attempt to challenge the prevailing social order.[108] To outsiders, the ideals that had driven the introduction of fair trade certification as a way to transform the market became much less visible.

The growing importance of the market over the course of the 1980s and 1990s did not result from some coup mounted by advocates for neoliberalism. The history of the fair trade movement in this era shows that activists critical of prevailing market practices had their own reasons for adopting market-oriented methods. Well before the fall of the Berlin Wall, world shop groups, the employees of alternative trading organizations, and the staff of development organizations like Solidaridad were considering a more 'business-like' approach to bring their ideals within reach. These considerations, however, did not push them to adopt the ideals of austerity, market liberalization, and maximized competition. A first reason for this shift in orientation was the growing distance between social movements and institutional politics. The failure of international bodies like UNCTAD and national governments in addressing global inequality led activists to attempt to transform the market not through institutional politics but by directly targeting market actors. As a wave of rightwing governments took office across Europe and in the United States, fair trade activists could expect still less willingness to cooperate with them.

Second, fair trade activists built on the experienced successes of earlier market-oriented interventions. Initially, they had primarily confronted companies which practiced 'unfair' trade. Over the course of the 1980s, activists wanted to go one step further: instead of pointing out which products and what behaviour were unacceptable to them, they sought to foster responsible attitudes amongst companies and consumers. As Chapter 5 will set out in greater detail, the attempts to collaborate with companies so that they would develop more equitable practices, flanked by continued criticism of unsustainable corporate behaviour, contributed to notions of corporate social responsibility becoming widely popular in recent years.[109]

This development was closely connected to a third factor driving market-oriented approaches. Even as the number of partners in the South increased, these interlocutors were severely affected by economic crises from the early 1980s onwards. Producers needed immediate support more than ever – support that the prevailing practices of fair trade activism could not deliver. Operating more professionally was one logical answer for activists who did not relish the movement's characteristic 'amateurism' and confinement to alternative circles. For them, the introduction of fair trade certification offered a chance to achieve several goals at once: it would increase the immediate economic impact for producers, expand the visibility and availability of fair trade, and put pressure on businesses and politicians to change prevailing market practices by leveraging fair trade's growing market share.

Enthusiasm for market mechanisms, then, could be found outside neoliberal circles. The market's appeal stemmed from the successes of a market-oriented approach, a lack of political alternatives, and a desire to bolster immediate impact. Moreover, fair trade certification was applied as part of a wider activist repertoire, which continued to include campaigns against corporate misbehaviour, political demonstrations and lobbying, and educational initiatives. Against this background, even activists critical of prevailing market practices were prepared to support market-oriented interventions. At the same time, their history highlights the presence of alternatives to the neoliberal view behind many attempts to implement market approaches. Contemporaries might have seen no overarching alternative to the market, but they did see many alternative ways to shape it.

5 CLOTHES
Activism in a Network Society

The personal computer became an essential tool for campaigning over the course of the 1990s, but its indispensable ubiquity did not diminish the utility of cargo bikes. A group of young protesters in the Dutch city of Sittard rode such a bike to a local outlet of the clothing chain C&A in April 1991. They had intended to set up a stall, but the branch's management had sniffed out their plan and successfully appealed to the city council to prevent it. The protesters thus parked their vehicle 10 metres from the store's entrance and fitted it with posters, flyers, and textiles drawn from the inventory of the local world shop. They hung a clothesline with dirty laundry and put up sandwich boards accusing C&A of exploiting textile workers – 'C&A's dirty laundry'. In the vicinity, they posted bills with critical statements like 'C&A doesn't suit me'.[1] A group of performing musicians from Ecuador also caught the attention of many passers-by. The nervous store manager invited a delegation of the protesters to have a cup of coffee but would not acknowledge any criticism of his employer.[2]

A letter containing an account of this action in Sittard reached the Amsterdam office of the Clean Clothes Campaign (CCC), with which the young protesters from Sittard were affiliated. 'We are now waiting for plans and initiatives by the CCC. (...) We are coming to Utrecht with 2–4 people, posters, and glue', its author wrote as a sign-off, looking forward to a planned national meeting of likeminded activists in Utrecht.[3] There and in the northern town of Assen, the campaign had started on 10 November 1990, mounting similar actions at C&A stores. The drive to 'Clean out the clothing world' intended to improve the working conditions of women in the clothing industry. In low-wage Asian and Eastern European sweatshops and in their illegal counterparts in Western Europe, women worked unsafe and insecure jobs for little pay. The initiators of the CCC had obtained information about large clothing chains like C&A which were selling clothes made by such women. They decided to first take aim at C&A because the company had the largest market share in the Netherlands and had earned a reputation as an adversary of trade unions.[4] The campaign's representatives asked C&A to disclose its procurement policy and to take responsibility for the production of the clothes the company sold. Other companies would be targeted in a second stage of the campaign.[5]

Clothes became an important subject in the fair trade movement during the 1990s. Textiles were some of the products that brought crucial questions to the fore about the relations between fair trade activism and mainstream companies. The complex production chain required for textile production, entailing the making of fabrics, design, sewing, marketing, distribution, and sales, illustrates the challenges faced by fair trade activists in addressing postcolonial globalization after the end of the Cold War. As this chapter highlights, textiles necessitated reflection on who the stakeholders of fair trade activism were. In the textiles industry, a focus on small farmers was not as straightforward as it was for products such as coffee or cocoa, because the product chain was more complex, with widespread exploitation in the processing stages in factories and workshops.[6] They also tested the consequences of the expansion of the fair trade activists' repertoire to a set of collaborative tactics.

The CCC emerged from earlier activities that a coalition of groups from the alternative milieu had directed against C&A. Feminist and Third World solidarity groups, along with the movements of the squatters and the alternative consumers, joined this cause at the end of the 1980s. The campaign's diverse origins are telling. It started as a loosely coordinated collaboration amongst groups criticizing the prevailing working conditions in the clothing industry. Many campaigns mounted by the CCC aimed to demonstrate solidarity with women employed under extremely precarious conditions.[7] The CCC's official introductory campaign denounced the working conditions of people producing clothes for C&A

in sweatshops in the Global South as well as the Netherlands.[8] Mirroring the shift in the global division of labour which took place around 1990, most subsequent actions denounced the exploitation of people in low-wage countries in Eastern Europe and the Global South. Companies like C&A cynically profited from international trade agreements which did not protect workers in these countries against malpractice.[9] The tone was outright aggressive at times: 'C&A clothes are contaminated! (...) Burn C&A's clothes!' a pamphlet distributed in 1990 raged. To the ears of store managers, this was not an empty threat, as in the 1980s the West German feminist group Rote Zora had committed several arson attacks at Adler clothing stores in solidarity with South Korean textile factory workers.[10]

As with Solidaridad during the 1980s, the pioneers of the CCC did not come from traditional strongholds of the fair trade movement such as the world shops and alternative trading organizations. Nonetheless, they, too, had manifold connections within the movement. With Max Havelaar they shared the assumption that they would have to go beyond the alternative milieu were there to be any significant improvement. Just as with the world shops, most activities were expressly directed at targets in the activists' immediate environment. The idea that women bore the brunt of unfair market practices had also been articulated in many world shop groups in the 1970s and 1980s. The CCC is thus inextricably connected to the longer history of the fair trade movement. But its evolution as a self-proclaimed 'network organization' spanning the globe marks a new phase in the history of postcolonial globalization. The emergence of digital communications, the end of the Cold War, and a new wave of global economic integration produced a novel situation which challenged fair trade activists to rethink their perspective and practices. It also enabled them to place cooperation between groups in different parts of the world on a new footing.

As people across the world struggled to make sense of global relations after the Cold War, challenges to the exploitation of workers in the clothing industry took on a changed appearance. Critiques of the exploitation of workers in the clothing industry were at least as old as industrialization itself. At the turn of the nineteenth century, textile workers in Great Britain smashed the looms of new factories in protest against the new working conditions these machines represented.[11] Protest was voiced not just by workers but by consumers and their organizations, too. Between 1898 and 1918, the American National Consumers' League promoted clothes which had been produced under hygienic conditions and for which white female workers had been paid fairly. By buying only clothes marked with the organization's 'white label', consumers could support this push for 'clean' and fair clothing.[12]

Fair trade advocates had also at times imported textiles from producers' groups to sell in gift shops and at other venues. Most prominently, jute products from the Jute Works project in Bangladesh had been a staple of fair trade activism in the 1970s and 1980s. The project had been established by the Catholic Christian Organization for Relief and Rehabilitation in collaboration with the Mennonite Central Committee (MCC) to help people in Bangladesh after the War of Independence had ravaged the country in 1971.[13] Their products had been marketed by alternative trading organizations in North America and Western Europe. In West Germany, 'Jute statt Plastik' had become a famed slogan, calling on consumers to substitute the plastic bags that epitomized mass consumer society with eco-friendly jute bags, which also supported marginalized producers.

By the end of the 1980s, challenges to the exploitation of workers in the clothing industry had a different complexion than heretofore. Activists no longer targeted working conditions close to home or far away exclusively, and they did not organize themselves in one specific region. Instead, the CCC set up a transnational network to address the abuses in the industry wherever they might be found.[14] In subsequent years, the campaign expanded into an organization which tried to improve the lives of people working in the clothing industry across the whole world, collaborating with more than 250 partners.

Digital communications became a crucial factor in facilitating processes of production and distribution as well as activist initiatives. The microprocessor had silently evolved into an influential presence, first changing the way many people went about their work. Personal computers entered offices and homes over the course of the 1980s. From 1995 onwards, the internet (largely via the World Wide Web) also became part of people's daily lives.[15] These technological innovations enabled incredibly rapid communications between distant parts of the world. Companies benefitted first and foremost. Financial institutions could transfer capital with ease, abetted by the deregulation of international financial markets since the 1970s.

The new technology also impacted everyday interactions. Social scientists were quick to note and interpret this change. In 1996, the sociologist Manuel Castells made the influential observation that a 'network society' was coming into existence. This phrase became a buzzword to point out the importance of digital infrastructure and the emergence of a web of relations between people all over the world. As a result of the rise of information technology, electronic communications became the most important form of communication. Geographic distance lost its importance – to someone communicating electronically, Tokyo was closer to Frankfurt than to the Japanese capital's suburbs.[16] Crucially, the networked vicinity between the financial capitals of Tokyo and Frankfurt was premised on unequal integration into this network society. Although networks of communication and trade spanned the globe, their diffusion was uneven. The history of fair trade activism highlights how people in different parts of the world did not have equal access to these technologies. These activists also appear to have adopted digital communications later than businesses and government institutions did. For most of the 1990s, telephones and fax machines were activists' technological mainstays, whereas email was much less common before the turn of the twenty-first century.

The dissolution of the Third World as a point of reference for solidarity activism posed a second challenge to fair trade activists, spurring them to rethink their transnational relations at the start of the 1990s. The waning of the Third World went beyond the loss of a vision of global order. The Third World, regarded as a socialism-inspired project of unaligned states venturing on their own courses independent of East and West, had become less popular during the 1980s. The successful economic development of the 'Asian tigers' of Singapore, South Korea, Hong Kong, and Taiwan demonstrated that development was possible through a combination of a free market and a strong state. In addition, over the course of the 1980s, socialist beacons such as Vietnam, Algeria, and Nicaragua became tainted in the eyes of much of the world.[17]

This demise of the Third World changed the common denominator of the fair trade movement. Until the end of the 1980s, most world shop activists, alternative trading organizations, and campaigning organizations like Oxfam or Solidaridad regarded themselves to be aligned with a 'Third World movement'. By the end of the 1990s, internal evaluations of fair trade organizations indicated that customers no longer related to the goal of advocating on behalf of the Third World.[18] As a result, understanding relations between people in different places became less straightforward. Notions like 'global citizenship' became popular but were notoriously vague. Everyone was a citizen of one world, now no longer divided into clear-cut blocs.[19]

The new networked digital communications, the dissolution of the Cold War order, and questions about the implications of these development gave rise to widespread talk of 'globalization'. 'You shouldn't forget this was long before globalization became a household notion and before the internet', Clean Clothes Campaign leader Ineke Zeldenrust remarked in 2007 as she looked back at her late-1980s activism.[20] If globalization is defined as a combination of global economic, political, and social relations accompanied by a consciousness of the worldwide span of those relations, then this was nothing new at the end of the 1980s. People had been trading goods globally for hundreds of years. Rising income levels, large-scale production, and improved means of transportation had expanded the range and number of products households could obtain since the late nineteenth century. Even though the effects of this expansion had been felt throughout the world, the Western European and North American countries were its main beneficiaries, particularly after the Second World War.

Despite these continuities, globalization presented itself in a new guise in the 1990s. The word itself had hardly been used until the beginning of the 1990s, when its frequency quickly soared in books and newspapers not just in English but also in German, Dutch, and other languages. The new awareness of global connectedness in a less clearly ordered world was often expressed via the word 'globalization' during the 1990s. In the United States, politicians like Bill Clinton used it in a positive sense. They presented globalization as a process that had proved that the American way of life would prevail and that the world would change for the better

Figure 5.1 Clean Clothes Campaign in Sittard in April 1991. Clean Clothes Campaign in Sittard. International Institute of Social History, archive Clean Clothes Campaign.

via global market integration and the dissolution of boundaries. On the European continent, the mood was less euphoric. Here, globalization was often regarded as something coming from the outside and posing a 'challenge' – also known as a problem.[21]

Sceptical observers lamented that worldwide technological, economic, and social interconnectedness would undermine the ability of national states to implement independent policies, as well as empower large companies and cause American culture to spread all over the world. The American fast-food chain McDonalds became a symbol of this dominance in the daily lives of people across the globe. The opening of its first Moscow branch on 31 January 1990 attracted global coverage: even in Russia, people could no longer resist the attractions of American culture. Two years later, the sociologist George Ritzer coined the term 'McDonaldization' to criticize the increasing impact of economic rationalization in the lives of people throughout the world.[22]

This pessimistic view was accompanied by doubts about whether ordinary citizens could influence the world's direction. Castells had postulated that in a network society, social movements could still take to the streets, but they were no longer finding a target for their protest. Social movements splintered. They momentarily zeroed in on isolated issues. The nation-states they had previously targeted no longer held the power in the age of electronic information. Power had become volatile and citizens were no longer capable of forcing change. Social movements could not join forces more effectively under these new circumstances, whilst their targets had become at least as agile as the activists.[23]

Other social scientists sounded more optimistic. The sociologist Martin Albrow pointed to the environmental activists who had confronted Shell in 1995. Attempting to prevent the company from sinking the oil storage buoy Brent Spar in a deep-sea ridge, they had benefitted from their newfound ability to coordinate campaigns across national borders.[24] Occupying the platform, spreading alarming news bulletins, and calling for a boycott of Shell's gas stations, Greenpeace's activists forced Shell to engage with notions of corporate social responsibility and spurred stricter regulation for the dumping of waste.[25] The political scientist Donatella della Porta likewise ventured that network societies offered social movements new resources, making it easier to rally people from across the world around a particular issue. Even if people agreed on one issue only, they could find allies anywhere in the world. Besides, new global political institutions and civic organizations would emerge, which would provide activists with new chances to exert their influence.[26]

The history of textiles highlights the tensions between different approaches to promote socio-economic equity which emerged within the movement in the late 1980s. After the introduction of fair trade-certified coffee around 1990, its pioneers looked for new products. Alternative trading organizations such SOS, GEPA, and Ten Thousand Villages had experience selling other commodities on a small scale. The engagement with regular trade through a combination of adversarial and collaborative means encouraged activists to explore the possibilities of confronting the textile industry. Clothing offered a chance to stir up a business sector in which exploitation of people and the environment was business as usual. In contrast to foodstuffs like coffee and bananas, clothing was a remarkably complex product.[27] The attempts to make the clothing industry fairer are uniquely suited to explore the consequences of a new phase in the history of globalization. They demonstrate the different ways the fair trade movement attempted to give producers a voice and the evolution of the movement's repertoire of action.

As the previous chapters have demonstrated, exchanges between marginalized groups and sympathetic activists led to a series of attempts to reform the structures of global trade. Contacts between activists from different parts of the world had nonetheless been sparse and often indirect. Fair trade advocates derived much of their information about geographically distant circumstances governing the lives of marginalized groups from books and brochures, newspaper articles, radio bulletins, television broadcasts, slideshow presentations, and guest lectures. Only a few representatives of development and alternative trading organizations regularly travelled to South America, Asia, and Africa. The visit by producer representatives in the framework of the workshops on alternative trade congresses in Noordwijkerhout in 1976 and in Vienna the following year provided rare opportunities for direct exchanges between producers and European activists at a time before such meetings became more frequent, starting in the late 1980s.

Individual producers became more visible in fair trade campaigns during the 1980s. Instead of vaguely sketched figures, recognizable individuals were depicted on packaging and action material. They continued to be clearly distinct from the activists themselves. The individuals depicted – usually men – were shown engaged in heavy labour. They were presented not as needy but as strong, self-conscious persons. They asked for justice and solidarity, not for help. This sort of representation aligned with the way Third World solidarity groups had regarded producers: regardless of the support they received from activists in Europe and North America, these figures were exemplary in both their self-reliance and their combativeness.

The idea that people in the South did not so much need help as deserve justice was closely related to the insistence on the crucial importance of human rights for anyone and everyone in the world. 'World shops are committed to dignified working condition in global trade', declared the staff of an Amsterdam world shop in 1997. Alongside their attention to fair prices, development, and the environment, world shops also strived for the 'equal treatment of men and women'.[28] Universal human rights had become an important foundation for the engagement of world shop members.

145 / Clothes: Activism in a Network Society

Figure 5.2 Poster advertising fair trade bananas issued for a Solidaridad campaign, c. 1996. International Institute of Social History.

It was undeniable that producers had lost some of their appeal as exemplary figures. Although still presented as individuals to be admired for their combativeness, joy, and work ethic, they no longer embodied hopes for emancipatory politics now that the 'Third World' was no longer a beacon. Moreover, partnerships between producers and activists were complicated in practice, as could be glimpsed in an interview with Max Havelaar's director Hans Bolscher in 1998. Looking back on the first ten years of the foundation, he concluded that it had been naïve in its early years: 'Ten years ago we simply assumed: make people receive fair prices, let them decide on how to spend their additional income themselves, and they will naturally catch up on their lagging development'. Without education and guidance, many partners were sidetracked by elementary mistakes, Bolscher ventured, apparently self-assured about the virtues of the 'developed' world.[29]

The fair trade movement attempted to improve the situation of people in the Global South. Its adherents shared a commitment to the ideals of equality, human rights, and self-reliance. Still, producers were under continual threat of being reduced to a supporting role because of a lack of communication and the imposition of distinct aims of 'development' by Northern partners – all the more so because the governments, companies, and consumers enabling change were located primarily in the North.[30] Yet the movement's expansion and new means of communication offered opportunities to change the balance within the movement.

The Voice of the Producer

The Clean Clothes Campaign developed a distinct vision of collaboration on equal terms, an approach which benefitted from the new means of communication that had recently become available. 'We are not negotiating, we are the microphone' is how Ineke Zeldenrust described the ideal the organization was attempting to put into practice. Protest in the Global North had to function as a mouthpiece for the grievances of textile workers. It was meant to bring companies to the table to discuss issues with the employees impacted by their policies.[31] The CCC thus presented itself as a 'network movement' of groups spanning the globe and pursuing the same aims.[32] Relations with people in the clothing industry were established with the help of partner organizations. Trade unions and solidarity groups working on behalf of countries like India, Bangladesh, and Sri Lanka were particularly important. Trade union contacts between North and South and the activities of solidarity committees in many cases hearkened back to the solidarity with the Third World which had blossomed in the 1960s. In this respect, too, the foundations for the initiatives which took off in the late 1980s had been laid much earlier.

The CCC ambitiously expanded its network internationally and in the Netherlands itself during the 1990s to operate more effectively. In the Netherlands, it made official its cooperation with world shops and alternative trading organizations. International partnerships were promoted first via an English-language newsletter (first published in 1993), then an international secretariat; the organization also actively searched for allies in other countries. Workshops with potentially interested groups in countries including Germany, France, Belgium, and England produced, in 1995, a crop of new relations. These events, in turn, provided access to trade unions representing workers in the clothing industry.[33] By 2001 the CCC had evolved into a network of around 200 organizations all over the world. Its newsletter was being sent to 2,500 groups. Those involved with the campaign indicated that the added value of cooperation was both psychological and practical. The international partnership gave them a sense of being part of an international movement and provided them with relevant information from all over the world. What they thus learned was useful for informing their own members and the broader public about abuses in the global clothing industry.[34]

The CCC came closest to realizing the ideal of being a microphone for textile workers via its 'urgent appeals'.[35] These messages were regarded as a way to pass on the immediate concerns of distressed workers. If an organization in the Clean Clothes network identified a specific case in which clothing workers' rights were violated, other organizations and groups within the network could be called upon to engage in solidarity actions. Such action would take place in the country hosting the headquarters of the relevant clothing company, for example. Activists in countries where large batches of the producers' clothes were being sold could also join the urgent appeal. These campaigns were improvised by design.[36]

The international secretariat played an essential role in these spontaneous actions. If a partner organization appealed – usually this would be a group engaged on behalf of workers' rights in Asia – the secretariat's staff would first establish whether there was an obvious relation to the clothing industry. If so, they would evaluate which companies were involved and which countries should therefore be considered to be sites of action. The secretariat would also discuss which actions the people initiating the appeal would deem sensible in support of their plight. Which demands did they want to make? With whom did they want to engage in dialogue? The networked nature of the CCC was clearly visible in the subsequent planning: decisions about the specific actions that partner organizations wanted to initiate in different countries were up to the claimants. The international secretariat depended on the commitment of the affiliated activists in different countries, who received information about the appeal through a mailing list. Sometimes the secretariat's staff would be in direct touch with contacts to enquire into their possibilities concerning specific appeals.[37]

The practice of the urgent appeal shows the strengths and weaknesses of networked activism. In 1999, for example, an Indonesian organization appealed to the international secretariat. Employees of a factory in Tanerang who had joined a new independent trade union had been targeted by the company's directors. After determining which companies did business with the factory, the secretariat passed along these companies' codes of conduct to the Indonesian activists. To support the local actions, the international secretariat also distributed the appeal within its network. It sent letters, mostly as faxes, to the boards of the companies involved, the relevant Indonesian ministry, and the Jakarta office of the International Labour Organization. These efforts led to a meeting attended by the company responsible for most of the factory's orders, a spokesperson for the CCC, and a representative of the Indonesian employees. This meeting had little effect, though. Inspectors visiting the site did not find any employees willing to confirm the complaints. The factory directors denied the accusations, dismissed most of the trade union's members, and watched contentedly as the other members terminated their contracts. Their departure made it hard for the activists involved to continue their campaign, because they were no longer receiving first-hand information about the factor's working conditions and could no longer campaign in the name of the factory's employees.[38]

Disconcerted by this outcome, CCC staff concluded that the networked structure was well equipped to signal issues but less adept at follow-through. The local partners were often unable to protect workers who spoke out and did not always have the adequate legal expertise to deal with the companies and regulations they were facing. Within the network, contacts between local trade unions and other partners could easily break down because the parties did not know each other well. The international secretariat coordinated so many individual actions that it risked losing track of the various issues, resulting in a lack of sustained pressure on the companies responsible for the abuses. The events in Tanerang were also a stark reminder that codes of conduct were effective only if they could be sufficiently monitored.[39]

Although the CCC came close to the ideal of a network made up of equal member organizations, considerable impediments remained. In the course of an evaluation, for example, the Bangladesh People's Solidarity Center communicated in 1998 that the CCC had too small a presence in the countries where textile production was predominantly located.[40] In the same evaluation, other participants from the Global South stated that they found it too taxing to take part in the network, pointing to language barriers and limited access to email. Some remarked that the network was too loosely knit, causing a lack of mutual understanding. Finally, some of the respondents felt that it was too focused on exposing exploitation in Asia, as if similar issues were not prevalent in the Global North as well.[41] In practice, moreover, the international secretariat held a privileged position as a node within the network. Many lines of communication ran through it, its members could muster a host of international relations, and information from a range of sources throughout the world was at its disposal. The imbalance was reinforced by global economic structures. The headquarters of clothing companies were usually located in rich Northern countries, and they could most effectively be pressured by consumers in their home regions.[42]

In the realm of fair trade certification, acknowledging the voice of the producer directly implicated the way certification was governed. Mexican coffee producers' engagement with Western European activists had instigated the introduction of certification, as Chapter 4 highlighted. The subsequent conflicts over the representation of producers in the certification system underline that better means of communication did not automatically result in more equal relations. Within the organizational structure of Max Havelaar, producers had held three seats on the board since its founding in 1988. Its German counterpart, Transfair, founded in 1992, did not anchor producer representation in this way. Its founders felt that this would complicate its establishment, an unwarranted view given the already ample disagreement amongst the European partner organizations.[43]

When Transfair and Max Havelaar decided to merge under the roof of Fairtrade Labelling Organizations (FLO) International in 1997, the future of producer representation was unclear.[44] FLO initially adhered to Transfair's policy, granting producers no voting rights in its governing bodies. Producers who had been represented within Max Havelaar therefore pleaded to use their membership in this organization as a way to make their voices heard in the international umbrella association.[45] The significance of this circumventing strategy waned when FLO subsequently started to include producer representatives in its governing bodies between 1997 and 2002. Recognizing that 'shared ownership' was complicated but fundamental to the credibility of fair trade certification, the national labelling organizations voted in 2006 to include producer organizations as full members of FLO.[46] Disputes over which producers should be eligible for fair trade certification would prove highly contentious in the years that followed. The United States' national labelling organization, Fair Trade USA, left the federation over this issue in 2011. Fair Trade USA wanted to broaden its criteria for certification so as to include more producer groups and expand collaboration with large multinational companies. Fairtrade International, as FLO renamed itself that same year, did not agree, pointing out that its stricter criteria were supported by the producer group members.[47]

The collaborations between producers and alternative trading organizations had traditionally been the most developed partnerships within the fair trade movement. Their relations also shifted as a result of the network's growth and the improved opportunities for communication. In 1987, representatives of alternative trading organizations and their suppliers met in West Berlin to discuss the future of their partnership. Individuals such as West German world shop activist and fair trade mail order pioneer Dieter Hartmann, Carl Grasveld of the Dutch foundation Stichting Ideële Import, and Traidcraft's Richard Adams had discussed closer collaboration within this network of producers and trading organizations since the early 1980s, but these initiatives had stalled due to a lack both of means and of a sense of urgency. During the Berlin conference, it transpired that a group of Western European trading agencies planned to set up their own federation: the European Fair Trade Association, as it has been known since 1987. Groups not part of this initiative had considerable reservations about it, and particularly about its effects on the unity of the movement. To prevent discord, Hartmann and his allies decided to find a federation that could embody the worldwide movement. The foundations of the International Federation for Alternative Trade (IFAT), nowadays known as the World Fair Trade Organization (WFTO), were thus also laid in 1987. Its members foregrounded, as a common denominator, justice and better living conditions for people in the Global South, the selling of products which highlighted unfair trade relations, reform of the structures of global trade, and the promotion of responsible corporate practice.[48]

IFAT's founders envisioned a platform for a movement-wide exchange of ideas and information which would strengthen ties within the movement. The attempt to realize closer collaboration was first directed at relations between North American and European activists. Up until the 1980s, fair trade activism in North America had mainly revolved around sales in gift shops and mail-order products from alternative trading organizations like Self-Help Crafts and SERVV. In Western Europe, world shops and similar forms of local activism had played a more substantial role as the grassroots bases for fair trade activism. During the 1990s, the movement's practices in the Global North converged around practices of importing and selling as well as certification.[49] As a result, the producers ended up in a remarkable position, as came to the fore during an international conference about alternative trade in West Berlin in 1988. Fair trade activists acted on behalf of producers and wanted them to be involved in the proceedings. Producer groups had – emphatically – been invited to participate. At the same time, the attendees from Bangladesh, Cape Verde, Guatemala, Haiti, India, Kenya, Mauritius, and Mexico were merely 'guests'. They were not included in the steering group which was put together to develop the international partnership.

A second international meeting initiated by the same group was hosted by Stichting Ideële Import in the Dutch seaport town of Noordwijk aan Zee in May 1989, just months before leaders from across the world would convene in the same town to fruitlessly discuss what they could do to address global warming. During the conference on 'alternative trade', it was mainly the representatives of European and North American organizations who took the floor. The founding of IFAT was made official during this conference. By then, the founders had recognized that producers had been too little involved, and they vowed to improve this situation. As a start, IFAT's statutes stipulated that anyone involved in fair trade could become a member of the organization.[50]

The ambitious plans for a global network fluttering across the tables during the conference left the Netherlands-based secretariat with an all but impossible task. The administrative burden of coordinating a global movement could not be shouldered by a handful of part-time employees.[51] Despite its difficult birth, IFAT would evolve into the umbrella organization embodying global partnership on equal terms. Representatives from Asia, Africa, and South America appointed representatives to participate at the next international conference. The first producer groups were officially admitted as members of the federation during this 1991 conference, held in Kilkenny, Ireland.[52] Producer representatives were subsequently appointed to IFAT's board. From 1991 to 1993, three out of a total of six members were nominated by producers.

A further sign of the shifting balance within the organization was the location of its 1993 conference: Manila, the capital of the Philippines. How laborious the alignment of ideals and practices of equal representation was became apparent during this fourth international meeting. In an official statement, producers declared that they felt like second-rate participants. Others had paid for them to attend, and the hotel where the conference took place felt far removed from everyday life in the Global South. Many attendees seemed to take little interest in the stories they wanted to share about their products. The way the organizations functioned, and how they could make their voices heard within them, had remained mysteries to most of them.[53]

Equal representation remained a work in progress within IFAT in the years that followed.[54] Producers established regional networks with distinct representation within the federation. In the second half of the 1990s, the publication of a newsletter in Spanish emphasized a more inclusive outlook. The fact that European organizations no longer self-evidently played first fiddle was apparent when a separate European section of IFAT was created in 2006, granted the same status as the Asian, African, and Latin American sections.

New technological possibilities contributed considerably to the transformation of IFAT into an organization in which people from all over the world could have a say. By enabling electronic voting, members could make their voices heard without undertaking expensive trips to conference venues. When the federation adopted the name WFTO in 2008, it had more than 400 members. NEWS!, the network of European world shops, became a member that same year.[55] Within the federation, the regional networks extended their cooperation. Particularly in the years 2006–2011, the African, Asian, and Latin American networks made a significant push to enhance their coordination and their influence within the federation.[56] Because the WFTO – aided by new means of communication – was able to represent partners from all over the world, it became a potential partner organization for entities like the European Union.

Tensions about how to acknowledge the voice of producers also surfaced around discussions over the movement's aims and priorities, particularly around the notion of sustainability. Since the late 1980s, debates about ideological preferences – ranging from revolutionary socialism to cautious reformism – had dominated such discussions. The dissolution of the Cold War division made the mental maps related to political alternatives obsolete. Instead, conflicts involving economic, social, and ecological concerns came to the fore. 'Sustainable development' was brought forth as an idea which could balance these dimensions. This notion gained widespread recognition during the 1980s, as a United Nations commission presided over by the Norwegian Gro Harlem Brundtland proposed the concept in its report, *Our Common Future*. Brundtland and the members of her commission put forward the claim that economic development would produce lasting results only if it were sustained by social and environmental conditions. Instead of either-or trade-offs setting economic interests against social and environmental policies, these realms had to be combined if there was to be a durable prosperity.[57]

Sustainability had an obvious appeal for many fair trade activists. The practices it entailed incorporated many of the activities they had engaged in since the 1950s. Fair trade activism readily aligned with calls for reconciling economic, social, and environmental concerns, particularly after activists had started emphasizing small-scale farming and local initiatives during the second half of the 1970s.[58] Although the histories of fair trade and environmental activism have been separated in most historians' accounts, to many contemporaries they were connected in everyday life.[59] Environmental campaigns had been amongst the actions enlisting the participation of many world shop members in Western Europe and North America. The principle that protecting the environment was crucial to preserving the livelihood of local communities was commonly held by many of their allies in the Global South. Sometimes the subjects were addressed through separate campaigns by the same people, sometimes they converged naturally. Thus, many world shops found it self-evident that they should sell recycled paper. Similarly, the coffee roaster Hans Lévelt found it incomprehensible that some organic coffee farmers did not care about the working conditions of their employees.

Although social and environmental issues thus often overlapped or even converged, the more professional outlook adopted by many civic organizations during the 1980s put pressure on such amalgams. National and transnational nongovernmental organizations specialized in distinct realms. For example, the environmental and the fair trade movement had both established certification initiatives. Within this context of specialization, integrating environmental concerns into the agenda of fair trade organizations could be difficult. Annette Bernd and Gerd Nickoleit argued for combining social and ecological criteria within the ranks of the German alternative trading organization GEPA in 1990. Their plea resulted in a European Fair Trade Association attempt to harmonize criteria from both strands of activism.[60] Bernd and Nickoleit expected such a synthesis to be readily achievable, because environmental and fair trade organizations shared an emphasis on product quality and a responsible way of living. But five years after a hopeful start, they had made little headway. Both eco- and fair trade labels had firmly established themselves in Europe – a merger was thus out of the question. The standards had been developed with a view of different producers and different products – small coffee farmers being the primary focus of fair trade activism in the 1990s, followed by banana and cocoa farmers as the decade went on. Both sides did consider integrating standards applied by their counterparts. But despite growing mutual understanding, fair trade advocates involved in the talks felt that the environmental organizations' commitment was probably not strong enough to stop them from abandoning social concerns if this meant preserving or furthering the success of their own initiatives.[61]

Sustainability proved a similarly combustible issue during IFAT's international conferences. Representatives from the South readily acknowledged the crucial importance of the environment, but people had to come first. Many producers, moreover, did not look forward to having to meet additional criteria within a system in which producers already bore the brunt of obligations whilst people in privileged circumstances were free to choose for themselves what to buy. During the 1993 IFAT conference in Manila, the contribution of producers to deforestation was discussed, for example. Because their impact was far outweighed by what was being done through the detrimental practices of large companies, the producer representatives did not feel their contribution was an issue. Debating the criteria for a product label during the same conference, the producers did seek to commit to impacting the environment as little as possible, but they declined to draw up firm requirements.[62]

Despite these initial reservations, the fair trade labelling organizations and the IFAT network would progressively incorporate the ideal of sustainable development, insisting that economic, social, and environmental interests could and should be reconciled. The Clean Clothes Campaign took a slightly different stance on the issue. Despite calling for 'clean' textiles, the network kept environmental issues at arm's length. Investigating which issues the organization was neglecting around 2000, many respondents specifically enquired about ecological impact.[63] Network members pointed to water pollution caused by garment production as an issue the CCC should address. Some also felt that the organization should engage with environmental organizations like Greenpeace on issues of greenwashing, pointing to Greenpeace's partnership with Nike. Hadn't the Campaign addressed similar collaborations within the fair trade movement?[64] Although these suggestions were readily acknowledged by all involved in discussions about the Campaign's future strategy, the members decided to leave environmental issues to those specializing in this field. As one of the participants from the Global South hopefully remarked: 'The environment is important but we cannot do everything and we should leave this to the relevant organizations, eventually they should come together'.[65]

'Mainstreaming' Reconsidered

Even as new technological and geopolitical circumstances changed relations within the fair trade movement, their relations to other actors also changed: a more adversarial stance yielded to more collaborative attitude. The transformation of the fair trade movement over the course of the 1990s and 2000s has usually been presented through the lens of 'mainstreaming'.[66] This notion describes a shift in involvement away from alternative markets and towards mainstream markets, primarily through product certification. The effects of this shift have been a divisive issue. Some observers lauded the new approach as a 'brilliant idea' with 'spectacular achievements'. Others mourned the loss of the alternative character and the politicized approach to fair trade.[67] Both sides, however, have paid excessive attention to the immediate economic dimension of fair trade certification. Recent research on 'mainstreaming' has tried to avoid this focus and to explore different mainstreaming strategies rather than adhering to a binary division between alternative and mainstream practices.[68] By assessing the evolution of fair trade as a movement, initiatives to transform the global marketplace during the 1990s and 2000s become part of a longer history of attempts to challenge prevailing market practices. If 'mainstreaming' is understood in this sense, certification appears as an expansion of the movement's repertoire of action. Certification, then, is here evaluated as an evolving activist practice for cooperating with companies.[69]

The introduction of product certification notwithstanding, addressing politicians involved in issues of global trade remained a staple of fair trade activists. The multifaceted ways they did so were evident around the eye-catching activist activities at the Seattle

Table 5.1 *The repertoire of fair trade activism*

Type of approach	Tactic	Examples
Adversarial	Negative publicity	Protest at C&A stores
		Demonstrations against WTO in Seattle, 1999
	Boycott	Boycott of Shell's gas station to protest Brent Spar's disposal
	Best practice	Trading activities by WFTO members, alternative trading organizations
		Tony's Chocolonely
		Fairphone
Collaborative	Lobbying	Fair trade delegation at WTO in Seattle, 1999
		Fair Trade Advocacy Office
	Certification	Fairtrade International
		Utz Kapeh
	Individual partnerships	Fair Wear Foundation
	Multi-stakeholder initiatives	Fair trade towns campaign
		Bangladesh Agreement

World Trade Organization (WTO) conference in 1999, marked by the violent confrontations of the 'Battle of Seattle'. Critics had taken aim at the Multilateral Agreement on Investment being discussed by the WTO, because it would grant corporations far-reaching rights for investments all over the world, which could then be leveraged against local regulations and rights. Activists feared this agreement would open the door to multinational companies acquiring hitherto public services like health care, water provision, and public transportation. Their actions at the conference provided a springboard for a worldwide movement for 'alter-globalization', which hosted its own international conferences. Many participants were, according to one observer, 'young, green, leftist, radical and wary of traditional ideologies'.[70]

Representatives of the fair trade movement could be found among the riotous activists as well as in the tidy halls of the summit meeting in Seattle. Close to the convention centre hosting the world leaders was the 'Fair Trade Fair' mounted by the human rights organization Global Exchange, a place where kindred groups from Europe and America could gather.[71] Several IFAT members also participated in the official WTO conference. A delegation had been invited to participate and viewed the occasion as a golden opportunity to lobby for the work of its members.[72] The proceedings were less tranquil than expected. Members of the delegation reported having to avoid tear gas and riots in their attempts to lobby for fair trade.[73] Having made their way in, the conference was delayed because of a bomb threat. World shop representatives Ellen Oomen and Klaus Wöldecke reported to the network of world shops about streets filled with activists who were singing, carrying banners through the streets, and hosting protest meetings and marches. They happily mentioned that the material that NEWS! had prepared stood out amongst the mass of posters, brochures, and flyers because it was printed in full colour. Facing activism which was more radical than expected, the world shop delegation decided to change their plans. One NEWS! representative would speak about the world shops' work at the conference's official reception. Others demanded that attention be given to the debt burden of many poor countries by joining a human chain wrapping around the congress site.[74]

Collaborative lobbying also became more important at the European level. The European Union's economic integration of its member states and its territorial expansion after the signing of the Maastricht Treaty in 1992 had immediate implications for the relations between European and non-European contingents of the fair trade movement. Grasping the new status quo, EFTA members set up an Advocacy Lobby Group to lobby in Brussels on behalf of fair trade.[75] Realizing the importance of such activities, FLO, IFAT, and EFTA eventually set up a joint Fair Trade Advocacy Office in Brussels in 2004.

Alongside political lobbying efforts, many activities by fair trade supporters directly targeted companies. At least partly motivated by the consumer campaigns of the 1970s and 1980s, many Western firms had embraced the idea of corporate social responsibility.[76] Fair trade activists seized on this self-fashioning by exposing malpractice which highlighted the gap between self-professed ideals and corporate behaviour. Campaigns by organizations like the Clean Clothes Campaign called attention to abuses such as the exploitation of coffee producers, unsafe working conditions, and child labour. At the same time, fair trade activists from the late 1980s onwards showed greater willingness to work with companies to do better. Activists thus ventured beyond the circle of committed fair trade advocates. This was not a preconceived strategy. The Max Havelaar certificate had emerged from the urge to sell more coffee on behalf of small coffee farmers with their backs against the wall. Similarly, attempts to improve the working conditions in the clothing industry led to the idea of a code of conduct for clothing companies.

The CCC arrived at a collaborative approach on its own accord. Over the course of the 1990s, members did not limit themselves to protesting but opted to work with companies to improve the working conditions in their chains of production. The influence of worker representatives bolstered the tendency to do more than just confront companies. Representatives of textile workers continuously stressed that boycotts resulted in companies terminating relationships with manufacturers in instances where missteps had been observed, leaving their workers out in the cold.[77] Such a cooperative approach was also important in providing consumers with practical alternatives. Responding to campaigns, buyers would often ask activists, 'Where can I buy clean clothes?'[78] The CCC developed a two-pronged approach: generating public pressure and offering to collaborate with companies to improve the working conditions across the whole of their production chains.

To promote fair behaviour amongst companies, the CCC began developing in 1992 a code of conduct which its staff dubbed the 'Charter of Fair Trade' (*Eerlijk Handels Handvest*; not to be mistaken for the International Fair Trade Charter issued in 2009 by a broader coalition of organizations). Within the ranks of the CCC, this charter was regarded as a way to promote change amongst companies. The demands had to be realistic, because otherwise they could easily be dismissed as naïve by these companies' representatives.[79] These conditions were discussed with trade union groups from India, the Philippines, Hong Kong, and Bangladesh. Based on their input, the charter called on companies to guarantee the right to organize, provide a wage high enough to cover basic needs, and assure equal pay for women and men. In addition, it demanded a safe and healthy workplace and that child labour be prohibited.[80]

To gauge the charter's viability, a draft was presented to commercial branch associations concerned with textiles in the Netherlands. Their reactions were mixed. Industry spokespersons, though welcoming attempts, were sceptical towards the obligations implied by supporting the charter. Would independent oversight entail extra costs? What would be the consequences of a company failing to meet the standards? The associations were only willing to advise their members to voluntarily address the issues mentioned.[81] Within the movement, the reception of the charter was also lukewarm. Trade unionists wanted to focus on child labour, whilst many fair trade activists did not regard the charter to be an urgent matter.[82]

The version of the CCC's Charter of Fair Trade that was eventually adopted in 1999 called on companies to pay fair wages and guarantee decent working conditions, respect their employees' civil rights, and refrain from employing children. A foundation – the Stichting Eerlijk Handels Handvest – would ascertain that participating businesses observed these rules.[83] They would commit to fair conduct in all of their operations. This went well beyond the existing collaborative practice of fair trade certification. That approach focused on paying a fair price to producers of mostly raw materials. By joining the Charter of Fair Trade initiative, companies accepted responsibilities that extended from the production to the sales of their products. At the same time, its initiators wanted to be realistic about the fact that not every participant would always be able to meet all conditions. They were looking for a way to admit companies which were working towards becoming 'fair' but were not there yet.[84]

The CCC's representatives who had pioneered this charter were disheartened to learn that companies were not exactly lining up to join the initiative. Many did respond, however. They formulated their own codes of conduct, in which they tried to sidestep prickly issues and usually avoided independent inspections. For the CCC, the best way forward appeared to be a close collaboration with civic organizations which could identify and publicize abuses.[85] Codes of conduct could be successful only if local workers knew what they entailed. Trade union partners had indicated that such codes were effective only if their organizations were allowed to stand up for the rights stipulated in the codes. Regular independent audits were also required.[86] The CCC's members therefore regarded successes in working with individual companies as first steps towards public regulation rather than an alternative to regulation.[87]

The Consequences of Collaboration

The expansion of collaboration, even involving fair trade organizations with similar intentions, could lead to difficulties in cooperative endeavours with consumers and businesses. Looking to broaden the reach of fair trade after Max Havelaar had entered the scene, Solidaridad's leader Nico Roozen and his team decided to introduce fair trade jeans on the market. If fair trade producers procured different kinds of products, they figured, they would avoid the pitfalls of dependence on a single commodity. Such a development also promised employment opportunities for more people and would move the cooperatives away from the exclusive production of raw materials.[88] High-quality jeans, however, demanded a degree of expertise and specialized equipment which the cooperatives involved did not possess. They would have to team up with more experienced manufacturers.[89] Kuyichi jeans, as the brand became known, were introduced in the Netherlands in 2001. The initiators had realized that it would be important to prove that the more complex chain of production did not detract from the 'fair' nature of the clothing. The solution Kuyichi had opted for was to ask its partners to commit to the SA8000 Standard, an international protocol for corporate social responsibility. It entailed minimal demands regarding working conditions, safety, the right to organize, and remuneration.

This decision did not sit well with representatives of the CCC. Partner organization had repeatedly reported that companies adhering to SA8000 protocols in practice nonetheless did not provide decent working conditions for their employees. The inspections leading up to certification were pre-announced and took place only once, making it relatively easy for companies to mislead inspectors. Because certification was not exacting in practice, certified products were given a bad name, the CCC's chairman Evert de Boer wrote to Nico Roozen in 2003.[90] De Boer found it incomprehensible that

Kuyichi did not join the Fair Wear Foundation, as the Charter of Fair Trade had been renamed. Kuyichi had claimed that the additional inspections demanded by the Fair Wear Foundation were too ambitious and that it could guarantee its own integrity. De Boer disagreed, pointing out that Kuyichi cooperated with mainstream companies to produce the fair trade jeans. Unwilling to verify its claims about corporate behaviour, the new fair jeans company was acting no differently than many other clothing businesses, according to De Boer.[91]

The CCC acknowledged the importance of initiatives like Kuyichi to develop a better alternative to current market practices.[92] At the same time, the Campaign's team feared that Kuyichi would undercut the Fair Wear Foundation by its refusal to join. The CCC's staff feared that others would think they approved of Kuyichi's methods if they did not speak out about their disagreements.[93] Kuyichi would eventually join the Fair Wear Foundation in 2013. How hard it was to put ideals into practice became evident when the foundation published its first reports about the company. In 2015, a report concluded that Kuyichi, though committed to socially responsible policies, needed to make significant improvements. Its self-ordained policies had not been implemented in all parts of its operations, not all suppliers were being actively monitored, and not everyone involved in producing the clothing was receiving fair remuneration.[94] These criticisms did not imply that Kuyichi did not take fair trade seriously. When volunteer researchers for the website Rank-a-Brand assessed the sustainability, corporate social responsibility, and transparency of Kuyichi in 2017, they awarded Kuyichi a B ('Well on the way'), a rarity amongst Dutch clothing companies at that time. Only two small German brands were given an 'A', whereas most well-known brands received Ds or Es, the lowest scores.[95]

To present consumers with an opportunity to join the effort to urge businesses to collaborate, a partnership with world shops and alternative trading organizations was a feasible option. Many of them had introduced clothing over the course of the 1990s, both as a new business opportunity and as a way to address the injustices of the global textile trade. World shops regularly supported actions by the CCC. Nonetheless, the partnership was slow to take off. This was due in part to different styles: traditionally, the CCC had employed an adversarial approach and had conveyed clear political messages, whereas many world shops and importers had adopted a more collaborative, businesslike outlook during the 1980s.[96] Second, the Campaign did not focus on the specific group of marginalized producers which had been front and centre for the world shops and alternative trading organizations since the demise of most of the leftist states in the late 1980s. The Charter of Fair Trade and other CCC initiatives, rather, stressed that companies had to take responsibility for the entire production chain involved in bringing their products to market. The successful expansion of fair trade to mainstream actors and markets since the 1980s supercharged this tension. The combination of new products, new partners, and a larger scale made it much more challenging to ascertain whether the whole product chain met the activists' expectations for fair trade.

As the reach of collaborative strategies like certification grew, the original focus on smallholder production became increasingly questionable. The CCC was frequently at odds with groups focused on the interests of small farmers. In 2003, the CCC clashed with representatives of Max Havelaar and FLO. Meeting that year, Clean Clothes' representatives urged their interlocutors to take the working conditions in the textile industry into account when introducing fair trade-certified cotton. But it was not easy to do so, because fair trade certification had not been applied to textile factories and did not include criteria which could be applied to these factories. Unable to come up with a more inclusive form of certification, FLO representative Olaf Paulsen proposed that it be communicated very clearly that only the cotton processed for the clothing was 'fair'. FLO would then work out a way to certify textile factories. Companies willing to commit to fair trade beyond what was required could insist on engaging suppliers which complied with the same SA8000 standard initially adopted by Kuyichi. To ensure that companies would not use certified clothing for window-dressing, Paulsen wanted them to accept a clause which stipulated that participating companies were not allowed to convey the impression that they complied with fair trade norms across the board.[97]

The CCC did not agree with this approach. Their objections were not limited to endorsement of the SA-8000 standards, which they had not found to be a guarantee of fair working conditions. CCC's Ineke Zeldenrust, Carole Crabbé, and Stefan Indermuehle insisted that companies which wanted to sell fair trade-certified clothes should be obliged to work towards acceptable working conditions across the entire product chain. Otherwise, these companies would – clause or no clause – use the product to polish their corporate reputation. Instead, CCC's representatives advocated that these firms be obliged to take corporate social responsibility seriously.[98]

The conflict was not resolved. By the end of 2004, the first socks made of fair trade-certified cotton were sold in France, and in Switzerland some months later. Again, members of the CCC enquired into the way the certification organization aimed to guarantee decent working conditions beyond cotton producers. To avoid any public confusion, Ineke Zeldenrust urged the organization to adopt the approach advocated by her organization. That way, the fair trade movement would speak with one voice regarding working conditions.[99] As other national FLO branches introduced fair trade textiles, however, it became clear that the differences were insurmountable. The CCC insisted that minimal working conditions be guaranteed across the entire product chain, whereas FLO's members prioritized improving the situation of marginalized producers.[100]

In the background, however, the focus on small farmers was becoming contentious within FLO's ranks, too. If the organization wanted to continue to expand its reach, they could not just focus on small farmers. Ever since the introduction of fair trade certification, there have been arguments about the status of plantation workers within the system. The question of whether these should also be included in the groups which fair trade certification aimed to support was all the more pressing because the fair trade tea marketed by alternative trading organizations originated from plantations. During the 1990s, another exception had been made for fair trade-certified bananas. If processed goods were to obtain a larger share of fair trade-certified marketing, a more fundamental reflection of the certification approach would be necessary.[101] Adding fuel to the fire, the certification of plantation-produced products was often the result of partnerships with multinational companies. Around 2005, Nestlé introduced 'Partner's Blend', which was certified by the British Fairtrade Foundation. At the same time, Fair Trade USA negotiated with Chiquita about certifying its bananas. These multinational companies had been significant adversaries of many fair trade activists in the North and South because of their operations in South America and Africa in particular.[102]

The labelling organizations gradually broadened their producer base, retaining an emphasis on agricultural products.[103] Certification was a result as well as a driver of new ways to engage with the business community. It opened up the field of fair trade by allowing any company complying with the criteria to offer fair trade products. Independent monitoring guaranteed that such companies were complying with fair trade guidelines. However, this approach also presented new problems. Monitoring was costly and hard to conduct in a satisfying manner.[104] As a result, commercial viability and principles constantly had to be weighed against each other. If fair trade certification raised the bar too high, the likelihood of expansion and widespread impact would diminish, some ambitious pioneers feared.[105] If the criteria were too lax, however, fair trade would lose its credibility.

This conflict flared up around the movement's flagship product. In 2003, the coffee roaster Hans Lévelt was one of those sounding the alarm. Lévelt, closely involved in the development of fair trade certification since the 1980s, now concluded that certification had been a boon for coffee farmers like the members of the Mexican cooperative UCIRI. Intermediary traders had been eliminated, a minimum price was guaranteed, and prefinancing and long-term buying obligations provided coffee producers stability. They retained a fair trade premium to improve the lives of people in their community. The market share of fair trade-certified coffee had stagnated, however. The introduction of new products suchlike bananas, tea, and fruit juices progressed with painful slowness. As an alternative, Lévelt outlined an approach which was closer to what was commonly practised in the coffee business. A fair relationship with coffee farmers implied that small coffee farmers with rough prospects should be advised to spend their time and energy on other ventures. Those who might plausibly establish a feasible business as coffee producers should be urged to become self-supporting as soon as possible, for example by limiting the timespan during which they could benefit from fair trade certification. Instead of support for development, transparency should become the key issue.[106]

Lévelts objections and proposal resonated with one of Max Havelaar's other pioneers, Nico Roozen. Because he felt Max

Havelaar had run its course, he joined a new initiative: Utz Kapeh. The new certificate had been developed with the support of Ahold, the mother company to a host of supermarket chains throughout the world. According to Roozen, this initiative presented the logical next step in making fair trade common practice. Large companies had become interested in corporate social responsibility and now had to be guided along this path. This implied a different approach and tone, according to Utz's advocates. Instead of Max Havelaar's demands, Utz formulated targets. There was no minimum price or development premium. Large plantations could also participate. Companies taking part in the certification scheme were obliged to contribute a pre-agreed sum which would be devoted to the improvement of agricultural techniques, mapping of the origins of the coffee traded, and work towards socially and environmentally responsible production.[107] In practice, farmers selling their coffee through Utz's channels earned slightly more than the market price, in part due to a system of rewards for proven quality. How much more they earned, and who actually received the gains, were not always clear. The prices also lagged behind those of the fair trade-certified coffee promoted by FLO and its members.[108]

The new initiative caused a rift between former allies, as the reaction of Solidaridad's Mexican partners made clear. 'Disappointment can never be a reason to flee to an alternative which is not sound' – such was Frans van der Hoff's fierce reaction to Utz Kapeh's announcement. He followed the developments around fair trade certification closely from Mexico on behalf of UCIRI. The new initiative he deemed 'villainous'. Qualifications like 'responsible' and 'sustainable' were not appropriate for a system which was 'slightly less indecent at best', he quipped. The new director of Max Havelaar, Stephan Peijenenburg, was equally infuriated, if less aggressive in his wording: 'Utz Kapeh is better than [regular coffee, PvD], but I wouldn't say they sell *certified responsible coffee*, as the package is announcing', he commented.[109]

Collaborative tactics induced a demand for transparency on behalf of partners who had not been traditionally committed to the movement's goals.[110] Certification by an independent third party was only one way to achieve such transparency. As the variety of ethical certification initiatives exploded over the course of the 1990s, the aim of transparency risked slipping out of reach.

Although some observers expressed dismay about the resulting confusion, supporters of fair trade could downplay the risks, because the different certificates, taken together, made up a larger market share, indicating that more consumers and companies were gradually embracing notions of ethical trade.

The attention to transparency also caused activists to evaluate their own work critically. How fair were the producers who obtained a certificate? Could alternative trading organizations and fair trade certification agencies guarantee that their partners were satisfying the criteria? 'Fair' products turned out not always to meet the activists' ambitions. This caused a shift in the rhetoric of many fair trade organizations, amongst them the CCC and the fair trade chocolate brand Tony's Chocolonely, established in 2005. Instead of presenting their products as entirely 'fair', they acknowledged that it was almost impossible for a company to offer products which could be labelled as such. Instead, they presented themselves as committed to improving social and ecological conditions within product chains in order to someday – perhaps – arrive at a situation which corresponded to their ideals. For example, Tony's Chocolonely went from claiming to sell 'slave-free chocolate' to stating that, through the buying and selling of its products, 'together we are making chocolate 100% slave-free'.[111]

These organizations no longer suggested that people could choose products which were 'fair' in an absolute sense. Instead, they presented their activism as a way to work *towards* genuinely fair trade. The introduction of a fair cell phone in 2013 by the pioneers of an Amsterdam-based company called Fairphone mounted a challenge to large electronics firms claiming that fair electronics was impossible in practice. It involved the public from the outset by blogging about the search for 'fair' suppliers of raw materials and manufacturers which could guarantee decent working conditions for future buyers. The public at large could gain insights into current market practices and the choices which had to be made in selecting suppliers and manufacturers.[112]

Local Collaboration

Collaborative approaches to fair trade also became part of local activism. Thousands of local groups had become integrated into a haphazard worldwide network. Local groups had provided the impetus for many campaigns by signalling injustices and providing local platforms for mobilization. At the end of the 1990s, people involved with the CCC proposed mobilizing local activists to bring fair trade onto the agenda of communal politics in a new way. 'On the whole, the government in the Netherlands is one of the largest consumers', they noted in a newsletter. If activists would press local governments to commit to fair trading practices in their procurement policies, companies would see a need to treat their employees decently. The CCC therefore developed a guide for those interested in such activities, outlining what a local campaign could look like. If the plan succeeded, local groups would engage in this new strand of fair trade activism across the country. If hospitals, fire brigades, and city cleaners wore fair clothing, others would soon enough follow suit.[113]

The proposal met with doubts within the CCC, but its advocates pointed to the success of local drives to create communities 'free from nuclear weapons' (*kernwapenvrij*) or 'anti-apartheid' towns. Although local councils could do little to affect international politics, such actions had led to fair amounts of publicity. Activists in the United States had also demonstrated that selective procurement could work well with government institutions.[114] The campaign's founders playfully dreamt of a country covered with signs for Clean Clothes Towns and a Clean Clothes Museum to commemorate the twentieth century's awful working conditions.[115] Volunteers went to work in several places. In 2002 Dutch world shops took up the idea.[116] The criteria to become a Clean Clothes Town were quite substantial. A municipality had to spend 70 per cent of its work-clothes budget on products of companies committed to an independent code of conduct in relation to working conditions and the environment. It had to appeal to local clothing stores to associate themselves with the Fair Wear Foundation and to support the activities of local groups around the issue of fair clothing. In the end, no municipality managed to meet these criteria.[117] The dream of a country covered with Clean Clothes Towns was soon in tatters.

Even as the Clean Clothes Towns did not materialize, fair trade towns were rapidly emerging. The inhabitants of the British town of Garstang had succeeded where the CCC had failed. Their

Figure 5.3 New Koforidua, the first fair trade town in Africa. Bruce Crowther.

town proclaimed itself a Fairtrade Town in 2001. In such a town, the municipality partnered with citizens and local businesses to trade fair products and direct public attention to the subject. The campaign rapidly spread across several countries. Ten years after the first Fairtrade Town was proclaimed, there were more than 500 such communities.[118] Notably, fair trade towns did not emerge only in the traditional strongholds of local fair trade activism in Western Europe. The global reach and common appeal the movement had obtained by the 2010s were discernible in the establishment of fair trade towns in Asia, Africa, and South America. In general, the resonance of this campaign indicated the availability of a range of fair trade products, a basic familiarity with the movement, and the willingness of companies and officials to engage in conversations about corporate social responsibility.[119]

Leveraging public procurement as a way to mainstream fair trade was an effective way of addressing public institutions in particular. It had the potential to enlist public institutions beyond mere declarations of support. In fact, the increasing turnover of fair trade products was to a large extent the result of purchases by public institutions and businesses. After exploring this strategy in relation to municipalities, fair trade supporters have applied it in a wide variety of context, as is evident in the emergence of Fair Trade Schools and Universities. Such campaigns also pressured businesses involved with similar products to engage with fair trade in order to be able to bid for contracts. This reinforced debates about which criteria were valid to establish whether a company was in fact acting responsibly. For example, the large coffee company Douwe Egberts took government institutions to court because their procurement policies left little room for products not certified by the FLO family.[120]

The enthusiasm for local activism had hardly disappeared, then. At the same time, however, world shops struggled, particularly in the Netherlands, the country where they had first been established. The first ten years after the introduction of certification, the number of shops had not been impacted by the wider availability of fair trade products and the ensuing competition with regular companies. In 1990 there had been 401 active world shop groups in the Netherlands, with an average of thirty volunteers per group. Their turnover was gradually increasing – particularly in small towns.[121] Many of their popular products, however, became ever more widely available.

Even though their position within the fair trade movement had changed due to the introduction of fair trade-certified products in many other shops, world shops continued to function as local platforms for activism around issues of global inequality. A survey amongst Dutch world shops in 2001 established that half of the groups collaborated with UNICEF, 39 per cent with churches, and 38 per cent with Amnesty International. Education remained a staple of their activities. Half of the groups worked with schools to draw pupils' attention to global inequality.[122] The need for such local hubs for activism gradually declined as online message boards, email lists, Facebook groups, and other social media platforms became more widespread in the first decade of the new millennium. Professional national and international campaigns also allowed local supporters to participate directly, as communication over distances had become considerably more convenient through the internet and email. World shops in Europe generally reacted in one of

Table 5.2 Total value of retail sales (in Euro) by FLO members based on the FLO Annual Reports, 2004–2009

Country	2004	2005	2006	2007	2008	2009
AUS/NZ	–	250,000	6,800,000	10,800	18,567,280	28,733,986
Austria	–	25,600,000	41,700,000	52,794,306	65,200,000	72,000,000
Belgium	13,605,000	5,000,000	28,000,000	3,500,000	45,780,141	56,431,496
Canada	1,753,6575	34,800,000	53,800,000	19,628,241	123,797,132	201,978,074
Czech Rep.	–	–	–	–	–	556,540
Denmark	13,000,000	14,000,000	23,200,000	39,559,534	51,220,106	54,436,609
Estonia	–	–	–	–	–	295,045
Finland	7,553,000	13,000,000	22,500,000	34,643,000	54,445,645	86,865,284
Rest of the world	–	–	–	–	130,722	18,099,255
France	69,670,360	19,100,000	166,000,000	210,000,000	255,570,000	287,742,792
Germany	57,500,000	70,900,000	110,000,000	141,686,350	212,798,451	267,473,584
Ireland	5,051,630	6,600,000	11,600,000	23,335,678	94,429,586	118,574,416
Italy	25,000,000	28,000,000	34,500,000	39,000,000	41,284,198	43,382,860
Japan	2,500,000	3,400,000	4,100,000	6,200,000	9,567,132	11,283,451
Latvia	–	–	–	–	–	153,500
Lithuania	–	–	–	–	–	315,380
Luxembourg	2,000,000	2,300,000	2,800,000	3,200,000	429,301	5,327,122
Netherlands	3,500,000	36,500,000	41,000,000	47,500,000	60,913,968	85,818,400
Norway	4,785,900	6,700,000	8,600,000	18,069,198	30,961,160	34,689,522

Table 5.2 (cont.)

Country	2004	2005	2006	2007	2008	2009
South Africa	–	–	–	–	–	458,075
Spain	–	300,000	1,900,000	3,928,213	5,483,106	8,030,724
Sweden	5,494,505	9,300,000	16,000,000	42,546,039	72,830,302	82,662,331
Switzerland	136,000,000	133,800,000	142,300,000	158,101,911	168,766,526	180,160,263
UK	205,556,621	276,800,000	409,500,000	704,314,576	880,620,304	897,315,061
USA	214,603,263	344,100,000	499,000,000	730,820,000	757,753,382	851,403,590
Total	814,856,854	1,132,700,000	1,623,300,000	2,160,547,846	2,954,368,442	3,394,187,360

Source: Mark Boonman, Wendela Huisman, Elmay Sarrucco-Fedorovtsjev, Terya Sarrucco, *A success story for producers and consumers: Fair trade facts & figures* (Culemborg; Dutch Association of World Shops, 2011), 52

Table 5.3 *Number of world shops in selected European countries, 1995–2007*

	1995	1998	2001	2005	2007
Belgium	200	227	250	295	296
France	54	67	88	165	145
Germany	700	700	700	800	836
Netherlands	380	395	400	412	426
Totals reported for Europe (EFTA-Yearbooks)	c. 3,000	c. 3,000	2,740	2,800	3,191

Source: EFTA-Yearbooks 1995–2007. Numbers for France include only Artisans du Monde-members.

two ways to this trend. Some focused more decidedly on selling fair trade products as their core activity. Others regarded the introduction of fair trade products in mainstream stores as an opportunity to devote themselves to campaigning and educational activities.

As multi-stakeholder initiatives like the Fair Trade Towns campaign proved effective on a local scale, fair trade activists attempted to transpose this approach to the international level. On 24 April 2013, the Rana Plaza complex in Bangladesh collapsed. More than 1,000 people who had been at work in the textile workshops in the building died, with about 2,500 injured. Although the authorities had warned of safety concerns, the textile workers had been pressured to continue to work in the complex. The CCC and its partners made a concerted effort to determine which companies were involved with the clothing manufactured in the building. These companies were then urged to compensate the families of the dead and injured. In addition, European and American clothing firms were pressed to sign the so-called Bangladesh Agreement in response to the catastrophe, guaranteeing independent oversight to safeguard the health and workplace safety of textile workers. In contrast to common practice, those companies signing the agreement were liable if the health and safety of employees proved to be at risk.[123] Although the Bangladesh Agreement arose from distressing circumstances, it did set a precedent on which activists hoped to model future attempts to hold companies to their promises of corporate responsibility.[124]

Fair Trade in a 'Network Society'

The limits of the postcolonial era came into view during the 1990s. Western European and North American companies had seized on post-1989 opportunities to relocate production to the Global South, which made an emphasis on North–South relations plausible for industries like textiles. At the same time, the dispersed networks of production and stretched chains of production and distribution made any spatial distinction tentative. Moreover, the networked structure of associations like the CCC offered activists the opportunity to expose local problems all over the world and to address them wherever they thought it appropriate to do so. Although access remained a problem, global communications in the internet age could be placed on a more equal footing than was the case with earlier forms of communications. The global network also gave activist networks more leverage than any single organization could achieve on its own. Coordinating campaigns nonetheless remained a challenge. The relations between activists were not very robust, and it was hard to sustain particular activities over a longer period. Whether the advantages outweighed the drawbacks differed significantly based on the objective, the product, and the actors addressed. On the whole, the extent to which fair trade initiatives have gained visibility and have made an impact on public and private actors since the 1990s underlines the extent to which social movements have been able to leverage these new conditions to their advantage.

The expansion of the fair trade movement during the 1990s and 2000s resulted from employing a range of tactics to promote fair trade's mainstreaming by companies, public institutions, and citizens. Their actions built on the previously established local footholds for fair trade activism and the repertoire of tactics developed by activists since the 1950s. They benefitted from, and in turn fostered, the growing acceptance of corporate social responsibility by businesses since the 1980s. Within this bundle of strategies, fair trade certification has drawn the most public and scholarly attention. This chapter has presented a broader perspective on certification, relating it to the broader repertoire of action and highlighting its evolution.

As for the development of this repertoire, the emphasis shifted towards approaches which demonstrated how companies could improve their practices. Collaborative tactics became predominant. The introduction of certification prompted the development of new collaborative instruments by making more fair trade products available. The inclusion of less committed actors within the network of fair trade activism generated additional pressure for transparency with regard to corporate practices. The widespread dissemination of fair trade has laid the foundations for recent attempts to set up multi-stakeholder initiatives to promote equitable socio-economic relations and protect the rights of workers not just on a local but also on a transnational level. The question of whether such initiatives should result in voluntary or rather legally enforceable agreements has become more pertinent as a result.

The end of the Cold War and the rise of digital communications also changed the relationships within the movement. Self-proclaimed 'network movements' like the CCC highlighted opportunities to build transnational coalitions and give voice to the grievances of workers and farmers from the Global South in particular. Despite this growing equity within the movement's everyday relations, the legacy of colonial inequalities remained discernible. Although people in Western Europe and North America became more aware of poverty and inequality remaining problems in their own vicinity, too, the idea remained that the global division of wealth could be mapped along a North–South divide. The sociologist Kathryn Wheeler concluded in 2012 that most fair trade buyers were driven by a sense of duty as global citizens towards less advantaged people elsewhere.[125] Prosperous people in the North continued to feel obliged to act in relation to less wealthy people in the South.

The end of the Cold War changed imaginations of a postcolonial future. Radical activists like the much-read Canadian author Naomi Klein complained that at the beginning of the new millennium hardly anyone was articulating an alternative to the free market.[126] This was true to an extent within the fair trade movement, too: the anticapitalistic strain of fair trade activism had gone quiet. But its dormancy did not imply that advocates of fair trade had accepted a preordained free market. They pursued activities to increase the market share and impact of fair trade products, bring companies to operate in a responsible fashion, and appeal to politicians to work to establish sustainable economic relations. These actions were underpinned by the idea that a more just economy was possible. At the dawn of the 21st century, fair trade activists deemed that small, practical steps provided the best means to move in that direction. Now that the clear-cut divisions between the first, second, and third worlds had receded and lines of communication were connecting people in startling new ways, the outlines of an equitable postcolonial world had become obscure.

CONCLUSION
Humanitarianism in the Era of Postcolonial Globalization

'Is fair trade finished?' asked the Indian writer Samanth Subramanian in *The Guardian* in 2019. Subramanian noted how fair trade had changed the way we shop, creating a 'virtuous triangle' of farmers and farming cooperatives, companies paying them a fair price, and consumers buying fair trade products. The successes had been remarkable in terms both of sheer numbers – products sourced from 1.66 million farmers and a plethora of widely recognized labels – and by highlighting that paying unfair prices should not just be business as usual. Fair trade had thus contributed to a 'world of heightened expectations of sustainability'. In this new world, however, companies were abandoning their commitment to fair trade certification. Instead, they took matters into their own hands, setting up their own codes of conduct and monitoring. This resulted in a proliferation of schemes and labels promoting sustainability. Given heightened expectations of sustainability and a mounting climate crisis, fair trade might actually have become problematic – by suggesting that if companies simply behaved a little better, the problems of our current social and environmental degradation could be solved.[1]

Subramanian's analysis posed crucial questions about the future of the fair trade movement. Fair trade certification, with its expectations regarding the 'virtuous triangle' of producers, companies, and consumers, had lost some of its appeal some thirty years after the introduction, in 1988, of Max Havelaar, the first fair trade label. Within the movement, too, the future of fair trade became more vividly contested during the 2010s. Individual fair trade pioneers and prominent organizations published retrospective accounts, accentuating a sense of transition.[2] In one such report, the German fair trade pioneer Gerd Nickoleit recounted a recent reunion with some of his comrades-in-arms at an international fair trade conference. The confident businesspeople now involved in the field made them feel like outsiders at the venue. 'No doubt, fair trade has come further and become more professional than we could ever have dreamt or even wanted during our sit-ins'.[3]

Nickoleit's remark was an apt expression of both amazement and uneasiness about the history of fair trade, and if we are to assess the movement as a whole, his ambivalence is revealing. Fair trade activism has endured over a period of seven decades, an astonishing feat for any social movement, all the more remarkable for a transnational network which was very loosely coordinated for most of its history. Over that period, fair trade advocates have publicized issues of global inequality in myriad settings, ranging from the world shops and supermarkets to meeting rooms and congress halls. However much admiration these accomplishments may occasion, it is offset by questions about their impact. The immediate effect on the people involved in the fair trade network over the years has been significant, not least for those producers who have been able to sustain or even increase their income, particularly after fair trade certification created opportunities for large-scale sales for certain producers. At the same time, many producers have indicated that they have not been able to sell enough of their products through fair trade channels and that participation in fair trade initiatives has not significantly improved their living conditions. Taking a broader view, the volume of fair trade sales remains a drop in the ocean of global trade. The unsustainable social and environmental effects of global trade that fair trade activists have attempted to address have not been meaningfully mitigated during the long period over which this activism has evolved.

Incorporating Collaboration

Can fair trade activists be held accountable for these disappointing results? The movement has continuously promoted fair trade, but its goals, repertoire, and networks have been transformed. An assessment of these transformations also delineates the conditions under which this history has played out. The evolution of the movement's goals is hardest to evaluate, as its advocates have always espoused a broad range of ideals and objectives. The inclusion of groups with very different agendas through common practices has been an important characteristic of the movement. Many fair trade pioneers in the 1950s and 1960s wanted to support marginalized groups such as refugees. Usually the assistance was envisioned as a temporary partnership aimed at attaining independence for its beneficiaries. As the histories of alternative trading organizations show, these intentions readily aligned with prevalent notions of development aid during the 1960s.

As the limitations of individual development projects became evident during this decade, most fair trade activists became united in a desire to reform the international trade system. Some argued that reform should be achieved through comprehensive measures to be taken by institutions like the United Nations Conference on Trade and Development and the European Economic Community. Others prioritized supporting countries and producer organizations which worked towards the realization of socialist or cooperative alternatives. The goal of global reform (or even revolution) was usually conceptualized within a distinct geographical imagination, which saw the Third World as the primary driver and beneficiary of change. The viability of this postcolonial framework gradually dissipated as new priorities emerged within and beyond the fair trade movement. The promotion of human rights, sustainable development, and, finally, a living income represented goals applicable beyond a specific geographic focus.

As the goals shifted, so did the repertoire of activities devoted to achieve them. At the outset, initiatives were aimed at supporting specific producer groups. Traditional humanitarian practices such as fundraisers, relief sales, and lectures predominated. As raising awareness about global inequality amongst the public in rich countries became a more pronounced goal during the late 1960s, it was supplemented by tactics for publicizing global inequality. Familiar actions such as demonstrations and marches were complemented by boycotts, workshops, and buycott campaigns. Once the scope of the movement widened, new instruments were developed to trade more effectively and on a larger scale. The fair trade movement's repertoire eventually expanded to include more collaborative tactics aimed at businesses in particular, but up through the present the movement has encompassed adversarial and collaborative initiatives alike. What seems notable in hindsight is that violent tactics seem largely absent. Even as producers resisting prevalent market practices often lived with the threat of violence, fair trade initiatives generally refrained from violent tactics. They only went as far as condoning blocking store entrances, stipulating the right to violent resistance in situations of autocratic oppression, and the use of shocking images. Incidental attacks on clothing stores in the 1980s appear to be the exception to this rule.

Certification has tended to obscure the broader repertoire of action of fair trade activism. Large and professional organizations like the fair trade labelling initiatives attract media attention, commission histories, and leave ample archival material for historians to work with. The work done by small producers and the campaigns of local volunteers are easily eclipsed. But to understand certification's emergence as well as its place within fair trade activism, it has to be considered as one form of action in a broader range. Pioneers of certification at Solidaridad, the Fairtrade Foundation, and Arbeitsgemeinschaft Kleinbauernkaffee had all deemed it a viable way to publicize and lobby for fair trade policies and corporate regulation whilst maximizing economic impact for producers in the short term. Yet certification yielded the unintended consequence of creating a physical distance between fair trade activists and the points of sale for fair trade products in supermarkets. These products, too, became less noticeably connected to the movement, their relation to fair trade was often reduced to a label on a package. As a result, fair trade organizations had to consider how the marketing of certified products could remain aligned with the movement's broader goals. As certification took off, sales figures could be taken as indicators of success. Fair trade advocates were increasingly confronted by researchers and journalists assessing their impact in strictly economic terms.

Frustration over the limitations of certification has been mounting since the early 2000s.[4] Fair trade advocates have devised refined approaches to certification in response. The scheme introduced by Utz (which joined Rainforest Alliance in 2018) focused on making the system more flexible and less expensive for potential partners from the business community. Utz's approach concentrated on incremental improvements and product quality, aiming to expand the range of businesses willing to involve themselves and thus make fair trade more attractive to producers, too. Whereas Utz's initiators wanted to broaden the scope of participants, producer organizations opted for a more exclusive approach in order to avoid greenwashing and to appeal to a sense of common purpose. At a conference in Tuxtla in 2006, the Small Producers Symbol was launched by a group of small producers from Latin America, which evolved into a worldwide network of small producers. At its launch, the producers tellingly stated that

> We are pleased to realize that the Fair Trade Concept has begun to be used more and more widely, but we are concerned that the concept may also have increasingly light weighted and distorted content, so we have decided to recall the original principles that gave rise to the fair trade system and to fight for them.[5]

In the same vein, fair trade enterprises from across the globe which had united under the banner of World Fair Trade Organization (WFTO) adopted an approach stipulating that the federation's members should ensure the fairness of their products' entire production chain.[6] Because many members were involved with handicraft products, fair trade certification through Fairtrade International's system was often not viable. WFTO therefore developed its own label, which was introduced during its international conference in Rio de Janeiro in 2013. The principles laid out for participants specified that fair trade should first and foremost be beneficial to 'economically marginalized groups'.[7] Instead of certifying individual products, WFTO's guarantee system was directed at verifying the compliance of businesses and organizations.[8]

In addition to improving certification systems one way or another, there has also been an exploration of complimentary approaches. Organizations such as the Clean Clothes Campaign have continued to prioritize campaigning for equitable social and economic relations rather than practising or certifying fair trade. Representatives of organizations involved with fair trade certification took to calculating at what price level farmers and workers could be assured of a 'living income' or a 'living wage'. These calculations made an important addition to the fair price and premium paid under certification, because the sale of fair trade-certified products could provide a decent living for fair trade producers only if their individual production levels were high enough, pricing accounted for producers' particular living conditions, and businesses and consumers were committed to buying these products on a large scale.[9]

The shift towards selling products and adopting collaborative tactics during the 1980s was in part a reaction to the circumstances the movement found itself in at that time. Certification countered activists' lack of influence in political negotiations about global trade. Selling products could also alleviate the pressures of various economic crises on many producers. As a result, the movement focused predominantly on enabling fair trade organizations to function rather than on changing trade policy more broadly. The recent attempts to improve and supplement fair trade certification played out under vastly different circumstances. The 1990s were the heyday of the liberalization of international trade. The shock of the 2008 financial crisis made it once again viable to attempt to regulate international trade through entities like the European Union. Catastrophes like the deaths of more than 1,000 factory workers after the collapse of the Rana Plaza complex in Bangladesh catalyzed attempts to force companies to safeguard working conditions and mitigate environmental impact across the entirety of their supply chains. Under these new circumstances, the Clean Clothes Campaign and its allies pushed for intergovernmental agreements on working conditions, resulting in agreements such as the Bangladesh Accord on Fire and Building Safety. In Brussels, the Fair Trade Advocacy Office, which had been pioneered by EFTA and supported by Fair Trade International and WFTO, gradually established itself as a hub of expertise in the field of global trade policies.[10]

The network of people, groups, and organizations advocating more equitable trade relations has also evolved strikingly over the seventy-year span of fair trade activism. The ascendancy of the fair trade movement has resulted in a larger, more specialized field of organizations, which function alongside the continued commitment of many local groups of volunteers. Fair trade activism had emerged as part of a wider coalition of initiatives revolving around issues of international solidarity, sustainable development, and the Third

World. At first, it had comprised a loosely knit association of producers as well as all kinds of civic initiatives in relatively prosperous countries. Although they were dominated by white, middle-class individuals, they integrated a broad range of age groups, ideological backgrounds, and geographical orientations. Their activities often took place in venues – fundraisers, discussion groups, and world shops – which encouraged a diverse set of relations.

By the early 1970s, the field consisted of loosely connected producer groups, campaigning organizations, alternative trade agencies, and world shops. Targeting businesses became more essential to fair trade activism from the 1970s onwards. Boycotting was supplemented by new tactics such as buycotting, setting up nonprofit ventures, and, eventually, certification. Certification agencies and a scattered field of likeminded social enterprises thus began entering the movement in the late 1980s. Fair trade gradually became a more distinct field of activism.[11] Over the course of the 1990s and 2000s, a group of producer organizations, alternative trade agencies, certification initiatives, campaigning outlets, and local groups identified more exclusively as a network of 'fair trade' advocates. As their scope and means of communication expanded, so generally have their sizes and degrees of professionalism.

The position of producers within this network has been particularly contentious. The overt paternalism which some of the early pioneers displayed towards producers, who purportedly had to be guided to achieve 'development', largely receded during the 1970s. Nominally, producers had the largest say in decisions about the movement's goals and repertoire, though this ideal was often hampered in practice due to faltering and indirect communication, unequal capabilities, and the divergent positions of producers. The sociopolitical imaginary of many activists, who tried to fit the producer groups into a global perspective neatly divided into a First, a Second, and a Third World or a Global North and South, could also blind them to the particularities of their situation.

The position of producers changed markedly due to the end of the Cold War and expanded access to digital communications. The end of the Cold War fragmented global relations and brought about the demise of solidarity activism supporting specific 'progressive' countries such as Vietnam, Tanzania, or Nicaragua. Under these new circumstances, the designation of who could count as a marginalized producer became predominantly a question of socio-economic rather than regional position, culminating in debates about including producer groups from the Global North alongside the traditional producer base of the movement.[12] As fair trade advocates across the world gained access to digital communications during the 1990s, direct exchanges and regular consultations became considerably easier. Initiatives such as the Clean Clothes Campaign have demonstrated the potential for mounting targeted campaigns with stakeholders throughout the world, aided by the possibilities of digital communications. They, too, however, struggle to sustain their initiatives and their supporting coalitions. Access to these means of communications is by no means equally distributed, with many marginalized groups struggling to participate in transnational exchanges on an equal footing. The privileged access to means of communication in more affluent circles is paralleled by the continued dominance of these circles in deciding which products are attractive and which ways to engage powerful political institutions and companies are most viable.

The relation between fair trade activists and businesses fundamentally shifted in the early twenty-first century. The long-term impact of boycotts, certifications, and other fair trade initiatives was evident from the fact that companies no longer held their responsibility to be solely to deliver good and affordable products to consumers. Activists had exposed the social and environmental degradation resulting from corporate malpractice and campaigned for change. In reaction, businesses had developed more elaborate concepts of corporate social responsibility and sustainable practices. Rather than debating whether such responsibilities applied to them, conflicts now arose over the extent to which businesses were responsible for the social and environmental impact of their operations and about how their activities should be regulated in this regard.

The fair trade movement thus found itself in a new position. Once having to operate outside of mainstream markets and confront companies from this external position, there were now ample opportunities for collaboration as well as many competing practices of fair trade. It was not just fair trade organizations like Fair Trade International, WFTO, Utz, and the Clean Clothes Campaign which promoted different approaches. Companies also increasingly introduced their own sustainability initiatives, which made it harder for the public to distinguish between serious commitment and 'window-dressing'. Opportunities to collaborate with companies also presented fair trade activists with new dilemmas about balancing impact through partnerships and preserving their credibility despite cooperating with actors whose principal commitments were not to fair trade. With partner companies invested in the current system of global trade, it was more challenging to communicate a transformative vision.

The expansion of the fair trade network, and of certification in particular, also put pressure on the movement. Although many campaigns benefitted from the professionalism and specialization it brought, the crucial position of individual producers and local volunteers was harder to appreciate and accommodate. Established national organizations and transnational umbrella organizations such as Fairtrade International and WFTO, by virtue of their expertise and funding, were able to initiate and promote activities and visions to much greater effect, for better and for worse. Public familiarity with fair trade-certified products meant that fair trade was frequently equated with certification, obscuring the broader movement and repertoire of action in which certification was rooted. For example, although world shop groups continued to play a pivotal role in mounting local fair trade towns campaigns, their significance was not as readily understood from an economic perspective. If fair trade was about selling fair trade-certified products, supermarkets were much more desirable than specialized shops. Similarly, organizations like Oxfam and the Clean Clothes Campaign which had long been part of the network of fair trade advocates became reluctant to identify themselves as supporters of 'fair trade', because they did not want to associate themselves too closely with certification as an instrument to promote this cause.

Humanitarianism Reconsidered

These ambivalent conclusions about the practices and effects of fair trade prompt important questions about the evolution of humanitarianism and postcolonial globalization since the 1950s. As a social history of globalization, the account of fair trade I have provided here foregrounds the impact of global economic integration, decolonization, and the emergence of digital communications on how people across the world have regarded and have attempted to shape global relations since the 1950s. The history of fair trade activism proposes that we reconsider the keystones of the history of humanitarianism in this era.

First, the history of fair trade reinforces the recent shift away from a Eurocentric perspective in the historiography of humanitarianism. Its history is not one of people in the North doing good for distant others. Many fair trade activists and influential organizations within the movement were indeed based in the Global North. However, ever since a group of women urged Edna Byler to sell their needlework in the 1950s, fair trade activism has been shaped through exchanges with producers, politicians, and intellectuals from the Global South who were committed to challenging global economic disparities. The resulting global coalitions were improvisatory, unstable, and often skewed because of advantages due to the availability of certain economic, political, and communicative opportunities for activists in the North. This book has been a portrait of the resulting tightrope act as these coalitions evolved and did their work. Based primarily on sources produced and held in repositories in Western Europe and the United States, this study can nonetheless discern the impact of marginalized groups. They initiated exchanges, cued particular ideas and practices, and criticized inequality not only in global relations but also within the fair trade movement. At the same time, the available material often lacks the necessary detail to fully allow a more nuanced and comprehensive account of marginalized groups and their contributions.

The mental maps we carry of humanitarianism represent a second dimension which the history of fair trade brings to the fore. During the early years of fair trade activism, marginal groups were markedly dispersed across the globe. Handicrafts producers from Appalachia in the US and from West Germany, disadvantaged children in Sicily – these people were within the scope of fair trade activists just as much as refugees in Hong Kong and Palestine were. Despite the importance of the Cold War's East–West divide, global inequality was predominantly framed along a South–North axis from the 1960s onwards. The shift towards localizing marginalized groups in the Global South, however, was rooted not in isolated concern over the living conditions of people in that part of the world but, rather, in a new global outlook. Inequality in the Global South was challenged on the ground that inequality was a global moral issue in a postcolonial world where all individuals had a legitimate claim to equality. The lack of economic and social opportunities which directly affected people in the South infringed on moral standards which were proclaimed to be universally applicable. But inequality was not solely an abstract moral consideration. Inequality in one part of the world was regarded as threatening the stability and prosperity of people across the globe, particularly during periods of geopolitical volatility. The exchange of commodities which had passed through the hands of 'underprivileged' people made these unequal relations tangible and thus more harrowing to comprehend. This mechanism was particularly salient when considering relished commodities such as coffee or chocolate – how could one enjoy these if others had to suffer so you could consume them?

The reframing of inequality along a North–South axis was reinforced by groups who regarded the so-called Third World as a beacon of hope. For virtually the entirety of the Cold War, the idea that this Third World could break out of the stalemate of the East–West contretemps found vocal advocates in the South and North alike. Such ideas likewise did not remain abstract matters but were rooted in concrete practices. Collecting items to send to Vietnam, or selling wine from Algeria or coffee from Nicaragua to financially support leftist governments: the connections these transactions embodied were tangible. A politically more moderate version of Third Worldism focused on support for groups which brought alternative economic approaches like cooperation into practice, amongst them the coffee farmers; cooperatives which would eventually emerge as the main partners for fair trade certification in the late 1980s.

Postcolonial globalization, then, was primarily imagined within the framework of relations between the North and South. Although the end of the Cold War brought down the curtain on Third Worldism, it did not dissolve the North–South framework. Fair trade activists in the 1990s focused on expanding the range of products traded and the number of countries in the South included in the system. The expansion of the fair trade network, improved means of communication, and the new wave of trade globalization in the 1990s gradually dissolved any distinct regional focus, resulting at first in the predominance of a wide range of distinct producer groups instead of more generalized views of 'people in the South'. In fact, as Western European and North American companies seized on the post-1989 opportunities to relocate production to the Global South, an emphasis on North–South relations became even more plausible for industries like textiles. The same process of hyperglobalization has slowly eroded any clear regional division between prosperous and poor or producer and consumer, as networks of production and consumption dispersed and inequalities in individual regions increased.

Third, the history of fair trade indicates the need to rethink how transnational networks have shaped humanitarian ideas and practices. During the postcolonial era, ties established during the colonial era through solidarity activism and missionary activities were crucial to the enabling of fair trade initiatives. Economic integration and digital communications set the conditions for the evolution of these loosely linked actors into a globally interconnected movement of producers, volunteers, professional nongovernmental organizations, and businesses. The spread of digital communications since the 1980s has offered unparalleled opportunities to forge networks spanning all parts of the globe. The exchanges between likeminded groups across the world, in turn, catalyzed attempts to operate in a more professionalized and specialized manner. Attempts at specialization were reinforced by the gradual expansion of fair trade organizations and the experiences gained by activists over the years. Arguably, these processes of transnational interconnection and professionalization are also applicable to the histories of many other humanitarian organizations.

The ways fair trade activism was shaped by the exchanges between actors across the world highlight the need to look beyond individual people and organizations to adequately grasp the history of humanitarianism. A host of organizations, groups, and individuals participated in fair trade activism. If not for this broad coalition, the movement would not have survived for as long as it did, nor would it have attracted such widespread attention. This shape-shifting network drove experimentation with new tactics because not every actor was equally invested in a single approach. The resulting creativity made the movement broadly appealing, since different activities could draw in various sorts of people and different groups could articulate overlapping yet diverging viewpoints. The collaborations and exchanges about ideas and means of activism transcended national borders – the transnational nature of humanitarian action is a necessity rather than a luxury. Such requisite cosmopolitanism, so to speak, makes the history of humanitarianism a particularly challenging subject because in telling any such history one must consider a flurry of people and actions in different places. Taking as a research subject a single field of activism, such as fair trade, human rights, or medical assistance, can provide a viable way forward.

Concentrating on a distinct commodity's contestation can provide a similar focus. Approaching the history of humanitarianism through the lens of one commodity can bring transnational assemblages, rather than a specific organization or national 'field', into view. This material dimension of humanitarianism is a fourth area that the history of fair trade encourages us to explore. Commodities have provided material linkages between people in different parts of the world. As the preceding chapters have shown, they delimited which circumstances and relations could, and which could not, be made visible. This made finding commodities which fit their agenda a fickle element of campaigning. In the case of fair trade activism, the North–South imaginary and the postcolonial impetus resulted in an emphasis on 'tropical' products, which were connected from the 1970s onwards to histories of colonial exploitation. Indeed, as fair trade advocates started to consider including producers from the North, the range of products under discussion expanded to include commodities such as milk and apple juice.

To direct attention to humanitarianism's material dimension is to go beyond the commodities which connected actors and messages and to consider the specific places where humanitarian activities take place. A world shop equipped as an action centre enabled the establishment of local networks oriented around overlapping issues such as trade justice, human rights, and the environment. Fair trade-certified products in supermarkets allowed for more everyday and fleeting practices of humanitarianism. This emphasis on material infrastructure extends as a matter of course to a consideration of the means of interaction within activist networks. As this book has shown, the new possibilities for communication offered by digital communications have been particularly influential for activist networks since the 1990s. The widespread availability of such technology has fundamentally changed the extent to which the movement could make good on its intent to furnish an equal exchange of views between different parts of the globe.

The history of fair trade, finally, highlights the importance of economic relations for humanitarianism. Market relations have often been separated from civic initiatives. Humanitarians challenged prevailing market practices and launched efforts to buy and sell on behalf of their causes. To achieve these aims, they had to obtain support from private donors or public institutions. Fair trade highlights how economic relations have also, at times, been more fundamentally intertwined with humanitarian action. Raised as an issue, the unequal economic relations denounced by intellectuals like Raúl Prebisch galvanized the humanitarian actions which came to constitute the fair trade movement. Fair trade pioneers understood economic relations to be subject to the politics and policies of states, intergovernmental organizations, and multinational corporations. Social, political, and economic issues were thus inextricably intertwined. On a personal level, people could connect through trade relations or leverage such relations to point out to others how their lives were enmeshed with those of people across the globe. Leveraging their power as producers and consumers was crucial to the repertoire of fair trade activism. But, once again, this power was not strictly economic in nature. Without activists' ability to organize and publicize, the economic means of mobilization would not have served their purpose.

Even as fair trade activism was taking off during the 1970s, a strain of globalization emerged which was more comprehensively based on free markets and offered marginalized groups even less protection than they had previously experienced. The inability of fair trade activism and other humanitarian initiatives to address the foundations of global inequality calls into question their capability to address economic relations. Were they unable to do so due to a lack of institutional influence and popular support, or does their failure also stem from the vantage point of this strand of postcolonial humanitarianism? Have notions about human rights, grassroots mobilization, and the power of consumers reinforced the existing market-based order rather than challenged it?

The differences amongst different actors within the fair trade movement regarding their goals and repertoire are readily apparent and thwart a clear-cut answer to these questions. Discussions over the extent of change needed to achieve a better world are at the heart of the history of humanitarianism. The preceding chapters have highlighted a continuous debate within the movement that pits charity against justice and aid against structural reforms. A closer analysis of these debates, however, revealed considerable overlap between the positions, which were then contrasted. Neither side neglected the importance of providing whatever aid was possible in the short term. Each was rooted in a view of how a better world could be achieved. Some believed it could be realized within the current economic framework if people would simply act more decently towards (distant) others. Most fair trade advocates asserted that changes in the prevailing economic order were necessary – either through developing alternative economic models or by working towards some form of socialism.

The repertoire of fair trade activism shows how such ideals can be integrated into everyday practices, whether this meant meeting regularly in a local world shop or buying fair trade products in a supermarket. It can happen that this kind of integration dilutes sociopolitical agendas because activism becomes submerged within routines. A risk of selling fair trade products in mainstream retail stores is that solidarity will be commodified: people may well feel that they are doing enough to address wrongs in the world by buying one package of coffee instead of another. All the while, the preeminence of their role as a consumer can buttress the notion that people are consumers first and foremost. This interpretation, however, neglects the extent to which everyday practices can keep a vision of a better world alive under desperate conditions. The possibility of making a small short-term difference has certainly enabled fair trade activism to sustain itself in the face of adverse circumstances. The long-term effects of its activities still remain elusive, however. They apparently have provided an important springboard for recent attempts to realize more far-reaching reforms in the economic system, including the introduction of due diligence legislation and calls for a reckoning with the colonial past.

Fair Trade after the Postcolonial Era

Presenting my research at a fair trade fair some years ago, my host shared her frustrations over a controversy amongst exhibitors at the market. Some participants had taken exception to the presence of regionally produced organic juices. Products from Western Europe surely did not belong next to ceramics made by indigenous potters from Latin America and textiles made by underprivileged women in Bangladesh? The organizers, for their part, felt that any product contributing to a more sustainable world should be showcased. Such discussions over the position of 'local fair trade' in the North have intensified in recent years. The gradual erosion of the idea that fair trade pertained exclusively to relations between the South and the North points towards the demise of the era of postcolonial globalization, a time when economic inequality was primarily defined in terms of postcolonial South–North relations.

A recent wave of activism addressing issues of inequality, racism, and decoloniality has reframed the issue of coloniality and taken it beyond the North–South axis. Within the network of fair trade advocates, the division between producers in the South and advocates in the North has steadily eroded over the last twenty years. Fair trade activism, it seems, will outlast the era of postcolonial globalization. Over the last twenty years, the spatial imagination of a North–South divide has gradually been undercut by the regional organization of producers within separate Asian, African, and Latin American networks. The expansion of fair trade and an increase in living standards in the South sparked attempts to sell fair trade products within the Global South as well as in the North. At the same time, the increasing levels of inequality within the North provoked discussions about whether to include its producers in fair trade initiatives. Claims to be included under the fair trade umbrella were put forth by groups of producers like small-scale farmers, who believed themselves marginalized. The integration of environmental, social, and economic concerns under the rubric of 'sustainability' made such claims more persuasive: Shouldn't small-scale farmers in the North receive the sort of support given to rural cooperatives in the South? Moreover, wouldn't it be preferable that people obtain their products from their own regions, so as to decrease the environmental impact of transporting goods and to strengthen regional ties?

The fair trade movement has been a primary exponent of humanitarianism in the era of postcolonial globalization. Measured against its own ambitions, the glass is currently half full at best.

The network has been able to sustain a group of producers through a series of economic crises. It has continued campaigning despite setbacks and challenging conditions. The broad acceptance of the notion of corporate responsibility can partly be ascribed to fair trade campaigns contesting corporate practices and providing companies with examples and opportunities to implement more socially and environmentally responsible behaviour. Yet the legacy of colonial inequality continues to inform global inequalities and is now impeding attempts to address climate change, as former colonies rightly point out that the primary responsibility here lies with the countries which historically have reaped most of the benefits of the activities causing climate change. The challenge of addressing global inequality is compounded by the emergence of new inequalities within societies in the North and the South alike over the last fifty years.

Under these new circumstances, the fair trade movement has to come up with a new interpretation of fair trade, one which does justice to the continued impact of colonial inequalities whilst acknowledging the need to address local inequalities. Will this new conception be a universalized notion of fair trade as a socially and environmentally responsible practice, applicable to any relation throughout the world? Or will it produce many localized versions of what fair trade entails in different places? Either way, the fair trade movement will continue to be an important barometer for how people, beyond the dictates of boardrooms and the discussions held in congress halls, are attempting to shape the history of globalization.

NOTES

Acknowledgements

1. Peter van Dam, 'No Justice without Charity: Humanitarianism after Empire', *The International History Review* 44, no. 3 (2022): 653–74.
2. Peter van Dam, 'Goodbye to Grand Politics: The Cane Sugar Campaign and the Limits of Transnational Activism, 1968–1974', *Contemporary European History* 28, no. 4 (2019): 518–34.
3. Peter van Dam, 'Challenging Global Inequality in Streets and Supermarkets: Fair Trade Activism since the 1960s', in *Histories of Global Inequality*, eds. Christian Olaf Christiansen and Steven L. B. Jensen (Cham: Palgrave Macmillan, 2019), 255–75.

Introduction

1. Vivian Hendriksz, 'The mad rush in Amsterdam vermittelt Gefühl von Sweatshop', https://fashionunited.de/nachrichten/mode/the-mad-rush-in-amsterdam-vermittelt-gefu-hl-von-sweatshop/2016051120137 (22 November 2019).
2. 'Fairtrade impact', www.fairtrade.net/impact (17 November 2023).
3. 'World Fair Trade Organization Annual Report 2022', https://wfto.com/wp-content/uploads/2023/09/Copy-of-AR-layout-final.pdf.pdf (17 November 2023).
4. 'A global network', https://cleanclothes.org/network (17 November 2023).
5. Olaf Bach, *Die Erfindung der Globalisierung: Entstehung und Wandel eines zeitgeschichtlichen Grundbegriffs* (Frankfurt am Main: Campus, 2013), 9–11.
6. Robbie Robertson, *The Three Waves of Globalization: A History of a Developing Global Consciousness* (London: Zed Books, 2003), 172.

7. Jürgen Osterhammel, *Die Verwandlung der Welt: eine Geschichte des 19. Jahrhunderts* (München: Beck, 2009); Roland Robertson and David Inglis, 'The Global "Animus": In the Tracks of World Consciousness', *Globalizations* 1, no. 1 (2004): 38–49.
8. Bill Schwarz, 'Actually Existing Postcolonialism', *Radical Philosophy*, no. 104 (2000): 16–24.
9. Jürgen Dinkel, Steffen Fiebrig, and Frank Reichherzer eds., *Nord/Süd: Perspektiven auf eine globale Konstellation* (Berlin: De Gruyter, 2020).
10. Odd Arne Westad, *The Global Cold War: Third World Interventions and the Making of Our Times* (Cambridge: Cambridge University Press, 2005); Steven L. B. Jensen, *The Making of International Human Rights: The 1960s, Decolonization and the Reconstruction of Global Values* (New York: Cambridge University Press, 2017).
11. Elizabeth Buettner, *Europe after Empire: Decolonization, Society, and Culture* (Cambridge: Cambridge University Press, 2016); Peo Hansen and Stefan Jonsson, *Eurafrica: The Untold History of European Integration and Colonialism* (London: Bloomsbury, 2014); Adom Getachew, *Worldmaking after Empire: The Rise and Fall of Self-Determination* (Princeton, New Jersey: Princeton University Press, 2019).
12. Maarten van den Bos and Chris Dols, 'King Customer: Contested Conceptualizations of the Consumer and the Politics of Consumption in the Netherlands, 1920s-1980s', *BMGN – Low Countries Historical Review* 132, no. 3 (2017): 94–114; Meg Jacobs, *Pocketbook Politics: Economic Citizenship in Twentieth-Century America* (Princeton: Princeton University Press, 2005).
13. Lawrence B. Glickman, *Buying Power: A History of Consumer Activism in America* (Chicago: University of Chicago Press, 2009).
14. Matthew Hilton, *Prosperity for All: Consumer Activism in an Era of Globalization* (Ithaca: Cornell University Press, 2009).
15. Cf. Geert Buelens, *De jaren zestig: Een cultuurgeschiedenis* (Amsterdam: Balans, 2018).
16. Kevin O'Sullivan, *The NGO Moment: The Globalisation of Compassion from Biafra to Live Aid* (Cambridge: Cambridge University Press, 2021); Dena Freeman, *Tearfund and the Quest for Faith-based Development* (Abingdon: Routledge, 2019); Heike Wieters, *The NGO CARE and Food Aid from America, 1945–1980* (Manchester: Manchester University Press, 2017); Matthew Hilton and Jean-François Mouhot eds., *The Politics of Expertise: How NGOs Shaped Modern Britain* (Oxford: Oxford University Press, 2013).

17. Hansjörg Siegenthaler, 'Geschichte und Ökonomie nach der kulturalistischen Wende', *Geschichte und Gesellschaft* 25, no. 2 (1999): 276–301; Hartmut Berghoff and Jakob Vogl, 'Wirtschaftsgeschichte als Kulturgeschichte: Ansätze zur Bergung transdisziplinärer Synergiepotentiale', in *Wirtschaftsgeschichte als Kulturgeschichte: Dimensionen eines Perspektivenwechsels*, ed. Hartmut Berghoff and Jakob Vogl (Frankfurt am Main: Campus, 2004), 9–41; Mark Bevir and Frank Trentmann, eds., *Markets in Historical Contexts: Ideas and Politics in the Modern World* (Cambridge: Cambridge University Press, 2004).

18. Matthew Anderson, *A History of Fair Trade in Contemporary Britain: From Civil Society Campaigns to Corporate Compliance* (Basingstoke: Palgrave Macmillan, 2015); Ruben Quaas, *Fair Trade: Eine global-lokale Geschichte am Beispiel des Kaffees* (Köln: Böhlau Verlag, 2015); Konrad Kuhn, *Entwicklungspolitische Solidarität: die Dritte-Welt-Bewegung in der Schweiz zwischen Kritik und Politik (1975–1992)* (Zürich: Chronos, 2011); Konrad J. Kuhn, *Fairer Handel und Kalter Krieg: Selbstwahrnehmung und Positionierung der Fair-Trade-Bewegung in der Schweiz 1973–1990*, 1. Aufl. (Bern: Ed. Soziothek, 2005); Markus Raschke, *Fairer Handel: Engagement für eine gerechte Weltwirtschaft* (Ostildern: Matthias-Grünewald-Verlag, 2009); Gavin Fridell, *Fair Trade Coffee: The Prospects and Pitfalls of Market-Driven Social Justice* (Toronto: University of Toronto Press, 2007); Jan van de Poel, '35 Jaar Oxfam-Wereldwinkels: Over groei en organisatorische vernieuwing', *Brood & Rozen* 11, no. 4 (2006): 7–25; Matthieu Gateau, 'Quelle(s) stratégie(s) de distribution pour les produits équitables ? Le cas français ou la difficile alliance entre logique militante et logique commerciale', *Économie et Solidarités* 37, no. 2 (2008): 109–22.

19. Sarah Lyon and Mark Moberg, eds., *Fair Trade and Social Justice: Global Ethnographies* (New York: New York University Press, 2010); Laura Raynolds, Douglas Murray, and John Wilkinson, eds., *Fair Trade: The Challenges of Transforming Globalization* (Abingdon: Routledge, 2007).

20. Laura Raynolds and Elisabeth Bennett, 'Introduction to Research on Fair Trade', in *Handbook of Research on Fair Trade*, ed. Laura Raynolds and Elizabeth Benett (Cheltenham: Edward Elgar Publishing, 2015), 3–23; Gavin Fridell, Zach Gross, and Sean McHugh, 'Why Write a Book About Fair Trade?' in *The Fair Trade Handbook: Building a Better World, Together*, ed. Gavin Fridell,

Zach Gross, and Sean McHugh (Halifax: Fernwood Publishing, 2021), 1–6.
21. Sidney G. Tarrow, *Power in Movement: Social Movements and Contentious Politics* (Cambridge: Cambridge University Press, 2011), 20–22; Margaret Keck and Kathryn Sikkink, *Activists Beyond Borders: Advocacy Networks in International Politics* (Ithaca: Cornell University Press, 1998), 2–29.
22. Erik Swyngedouw, 'Neither Global nor Local: "Glocalization" and the Politics of Scale', in *Spaces of Globalization: Reasserting the Power of the Local.*, ed. Kevin R. Cox (New York: Guilford Press, 1997), 137–64; Doug MacAdam, Sidney Tarrow, and Charles Tilly, *Dynamics of Contention*, Cambridge Studies in Contentious Politics (Cambridge: Cambridge University Press, 2001), 331–37; Saskia Sassen, 'The Many Scales of the Global: Implications for Theory and for Politics', in *The Postcolonial and the Global*, ed. Revathi Krishnaswamy and John C. Hawley (Minneapolis: University of Minnesota Press, 2008), 82–93.
23. Angelika Epple, 'Lokalität und die Dimensionen des Globalen. Eine Frage der Relationen', *Historische Anthropologie* 21, no. 1 (2013): 4–25.
24. 'The Third World' in this book is used where historical actors refer to this mental division of the world.
25. Claudia Olejniczak, *Die Dritte-Welt-Bewegung in Deutschland: konzeptionelle und organisatorische Strukturmerkmale einer neuen sozialen Bewegung* (Wiesbaden: DUV, 1999); Claudia Olejniczak, 'Dritte-Welt-Bewegung', in *Die Sozialen Bewegungen in Deutschland seit 1945: Ein Handbuch*, eds. Roland Roth and Dieter Rucht (Frankfurt am Main: Campus, 2008), 319–45; Luuk Wijmans, 'De solidariteitsbeweging. Onverklaard maakt onbekend', in *Tussen verbeelding en macht. 25 jaar nieuwe sociale bewegingen in Nederland*, eds. Jan Willem Duyvendak et al. (Amsterdam: SUA, 1992), 121–40; Jan van de Poel, 'Solidarity without Borders? The Transnational Integration of the Flemish Solidarity Movement', *Belgisch Tijdschrift voor Filologie en Geschiedenis/Revue Belge de Philologie et d'Histoire* 89, no. 3–4 (2011): 1381–1404; Dieter Rucht, 'The Transnationalization of Social Movements: Trends, Causes, Problems', in *Social Movements in a Globalizing World*, eds. Donatella Della Porta, Dieter Rucht, and Hanspeter Kriesi (Houndmills: Macmillan, 1999), 206–22; Donatella della Porta Della Porta et al., *Globalization From Below: Transnational Activists And Protest Networks* (Minneapolis: University of Minnesota Press, 2006).

26. Schwarz, 'Actually Existing Postcolonialism'; Erik Tängerstad, '"The Third World" as an Element in the Collective Construction of a Post-Colonial European Identity', in *Europe and the Other and Europe as the Other*, ed. Bo Stråth (Brussel: Peter Lang, 2000), 157–93.
27. Westad, *Global Cold War*.
28. Robert Gildea, James Mark, and Niek Pas, 'European Radicals and the "Third World": Imagined Solidarities and Radical Networks, 1958–73', *Cultural and Social History* 8, no. 4 (2011): 449–71; Quinn Slobodian, *Foreign Front: Third World Politics in Sixties Germany* (Durham: Duke University Press, 2012); Samantha Christiansen and Zachary A. Scarlett, eds., *The Third World in the Global 1960s* (New York: Berghahn Books, 2013); Kim Christiaens, 'Between Diplomacy and Solidarity: Western European Support Networks for Sandinista Nicaragua', *European Review of History: Revue Européenne d'histoire* 21, no. 4 (2014): 617–34; Christoph Kalter, *The Discovery of the Third World: Decolonization and the Rise of the New Left in France, c.1950–1976* (Cambridge University Press, 2016).
29. Claus Offe, 'New Social Movements: Challenging the Boundaries of Institutional Politics', *Social Research* 52, no. 4 (1985): 817–68; Jan Willem Duyvendak et al. eds., *Tussen verbeelding en macht: 25 jaar nieuwe sociale bewegingen in Nederland* (Amsterdam: SUA, 1992); Marc Hooghe, 'Een bewegend doelwit: De sociologische en historische studie van (nieuwe) sociale bewegingen in Vlaanderen', *Belgisch Tijdschrift voor Nieuwste Geschiedenis* 34, no. 3 (2004): 331–57.
30. Mark Berger, 'After the Third World? History, Destiny and the Fate of Third Worldism', *Third World Quarterly* 25, no. 1 (2004): 9–39.
31. Benjamin Möckel, 'Consuming Anti-Consumerism: The German Fairtrade Movement and the Ambivalent Legacy of "1968"', *Contemporary European History* 28, no. 4 (2019): 550–65; Wouter Mensink, *Kun je een betere wereld kopen? De consument en het fairtrade-complex* (Amsterdam: Boom, 2015); Fridell, *Fair Trade Coffee*; Frank Trentmann, 'Before "fair trade": empire, free trade, and the moral economies of food in the modern world', *Environment and Planning D: Society and Space* 25, no. 6 (2007): 1079–102.
32. Peter van Dam, 'In Search of the Citizen-Consumer: Fair Trade Activism in the Netherlands since the 1960s', *BMGN – Low Countries Historical Review* 132, no. 3 (2017): 139–66.
33. Ruth Oldenziel and Liesbeth Bervoets, 'Speaking for Consumers, Standing up as Citizens: The Politics of Dutch Women's Organization and the Shaping of Technology, 1880–1980', in *Manufacturing*

Technology, Manufacturing Consumers: The Making of Dutch Consumer Society, ed. Adri Albert de la Bruhèze (Amsterdam: Aksant, 2009), 41–71; Ruth Oldenziel and Mikael Hård, *Consumers, Tinkerers, Rebels: The People Who Shaped Europe* (Houndmills: Palgrave Macmillan, 2013); Frank Trentmann, 'Citizenship and Consumption', *Journal of Consumer Culture* 7, no. 2 (2007): 147–58; Frank Trentmann, *Free Trade Nation: Commerce, Consumption, and Civil Society in Modern Britain* (Oxford: Oxford University Press, 2008).

34. Glickman, *Buying Power*.
35. Tad Skotnicki, *The Sympathetic Consumer: Moral Critique in Capitalist Culture* (Stanford: Stanford University Press, 2021), 1–24, 125–39.
36. Matthew Hilton et al., 'History and Humanitarianism: A Conversation', *Past & Present* 241, no. 1 (1 November 2018): e1–38; Kevin O'Sullivan, Matthew Hilton, and Juliano Fiori, 'Humanitarianisms in Context', *European Review of History: Revue Européenne d'histoire* 23, no. 1–2 (2 January 2016): 1–15; Johannes Paulmann, 'Conjunctures in the History of International Humanitarian Aid during the Twentieth Century', *Humanity: An International Journal of Human Rights, Humanitarianism, and Development* 4, no. 2 (2013): 215–38.
37. Michael Barnett and Janice Gross Stein, 'The Secularization and Sanctification of Humanitarianism', in *Sacred Aid: Faith and Humanitarianism* (Oxford, 2012), 3–36; Jeffrey Cox, 'From the Empire of Christ to the Third World: Religion and the Experience of Empire in the Twentieth Century', in *Britain's Experience of Empire in the Twentieth Century*, ed. Andrew Thompson (Oxford: Oxford University Press, 2012), 76–122; Peter Stamatov, *The Origins of Global Humanitarianism: Religion, Empires, and Advocacy* (New York: Cambridge University Press, 2013); Freeman, *Tearfund*; Daniel Maul, *The Politics of Service: US-amerikanische Quäker und internationale humanitäre Hilfe 1917–1945* (Berlin: De Gruyter, 2021); O'Sullivan, *The NGO Moment*.
38. Timothy J. LeCain, *The Matter of History: How Things Create the Past* (Cambridge: Cambridge University Press, 2017); Nick J. Fox and Pam Alldred, 'Social Structures, Power and Resistance in Monist Sociology: (New) Materialist Insights', *Journal of Sociology* 54, no. 3 (2018): 318–21.
39. Fridell, *Fair Trade Coffee*; Quaas, *Fair Trade*, 30–32; Benjamin Möckel, 'The Material Culture of Human Rights: Consumer Products, Boycotts and the Transformation of Human Rights

Activism in the 1970s and 1980s', *International Journal for History, Culture and Modernity* 6, no. 1 (2018): 76–104.
40. Cf. Anderson, *A History of Fair Trade*, 23–28.

1 Handicrafts

1. Julie L. Holcomb, 'Blood-Stained Sugar: Gender, Commerce and the British Slave-Trade Debates', *Slavery & Abolition* 35, no. 4 (2014): 611–28.
2. Kathryn Kish Sklar, 'The Consumers' White Label Campaign of the National Consumers' League, 1898–1918', in *Getting and Spending: American and European Consumption in the Twentieth Century*, eds. Susan Strasser, Charles McGovern, and Matthias Judt (New York: Cambridge University Press, 1998), 17–35.
3. Glickman, *Buying Power*, 61–90.
4. Cf. John Wilkinson, 'Fair Trade: Dynamic and Dilemmas of a Market Oriented Global Social Movement', *Journal of Consumer Policy* no. 30 (2007): 219–39.
5. Cox, 'From the Empire of Christ to the Third World', 78–79, 103–5.
6. Steven M. Nolt, 'Self-Help Philosophy and Organizational Growth: The Origins and Development of SELFHELP Crafts, 1946–1970', *Pennsylvania Mennonite Heritage*, October 1991, 18.
7. News Service, 29 January 1971, M[ennonite] C[entral] C[ommittee] [Archives], Box 12, Folder 23; Nolt, 'Self-Help Philosophy and Organizational Growth', 20.
8. Anne Giesbrecht to Bill Snyder, 31 October 1963, MCC, Box 189, Folder 110/177.
9. William T. Snyder to Anne Giesbrecht, 12 November 1963, MCC, Box 189, Folder 110/177.
10. Westad, *Global Cold War*.
11. News Service, 29 November 1974, MCC, Box 230, Folder 137/89; Nolt, 'Self-Help Philosophy and Organizational Growth', 26.
12. Policy guidelines for needlework and crafts program, October 1967, MCC, Box 12, Folder 23; Nolt, 'Self-Help Philosophy and Organizational Growth', 21–26.
13. Theo A. Tschuy to W. Ray Kyle, 8 November 1961, SERVV [archive], [Brethren Historical Library and Archive, Elgin], Box 6, folder 26.
14. 'Shopping the world in Maryland', *Sunday Baltimore American*, SERVV, Box 6, folder 26.

15. W. Ray Kyle to Doris E. Caldwell, 15 March 1962, SERVV, Box 6, folder 26.
16. Correspondence with producers, SERVV, Box 6, folder 26.
17. Simon Jelsma, *Bezit en vrijheid: Een reeks pleinpreken* (Bussum: Brand, 1957), 35–37.
18. Maggie Black, *A Cause for Our Times: Oxfam – the First 50 Years* (Oxford: Oxfam, 1992), 1–2, 9–14.
19. Black, 15, 20–30.
20. Black, 40.
21. Black, 32–34.
22. Oxford committee for famine relief, gift shops sub-committee, Home Industries, 20 March 1964, [Bodleian Library, Oxford], Oxfam [Archives], TRD/4/1/1.
23. Lynn ten Kate, Purchase of handicrafts, 9 March 1966, Oxfam, TRD/4/1/1.
24. Oxford committee for famine relief, gift shop sub-committee, 2 July 1965, Oxfam, TRD/4/1/1.
25. Black, *A Cause for Our Times*, 30, 34.
26. Anderson, *A History of Fair Trade*, 26.
27. Report of the special gift shop sub-committee set up by the executive committee, 204–67, Oxfam, TRD/4/1/1.
28. Report of the special gift shop sub-committee set up by the executive committee, 204–67, Oxfam, TRD/4/1/1.
29. The future development of Oxfam Gift Shops, 1969, Oxfam, TRD/4/3/9.
30. Anderson, *A History of Fair Trade*, 25–27.
31. Black, *A Cause for Our Times*, 85–92.
32. Bertrand Bissuel and Michael Castaing, 'L'abbé Pierre, fondateur d'Emmaüs, est mort', *Le Monde*, 23 January 2007 (trans. Mark K. Jensen, https://web.archive.org/web/20110926214008/http://www.ufppc.org/us-a-world-news-mainmenu-35/5614/ [29 August 2022]); 'Abbé Pierre', https://emmaus.nl/over-emmaus/abbe-pierre/ (29 August 2022).
33. The Bangladesh Model, 18 June 1985, MCC, roll 70, 1985; Joe Osman, *Traidcraft: Inspiring a Fair Trade Revolution* (Oxford: Lion Hudson, 2020) 16–19; Kuhn, *Fairer Handel und Kalter Krieg*, 82–111.
34. Magali Zimmer, 'Des échances économiques au service d'un changement global: Le context d'émergence d'Artisans du monde', *Le sociographe* no. 5 (2015): 97–113; Gateau, 'Quelle(s) stratégie(s) de distribution pour les produits équitables?'.

35. SOS was founded in 1959 as Komitee Steun Onderontwikkelde Streken, renamed Stichting Steun Ontwikkelings Streken in July 1959. It renamed itself Stichting Ontwikkelings-Samenwerking in 1973, SOS-Wereldhandel in 1977, and Fair Trade Organisatie in 1994 and is currently operating as Fair Trade Original, a name it adopted in 2005.
36. 'Stichting S.O.S. start acties voor missie in Nyassaland', *Limburgs Dagblad*, 6 December 1962, 7.
37. Quaas, *Fair Trade*, 61–67.
38. Paul Arnold, '"Went v'r jet dunt dan dunt v'r jot!" De geschiedenis van de Kerkraadse Stichting Steun Onderontwikkelde Streken, later S.O.S. Wereldhandel, 1959–1986', *Studies over de Sociaal-Economische Geschiedenis van Limburg* 46 (2001): 14–17.
39. 'SOS streeft naar ontwikkelingshulp op zakelijke basis', *Limburgs Dagblad*, 15 September 1967, 1.
40. Paul Meijs, *Ontwikkelingsstrategie van S.O.S. Derde Wereld-handel voor de periode 1970–1980* (Kerkrade: Stichting Ontwikkelings-Samenwerking Wereldhandel, 1971), 33–34.
41. Meijs, 35.
42. Meijs, 44.
43. The Haslemere Declaration Group, *The Haslemere Declaration* (London: The Haslemere Committee, 1968): 4.
44. Piet Reckman, *Je geld of je leven* (Baarn: Anthos, 1968), §61.
45. Black, *A Cause For Our Times*, 85–87, 160–62.
46. Hans Beerends, *De derde wereldbeweging: Geschiedenis en toekomst* (Den Haag: Novib, 1992): 18, 41.
47. Hans Beerends and Marc Broere, *De bewogen beweging: een halve eeuw mondiale solidariteit* (Amsterdam, 2004): 139.
48. Olejniczak, 'Dritte-Welt-Bewegung', 321–22.
49. Samuel Moyn, *The Last Utopia: Human Rights in History* (Cambridge: Belknap Press, 2010); Kevin O'Sullivan, 'The Search for Justice: NGOs in Britain and Ireland and the New International Economic Order, 1968–82', *Humanity* 6, no. 1 (2015): 173–87.
50. Hilton et al., 'History and Humanitarianism'.
51. Lynn Hunt, *Inventing Human Rights: A History* (New York: Norton, 2007); Jan Eckel, 'Utopie der Moral, Kalkül der Macht: Menschenrechte in der globalen Politik seit 1945', *Archiv für Sozialgeschichte* 49 (2009): 437–84; Stefan-Ludwig Hoffmann, 'Human Rights and History', *Past & Present* 232, no. 1 (1 August 2016): 279–310; Stefan-Ludwig Hoffmann, 'Introduction: Genealogies of Human Rights', in *Human Rights in the Twentieth Century*, ed. Stefan-Ludwig Hoffmann (Cambridge: Cambridge University Press, 2010), 1–26.

52. Hilton et al., 'History and Humanitarianism', e15–16; Johannes Paulmann, 'Conjunctures in the History of International Humanitarian Aid during the Twentieth Century', *Humanity: An International Journal of Human Rights, Humanitarianism, and Development* 4, no. 2 (2013): 216.
53. Maarten Kuitenbrouwer, 'Nederland Gidsland? De ontwikkelingssamenwerking van Nederland en gelijkgezinde landen, 1973–1985', in *De geschiedenis van vijftig jaar ontwikkelingssamenwerking 1949–1999*, ed. Jan Nekkers, Peter Malcontent, and Peer Baneke (Den Haag: Sdu Uitgevers, 1999), 183–200; Peter van Dam and Wouter van Dis, 'Beyond the Merchant and the Clergyman: Assessing Moral Claims about Development Cooperation', *Third World Quarterly* 35, no. 9 (2014): 1636–55.
54. Ulf Teichmann and Christian Wicke, '"Alte" und "Neue soziale Bewegungen": Einleitende Bemerkungen', *Arbeit – Bewegung – Geschichte: Zeitschrift für historische Forschung* 17, no. 3 (2018), 11–19.
55. Olejniczak, *Die Dritte-Welt-Bewegung*, 35.
56. Wijmans, 'De solidariteitsbeweging', 121–22.
57. Kuhn, *Entwicklungspolitische Solidarität*, 11.

2 Sugar

1. ANP Radiobulletin 03-12-1968, berichtnummer 71 K[oninklijke] B[ibltiotheek The Hague], ANP Radiobulletins Digitaal 1937–1984.
2. 'Perscommuniqué Rietsuikeraktie 1968', private archive Paul van Tongeren.
3. 'Rietsuiker – Engeland', *Sjaloom: Maandblad* 8, 1 (1971), 7.
4. Kiran Klaus Patel, 'Widening and Deepening? Recent Advances in European Integration History', *Neue Politische Literatur* 64, no. 2 (2019): 327–57.
5. Timothy Scott Brown, *West Germany and the Global Sixties: The Antiauthoritarian Revolt, 1962–1978*, New Studies in European History (Cambridge: Cambridge University Press, 2015); Kim Christiaens, 'Voorbij de 1968-Historiografie?', *Tijdschrift voor Geschiedenis* 128, no. 3 (2015): 377–406; Christiansen and Scarlett, *The Third World in the Global 1960s*; Gerd-Rainer Horn, *The Spirit of '68: Rebellion in Western Europe and North America, 1956–1976* (Oxford: Oxford University Press, 2007).
6. Patrick Pasture, *Christian Trade Unionism in Europe since 1968. Tensions between Identity and Practice* (Aldershot: Brookfield, 1994); Jelle Visser, 'Learning to Play: The Europeanisation of Trade Unions',

in *Working-class Internationalism and the Appeal of National Identity. Historical Debates and Current Perspectives on Western Europe*, eds. Patrick Pasture and Johan Verberckmoes (Oxford: Berg, 1998), 231–57.
7. Alasdair R. Young, 'European Consumer Groups. Multiple Levels of Governance and Multiple Logics of Collective Action', in *Collective Action in the European Union. Interests and the New Politics of Associability*, ed. Justin Greenwood and Mark Aspinwall (London: Routledge, 1998), 149–75; Hilton, *Prosperity for All*.
8. Douglas R. Imig and Sidney G. Tarrow, *Contentious Europeans: Protest and Politics in an Emerging Polity* (Lanham: Rowman & Littlefield, 2001), 7.
9. Vijay Prashad, *The Darker Nations. A People's History of the Third World* (New York: New Press, 2007), 3–50.
10. Berger, 'After the Third World?'; Stella Krepp, 'Weder Norden noch Süden: Lateinamerika, Entwicklungsdebatten und die "Dekolonisierungskluft", 1948–1973', in *Nord/Süd: Perspektiven auf eine globale Konstellation*, ed. Steffen Fiebrig, Jürgen Dinkel, and Frank Reichherzer (Berlin: De Gruyter, 2020), 109–34.
11. Prashad, *Darker Nations*, 102–3; Ian Taylor and Karen Smith, *United Nations Conference on Trade and Development (UNCTAD)* (London: Routledge, 2007), 6–9.
12. Karl P. Sauvant, *The Group of 77. Evolution, Structure, Organization* (New York: Oceana Publications 1981): 1; Mourad Ahmia ed., *The Collected Documents of the Group of 77. Volume IV: Environment and Sustainable Development* (New York: Oxford University Press, 2012), 5–7.
13. Sönke Kunkel, 'Zwischen Globalisierung, internationalen Organisationen und "Global Governance": Eine kurze Geschichte des Nord-Süd-Konflikts in den 1960er und 1970er Jahren', *Vierteljahrshefte für Zeitgeschichte* 60, no. 4 (2012): 555–77; idem, 'Contesting Globalization: The United Nations Conference on Trade and Development and the Transnationalization of Sovereignty', in *International Organizations and Development, 1945–1990*, ed. Marc Frey, Sönke Kunkel, and Corinna R. Unger (Houndmills: Palgrave Macmillan, 2014), 240–58; Steffen Fiebrig, 'Unequal Exchange? Post-koloniale Wirtschaftsordnung, Handelsliberalisierung und die UNCTAD', in *Nord/Süd: Perspektiven auf eine globale Konstellation*, ed. Steffen Fiebrig, Jürgen Dinkel, and Frank Reichherzer (Berlin: De Gruyter, 2020), 135–70.
14. 'Radioverslag van onze speciale correspondent D. Scherpenzeel 189-3-68', *Informatie-bulletin UNCTAD-2* (1968) 22.
15. Reckman, *Je geld of je leven*, 101.

16. Gildea et al., 'European Radicals and the "Third World"'.
17. Westad, *The Global Cold War*; Giuliano Garavini, *After Empires: European Integration, Decolonization, and the Challenge from the Global South, 1957–1985* (Oxford: Oxford University Press, 2012); Peter van Dam, 'Moralizing Postcolonial Consumer Society: Fair Trade in the Netherlands, 1964–1997', *International Review of Social History* 61, no. 2 (2016): 223–50.
18. Reckman, *Je geld of je leven*, 50, 53.
19. Ulbe Bosma, *The World of Sugar: How the Sweet Stuff Transformed Our Politics, Health, and Environment over 2,000 Years* (Cambridge: Harvard University Press, 2023), 3, 19–20.
20. Ulbe Bosma, *The Sugar Plantation in India and Indonesia: Industrial Production, 1770–2010* (New York: Cambridge University Press, 2013); Sidney W. Mintz, *Sweetness and Power: The Place of Sugar in Modern History* (New York: Viking, 1985).
21. Holcomb, 'Blood-Stained Sugar'.
22. H. M. de Lange, *Rijke en arme landen: een verantwoordelijke maatschappij in mondiaal perspectief* (Baarn: Wereldvenster, 1967), 68–70.
23. Werkgroep Rietsuikeraktie 1968 – notulen van 8 augustus en agenda voor 15 augustus, R[egionaal] H[istorisch] C[entrum] Z[uid]-O[ost] U[trecht], Sjaloom, T00248, file 117.
24. Anderson, *A History of Fair Trade*; Fridell, *Fair Trade Coffee*; Mark Hudson, Ian Hudson, and Mara Fridell, *Fair Trade, Sustainability and Social Change* (Houndmills: Palgrave Macmillan, 2013).
25. Eduard van Hengel, *Suikerraffinement: Rietsuikeraktie 1968* (Amsterdam: Sekretariaat Rietsuikeraktie, 1968) back matter.
26. Aktiesuggesties, RHCZU, Sjaloom, T00248, file 117.
27. Van Hengel, *Suikerraffinement* front matter.
28. Van Hengel, 14.
29. Tekst van het programma 'zin en tegenzin' op zondagavond 13 oktober 1968. Onderwerp: rietsuikeractie, RHCZOU, Sjaloom, T 00248, file 117.
30. Cf. Piet Reckman, *Riet. Het verhaal van de suiker* (Baarn: Anthos, 1969).
31. J. J. Eshuis, F. C. de Jong, and G. J. de Gilde, *Suiker en de ontwikkelingslanden: Bietsuiker-produktie een gezonde zaak* (Rotterdam: Ned. Suikerindustrie, 1968), 27–31.
32. Paul van Tongeren, 'Schrijven over buitenlandse contacten', January 1969, RHCZOU, Sjaloom, T 0248, file 117.
33. 'Cane sugar campaign in the Netherlands', December 1970, private archive Paul van Tongeren.

34. 'Rietsuiker en de wereldraad', *Sjaloom: Maandblad* 6, no. 6 (1969): 7.
35. Participants who have accepted the invitation [1970]. I[nternational] I[nstitute] [of] S[ocial] H[istory], X min Y, folder 69: 1969–1972.
36. Henk Biersteker and Huub Coppens, *Towards Internationalised Development Action. Report of the International Working-congress of Action-groups on International Development* (The Hague: Novib, [1970]).
37. Ibid., 88.
38. Ibid., 87–89.
39. Ibid., 90, 105–6.
40. International working-congress of action groups on international development, circular letter no 1, 12 May 1970, IISH, X min Y, folder 69: 1969–1972.
41. J. van Vlijmen, International working-congress of action groups on international development, circular letter no 1, 12 May 1970, IISH, X min Y, folder 70: 1970–1975.
42. Huub Coppens, Circular letter no 6, 14 August 1970, IISH, X min Y, folder 70: 1970–1975.
43. Huub Coppens, circular letter no 7, 1 October 1970, IISH, X min Y, folder 70: 1970–1975.
44. Black, *A Cause for Our Times*, 156, 160–62.
45. Europe '73 Programme, B[odleian] L[ibrary], Oxfam, CPN/4/4/1, folder 1.
46. Oxfam Director to Group Members, 1972, BL, Oxfam, CPN/4/4/1, folder 1.
47. Letter by Margaret Sargent, [1972], BL: Oxfam, CPN/4/4/1, folder 1.
48. Draft reply for Margaret Sergeant, [1972], BL: Oxfam, CPN/4/4/1, folder 1.
49. Paul van Tongeren, 'Rietsuikeractie slaat ook in andere landen aan', *Groene Amsterdammer*, 2 January 1971, 4.
50. Clifford Longley, 'How the cane sugar lobby is preparing for battle', *The Times*, 15 February 1971, 12.
51. Cf. 'Marching with the sugar workers', *The Times*, 19 October 1973, 18.
52. Clifford Longley, 'How the cane sugar lobby is preparing for battle', *The Times*, 15 February 1971, 12.
53. Huub Coppens, circular letter no 8, 4 November 1970, IISH, X min Y, folder 70: 1970–1975.
54. Huub Coppens, circular letter no 8, 4 November 1970, IISH, X min Y, folder 70: 1970–1975; 'Engeland noord-zuid', *Sjaloom: Maandblad* 8, no. 1 (1971): 7.

55. Alex May, 'The Commonwealth and Britain's Turn to Europe, 1945–73', *The Round Table* 102, no. 1 (2013): 29–39; Michael Franklin, *Joining the CAP: The Agricultural Negotiations for British Accession to the European Economic Community, 1961–1973* (Bern: Peter Lang, 2010), 211–34, 320–21.
56. 'Riet-biet-suiker. Ontwikkelingslanden voor pressie van rijke landen gezwicht', *Sjaloom: Maandblad* 8, no. 7 (1971): 10.
57. 'Keeping them poor', *The Times*, 6 December 1972, VIII; Haslemere Declaration Groups/Third World First, *Sugar today, jam tomorrow? A study of the sell-out over Commonwealth sugar in the Common Market negotiations* (London [1972]).
58. 'Politics of sugar', *The Times*, 16 October 1973, 17; 'Marching with the sugar workers', *The Times*, 19 October 1973, 18. Cf. 'Tate & Lyle Sugar Workers Strike', British Pathé, www.britishpathe.com/video/tate-lyle-sugar-workers-strike/ (last visited 20 August 2014).
59. Huub Coppens, circular letter no 8, 4 November 1970, IISH, X min Y, folder 70: 1970–1975; Piet Reckman, *Rohr: Die Geschichte Zuckers* (Nürnberg: Stein, 1970).
60. *Aktion Selbstbesteuerung* constituted a West-German self-tax initiative. Its aim was to make an individual donation for development projects calculated by subtracting the percentage the country of residence was in fact paying for development aid by the percentage it should pay for development and applying the difference to personal income. The 1970 international congress in Egmond aan Zee had been hosted by its Dutch counterpart X min Y.
61. W. Gebert, 'Wirken Sie mit an der Planung und Vorbereitung der internationalen Rohrzuckerkampagne', April 1971 [Universitätsbibliothek Basel].
62. W. Gebert, 'Wirken Sie mit'.
63. 'Sjaloom-Duitsland', *Sjaloom: Maandblad* 5, no. 11 (1968): 8. Initiatives in the Ruhr area were promoted at the University of Bochum. Cf. Hans-Eckehard Bahr ed., *Politisierung des Alltags: Gesellschaftliche Bedingungen des Friedens* (Darmstadt: Luchterhand, 1972); Hans Jürgen Schultz ed., *Von Gandhi bis Câmara. Beispiele gewaltfreier Politik* (Stuttgart: Kreuz, 1971).
64. Ernst Schmied, *Wandel durch Handel. Die Aktion Dritte Welt Handel, ein entwicklungspolitisches Lernmodell* (Stuttgart: AEJ, 1978), 153–54. Ironically, members of *Aktion 3. Welt Handel* had to devote much of their time to clarifying the relations with the Dutch organization *SOS Wereldhandel*, which provided local fair trade initiatives with products from developing countries.

65. Ulrich Willems, *Entwicklung, Interesse und Moral: Die Entwicklungspolitik der Evangelischen Kirche in Deutschland* (Opladen: Leske + Budrich, 1998), 298–99.
66. Cf. Konstanze Kemnitzer, *Der ferne Nächste: Zum Selbstverständnis der Aktion 'Brot für die Welt'* (Stuttgart: Kohlhammer, 2008).
67. *40 Jahre Aktion Selbstbesteuerung. Friede durch gerechte Entwicklungspolitik* (Stuttgart: Aktion Selbstbesteuerung, 2009) 4–5.
68. Protokoll: Deutscher Bundestag, 193. Sitzung, Bonn, Freitag den 16. Juni 1972, 11285.
69. 'Argumenten tegen de rietsuikeraktie', *Wereldwinkelbulletin* 2, no. 4 (1971): 3–4.
70. Discussiestuk Wageningen September 1971, RHCZOU, Sjaloom, T00248, file 130.
71. Felix Spies, 'Das Süße Fieber', *Die Zeit*, no. 49 (1974): 35.
72. 'Welthandel unter Druck', *Der Spiegel* 26, no. 18 (1972): 48–50.
73. Mia Goos and Willem van het Hekke, *Wereldwinkels en produkten. Theorie & praktijk* (Utrecht: Landelijke Vereniging van Wereldwinkels, 1977): 60.
74. Service and communications centre development action groups, Den Haag, 'Report of the strategy consultation for Action on Development', Dworp, Belgium, 18–21 November 1971, IISH, X min Y, folder 69: 1969–1972.
75. Henk van Andel, circular letter no 12, 20 April 1972, IISH, X min Y, folder 70: 1970–1975.
76. Henk van Andel, circular letter no 16, April 1973, IISH, X min Y, folder 70: 1970–1975.
77. Harry Neyer, 'Aktionsgruppen auf dem Weg zu internationaler Kooperation', *E+Z – Entwicklung und Zusammenarbeit* 13, no. 1 (1971): 17.
78. Strategy consultation for action on development, Dworp, Belgium, 18–21 November 1971. Action-model 3: Denmark, IISH, X min Y, folder 69: 1969–1972.
79. Henk van Andel, circular letter no 19, February 1973, IISH, X min Y, folder 70: 1970–1975.
80. Neyer, 'Aktionsgruppen auf dem Weg zu internationaler Kooperation'.
81. Cf. Epple, 'Lokalität und die Dimensionen des Globalen'; Swyngedouw, 'Neither global nor local'.
82. David Kuchenbuch, '"Eine Welt": Globales Interdependenzbewusstsein und die Moralisierung des Alltags in den 1970er und 1980er Jahren', *Geschichte und Gesellschaft* 38, no. 1 (2012): 162.

83. van Dam, 'Moralizing postcolonial consumer society', 237; Tehila Sasson, 'Milking the Third World? Humanitarianism, Capitalism, and the Moral Economy of the Nestlé Boycott', *The American Historical Review* 121, no. 4 (2016): 1196–224; Quaas, *Fair Trade*, 185–241.

3 Paper

1. Strategy-consultation for action on development, Dworp, Belgium, 18–21 November 1971: The basis for collaboration, IISH, X min Y, folder 69: 1969–1972
2. Service and communications centre development action groups, Den Haag, 'Report of the Strategy Consultation for Action on Development', Dworp, Belgium, 18–21 November 1971, IISH, X min Y, folder 69: 1969–1972.
3. Strategy-consultation for action on development, Dworp, Belgium, 18–21 November 1971: The commonwealth sugar campaign, IISH, X min Y, folder 69: 1969–1972; Strategy consultation for action on development, Dworp, Belgium, 18–21 November 1971, Action-model 3: Denmark, IISH, X min Y, folder 69: 1969–1972.
4. Christopher R. W. Dietrich, 'Mossadegh Madness: Oil and Sovereignty in the Anticolonial Community', *Humanity* 6, no. 1 (2015): 63–78.
5. Donella H. Meadows et al., *The Limits to Growth; A Report for the Club of Rome's Project on the Predicament of Mankind* (New York: Universe Books, 1972), 9–10.
6. Matthew Connely, 'Future Shock: The End of the World As They Knew It' in *The Shock of the Global: The 1970s in Perspective*, ed. Niall Ferguson (Cambridge: Belknap, 2010), 337–50.
7. Edward Goldsmith and Robert Allen, *A Blueprint for Surival* (Harmondsworth: Penguin, 1972). Cf. Maarten Hajer, *The Politics of Environmental Discourse: Ecological Modernization and the Policy Process* (Oxford: Oxford University Press, 1995), 80–87.
8. Duco Hellema, *Nederland en de jaren zeventig* (Amsterdam: Boom, 2012), 11–16.
9. Duyvendak, *Tussen verbeelding en macht*, 262.
10. John Toye, 'Assessing the G77: 50 Years after Unctad and 40 Years after the Nieo', *Third World Quarterly* 35, no. 10 (2014): 1759–74.
11. Gien van Warmerdam, 'En het begon in Breukelen: De geschiedenis van Wereldwinkel Breukelen 1969–2009', *Tijdschrift Historische Kring Breukelen* 24, no. 2 (2009): 48–49.
12. Verslag vergadering 12-11-1969, private archive Paul van Tongeren.

13. Goos and Van het Hekke, *Wereldwinkels en produkten*.
14. Paul van Tongeren and Ben ter Veer, *28 mondiale aktiegroepen in Nederland* (Voorburg: X min Y, 1971): 76–84.
15. Afschrift notariële akte, RHCOU, Sjaloom, T 0248, file 130. The organization had actually already taken up its first activities in May of the same year.
16. 'Landelijke Stichting Wereldwinkel', *Kosmodok* 3, no. 8 (1970): 1–2.
17. Beerends et al., *Anders nog iets?* (Amersfoort: De Horstink, 1979), 9–10.
18. Ibid.
19. For example, see the IKOR-broadcast Kenmerk on 25 November 1970, the AVRO-broadcast *Wie zeggen de mensen dat ik ben* on 19 December 1971, and the NOS-broadcast *Werkwinkel* on 17 February 1974.
20. Koninklijke Bibliotheek, ANP Radiobulletins Digitaal 1937–1984: ANP Radiobulletin 07-12-1970, berichtnummer 45; 'Hervormde wereldwinkels', *Sjaloom: Maandblad* 8, no 1. (1971): 12; Handelingen van de vergadering van de generale synode der Nederlandse Hervormde Kerk op 18, 19 en 20 februari 1974 in centrum Hydepark te Doorn, pkn-acta.digibron.nl (2 December 2013).
21. 'Van de redactie', *Wereldwinkel Bulletin* 3, no. 3 (1972): 1.
22. Quaas, *Fair Trade*, 83–91.
23. Raschke, *Fairer Handel*, 47–57.
24. Konrad Kuhn, '"Handelsförderung ist notwendig und problematisch zugleich": Die Entstehung des fairen Handels als neue Handels- und Unternehmensform', in *Dienstleistungen. Expansion und Transformation des 'Dritten Sektors' (15.-20. Jahrhundert)*, ed. Hans-Jörg Gilomen (Zürich, 2007), 114–16.
25. z.B. *Kaffee Ujamaa. Dossier zur Verkäuferschulung* [1975] 49–51, S[chweizerisches] S[ozialarchiv], 81.1 Z*F QS: 1970–1999.
26. NOS broadcast *Werkwinkel* on 17 February 1974. Archive Beeld & Geluid, Hilversum: Document ID 30324.
27. Ibid.
28. 'Derde wereld winkel', *Nesbic-bulletin* 4, no. 12 (1969): 327–28.
29. Beerends e.a., *Anders nog iets?*, 9.
30. Verslag landelijke vergadering 21-2-1970, private archive Paul van Tongeren.
31. Vergadering stuurgroep 2-3-1970, private archive Paul van Tongeren.
32. Van de Poel, '35 Jaar Oxfam-Wereldwinkels', 9–11.
33. Gilbert aan de provinciale Oxfam-centra in Gent, Brugge en Roeselaere, 26 November 1974, Amsab[-Institute of Social History], O[xfam] W[ereldwinkels], 251/0185.

34. Van de Poel, '35 Jaar Oxfam-Wereldwinkels', 11.
35. Ibid., 1–3.
36. Ibid., 3.
37. Kuchenbuch, '"Eine Welt"', 161.
38. Eileen Candappa and Harry Haas, *Herzhafte Mahlzeit: Ein asiatisches Kochbuch für Gastfreundlichen Menschen* (Frankfurt am Main: Beratungsstelle für Gestaltung, 1976), Einführung.
39. Ibid., 4, 42.
40. Eileen Candappa and Harry Haas, *Gemeinsam kochen: Ein Werkbuch für Familien und Gruppen* (Frankfurt am Main: Beratungsstelle für Gestaltung, 1977), 71–72.
41. Verein Erste Welt-Dritte Welt, *Bewusst kochen – herzhaft essen: 60 Rezepte für eine begrenzte Welt* (Wuppertal: GEPA, 1978): 2.
42. 'Wereldwinkel bestaat kwart eeuw', *Nieuwsblad van het Noorden*, 12 February 1994, 30.
43. Van Warmerdam, 'En het begon in Breukelen', 49–51.
44. 'Suriname-aktie in het najaar', *Wereldwinkel Bulletin* 4, no. 4 (1973): 3.
45. 'Suriname-aksie '73', *Wereldwinkel Bulletin* 4, no. 5 (1973): 2.
46. Evaluatieweekend 16–17 februari. Verslag plenaire vergadering zaterdag. [1974] Over wenselijkheid van landelijke acties, ervaringen met Suriname-actie, IISH, Wereldwinkel Amstelveen, box BA/CSD vrz 53.2, file DOS/46.
47. Evaluatieweekend 16–17 februari. Verslag plenaire vergadering zaterdag. [1974] Over wenselijkheid van landelijke acties, ervaringen met Suriname-actie, IISH, Wereldwinkel Amstelveen, box UBA/CSD vrz 53.2, file DOS/46.
48. Van gewest tot gewest. Rapport over het gewestelijk medewerkersprojekt, IISH, Wereldwinkel Amstelveen, box UBA/CSD vrz 53.2, file DOS/47.
49. 'Een politieke succes story', *Vrij Nederland*, 18 March 1972, 3; 'Het pragmatisch doordouwen van het Angola-comité', *De Groene Amsterdammer*, 18 March 1972.
50. Koffie-Aktie. Boontje komt om zijn loontje. Koffiebulletin nr. 2, RHCZOU, Sjaloom, file 114.
51. 'Een politieke succes story', *Vrij Nederland*, 18 March 1972, 3.
52. 'Kruidenier meet zich met actiegroep', *de Volkskrant*, 22 September 1973.
53. 'Boycotactie verliep soepel', *Wereldwinkel Bulletin*, no. 4 (1973): 7.
54. 'Boycotactie verliep soepel', *Wereldwinkel Bulletin*, no. 4 (1973): 8.
55. 'In een vrij land …', *De Telegraaf*, 1 September 1973.
56. 'Albert Heijn-oorlog tegen Angola-comité', *De Telegraaf*, 1 September 1973, 2.

57. 'Albert Heijn capituleert', *Nederlands Dagblad*, 15 October 1973, 1.
58. 'Angola Comité: "Consument oko politiek bewust"', *De Tijd*, 13 October 1973, 1.
59. *Beleidsdiskussie wereldwinkels '78* (Utrecht 1978), 23, IISH, Bro 2453/6 fol.
60. Joseph S. Nye and Robert O. Keohane, 'Transnational Relations and World Politics: An Introduction', *International Organization* 25, no. 3 (1971): 329–49; Piet Reckman, *De Multinationale* (Odijk: Sjaloom, 1976).
61. Niall Ferguson, 'Crisis, What Crisis? The 1970s and the Shock of the Global', in *The Shock of the Global: The 1970s in Perspective*, ed. Niall Ferguson (Cambridge: Cambridge University Press, 2010), 1–21; Reckman, *De multinationale*, 9.
62. 'Aktiviteiten van de actiegroep BOA', *Wereldwinkel Bulletin* 7, no. 2 (1976): 3; 'Verslag Boycot Outspan Aktie', *Wereldwinkel Bulletin Voorschoten*, no. 22 (1977): 4–5; 'Boycot Chileens fruit', *Wereldwinkel Bulletin* 7, no. 2 (1976): 18, 23; 'Consumentenboycot Granny Smith', *Wereldwinkel Bulletin* 8, no. 4 (1977): 12.
63. Dorothy Friesen and Gene Stoltzfus, MCC Indonesia, April 1977, MCC, Box 8, Folder 24.
64. Paul Leatherman, 'Is Self-Help Promoting Consumerism?', January 1978, MCC, Box 8, Folder 24.
65. Neil Janzen, Self-Help Study, 1979, MCC, Box 8, Folder 24.
66. Wereld-winkel. [ca. 1970]. RHCZOU, Sjaloom, T 00248, file 130.
67. Verhouding wereldwinkels – S.O.S., May 1974, IISH, L[andelijke] V[ereniging] v[an] W[ereldwinkels], file Externe Kontakten SOS, uittreksels '72-.
68. Stichting SOS aan wereldwinkeliers, 30 December 1970. IISH, LVVW, file Externe Kontakten SOS, uittreksels '72-.
69. Tussenrapport betreffende struktuur en werkwijze centrale wereldwinkels en verhouding wereldwinkels SOS, 2 June 1971, IISH, LVVW, file Externe Kontakten SOS, uittreksels '72-.
70. Landelijke Stichting Wereldwinkel, 'Plan tot de vorming van een kosmopolitieke koöperatie', RHCZOU, Sjaloom, T 00248, file 130.
71. Kosmo-koöp/eindverslag van de werkgroep, 26 November 1971, IISH, LVVW, file Externe Kontakten SOS, uittreksels '72-.
72. Verhouding wereldwinkels – S.O.S., May 1974, IISH, LVVW, file Externe Kontakten SOS, uittreksels '72-. Vgl. Beerends, *Anders nog iets?*, 9–10.
73. Meijs, *Ontwikkelingsstrategie van S.O.S*, 2.
74. Ibid., 12.
75. Black, *A Cause for Our Times*, 165–66.

76. Roy Scott, 'What, why, how. Bridge summarized', 1 March 1973, SS, Claro 1010.11.
77. Anderson, *A History of Fair Trade*, 29–33.
78. Meijs, *Ontwikkelingsstrategie van S.O.S.*
79. Ibid., 44.
80. Quaas, *Fair Trade*, 147–51.
81. Thomas Vatter, Kurzporträt OS3/Importzentrale, SS, Claro, 1011.11.
82. There was even talk of a 'hausse' of conferences in 1976; see: Paul Meijs to Jan Hissel, 23 April 1976, Amsab, OW, 251/1165.
83. 'De grote internationale handelskonferenties hebben nog nooit iets uitgehaald ...', *Wereldhandel*, no. 16 (1976): 2–4.
84. Summary Report: International Workshop on 3rd World Producers & Alternative Marketing Organisations, Frankfurt am Main, 10–11 July 1975, SS, Claro, 1011.11.
85. An overview of the producers who attended the meeting can be found in: 'Deelnemers alternatieve handelstentoonstelling koninklijk instuut voor de tropen, Amsterdam', *Wereldhandel*, no. 16 (1976): 5–7.
86. 'S.O.S. organiseert Internationaal alternatief handelskongres van 3 tot 10 september 1976 in Noordwijkerhout', *Wereldhandel*, no. 16 (1976): 1.
87. 'Veranderen handelsstructuur zou "zwevend idealisme" zijn', *Nederlands Dagblad*, 30 July 1976, 5.
88. 'Omzet wereldwinkels naar 7 miljoen', *Het Vrije Volk*, 29 July 1976, 21.
89. Summary – report on the International Workshop on Third World Producers and Alternative Marketing Organizations, 3–10 September 1976, private archive Fair Trade Original.
90. International workshop of Third World Producers and Alternative Marketing Organisations, Vienna, Austria. 28 April–4 May 1977, SS, Claro, 1011.11.
91. Verslag internationale bijeenkomst Parijs, 4–5 juni 1977, IISH, LVVW, file Externe kontakten Internationale Bijeenkomsten tot 1991 18.1.
92. 'Nog enkele opmerkingen over de internationale bijeenkomst te Parijs', IISH, LVVW, file Externe kontakten Internationale Bijeenkomsten tot 1991 18.1.
93. 'Derde internationale bijeenkomst van wereldwinkeliers uit Europa', *Wereldwinkel Bulletin*, no. 9 [May] (1978): 21.
94. Anderson, *A history of fair trade*; Quaas, *Fair Trade*.
95. 'Derde internationale bijeenkomst van wereldwinkeliers uit Europa', *Wereldwinkel Bulletin*, no. 9 [May] (1978): 21; Invitation Third International Conference of World Shop Organisations, 7 March 1978, IISH, LVVW, file Externe kontakten Internationale Bijeenkomsten tot 1991 18.1.

96. 'Internationale bijeenkomst, het onverwachte gebeurd', *Ontzet* 14 (1983) 1 [januari], 7–8; 6° Coordination Europeene – Strasbourg 27.28.29 Mai 83, Amsab, OW, 251/1053.
97. De Wereldwinkelbeweging in West-Europa: Enkele gegevens [1989?], Amsab, OW, 251/1128.
98. 'De thee-aktie van de wereldwinkel v.u.', *Wereldwinkel Bulletin* 5, no. 9 (1974): 5.
99. 'Sarvodaya Thee – Zinvol symbool?', *Wereldwinkel Bulletin* 6, no. 2 (1975): 5.
100. Matthew Anderson, '"Cost of a cup of tea": Fair Trade and the British Co-operative Movement, c. 1960–2000', in *Consumerism and the Co-operative Movement in Modern British History: Taking Stock*, eds. Lawrence Black and Nicole Robertson (Manchester: Manchester University Press, 2009), 240–59.
101. 'Sarvodaya Thee – Zinvol symbool?', *Wereldwinkel Bulletin* 6, no. 2 (1975): 6.
102. Verslagen van contactvergaderingen met Magasins du Monde. Amsab, OW, 251/0764.
103. 'Vijf jaar stichting ideële import', *Ideële import informatiekrant* 1, no. 4 (1981): 5.
104. Folder 'Stichting Ideele Import: een handelsagent voor derde wereldlanden', IISH, Bro 4006/6; 'Lelijke eend vangt tonijn met een hengel', *Ideële import informatiekrant* 5, no. 4 (1985): 4.
105. Annet Lingen and Betty Scheper, *De resultaten van de enquete onder de wereldwinkels april-juni 1983*, IISH, LVVW, file Externe kontakten NCO Plenaire tot 1990, 18.10.
106. Duyvendak, *Tussen verbeelding en macht*, 74–75.

4 Coffee

1. John Bowes, *The Fair Trade Revolution* (London: Pluto, 2011); Harriet Lamb, *Fighting the Banana Wars and Other Fairtrade Battles: How We Took on the Corporate Giants to Change the World* (London: Rider, 2008); Frans Van der Hoff and Nico Roozen, *Fair Trade: het verhaal achter Max Havelaar-koffie, Oké-bananen en Kuyichi-jeans* (Amsterdam: Van Gennep, 2001).
2. Michael Barratt Brown, *Fair Trade: Reform and Realities in the International Trading System* (London: Zed Books, 1993); Gavin Fridell, 'The Fair Trade Network in Historical Perspective', *Canadian Journal of Development Studies* 25, no. 3 (2004): 411–28; Daniel Jaffee, 'Weak Coffee: Certification and Co-optation in the Fair Trade Movement', *Social Problems* 59, no. 1 (2012):

94–116; Hudson et al., *Fair Trade, Sustainability and Social Change*.
3. Jeffry A. Frieden, *Global Capitalism: Its Fall and Rise in the Twentieth Century* (New York: Norton, 2006), 372–76; Gillian Hart, 'Geography and Development: Development/s beyond Neoliberalism? Power, Culture, Political Economy', *Progress in Human Geography* 25, no. 4 (2001): 649–58.
4. Cf. Quinn Slobodian, *Globalists: The End of Empire and the Birth of Neoliberalism* (Cambridge: Harvard University Press, 2018); Bram Mellink and Merijn Oudenampsen, *Neoliberalisme: Een Nederlandse geschiedenis* (Amsterdam: Boom, 2022).
5. Francis Fukuyama, *The End of History and the Last Man* (New York: Free Press, 1992).
6. Duco Hellema and Margriet van Lith, *Dat hadden we nooit moeten doen: de PvdA en de neoliberale revolutie van de jaren negentig* (Amsterdam: Promotheus, 2020).
7. Cf. Stolle and Micheletti, *Political Consumerism: Global Responsibility in Action* (New York: Cambridge University Press, 2013), 207–9.
8. 'Internationale bijeenkomst, het onverwachte gebeurd', *Ontzet* 14, no. 1 [January] (1983): 7–8.
9. Lingen and Scheper, *De resultaten van de enquête onder de wereldwinkels*.
10. Jan Willem Duyvendak and Menno Hurenkamp, *Kiezen voor de kudde: Lichte gemeenschappen en de nieuwe meerderheid* (Amsterdam: Van Gennep, 2004); Peter van Dam, *Religion und Zivilgesellschaft: Christliche Traditionen in der niederländischen und deutschen Arbeiterbewegung (1945–1980)* (Münster: Waxmann, 2010).
11. Provisional report sixth meeting of the ICDA, April 1977, IISH, X min Y, folder 71: 1978. Cf. Andrea Franc, *Von der Makroökonomie zum Kleinbauern: Die Wandlung der Idee eines gerechten Nord-Süd-Handels in der schweizerischen Dritte-Welt-Bewegung (1964–1984)* (Berlin: De Gruyter, 2020): 152.
12. Reckman, *Je geld of je leven*, §20.
13. Ibid., 8.
14. 'Wordt Juan Valdez oud?', *Maandblad Sjaloom* 6, no. 3. (1969): 14–15.
15. 'Voor een kwartje de wereld rond', *De Groene Amsterdammer*, 8 May 1971.
16. Spaardoosje koffieaktie, RHCZOU, Sjaloom, T 00248, file 114.
17. Café Solidaridad, SS, 81.1 Z*F QS: 1970–1999; Kuhn, *Fairer Handel und Kalter Krieg*, 25–26.

18. 'Angola koffie-aktie Nederland: een voorbeeld?', *Sjaloom: Maandblad* 9, no. 3 (1972): 12.
19. Kuhn, '"Handelsförderung ist notwendig und problematisch zugleich"', 115–16; Quaas, *Fair Trade*, 143–46.
20. 'Koffie uit Tanzania', *Wereldwinkel Bulletin* 6, no. 5 (1975): 24–25.
21. Jan C. Breitinger, '"Ujamaa Revisited": zur entwicklungstheoretischen Verankerung und politischen Wahrnehmung eines spezifisch tansanischen Entwicklungsmodells', *Comparativ* 23, no. 1 (2013): 89–111; 'Koffie uit Tanzania', *Wereldwinkel Bulletin* 6, no. 5 (1975): 24–25.
22. Quaas, *Fair Trade*, 135; 'Indio Koffie Guatemala', *Wereldhandel*, no. 3 (1973): 1.
23. Quaas, *Fair Trade*, 188–90.
24. Kort verslag van het gesprek tussen Hans Verhoef en Carl Grasveld (st. id. import), 14 November 1979, IISH, LVVW, file Externe kontakten S.I.I. 18.3.
25. Quaas, *Fair Trade*, 213–18, 226–27.
26. *The Provisioner* 1, no. 1 (1985).
27. Verslag werkgroep maatschappijvisie van 16 December 1982, Amsab, OW, 251/0147.
28. Reakties maatschappijvisie juni 1984, Amsab, OW, 251/0147.
29. Produktenverkoop in diskussie: een bundeling van artikelen en gesprekken, ontstaan rond de kwartaalbijeenkomst van het team van gewestelijk mederk-st-ers van de wereldwinkels, January 1986, Amsab, OW, 251/0155; Helpt produktenverkoop?, 24 September 1986, IISH, LVvW, 37.
30. Verslag workshop 'Professionalisierung' tijdens de internationale bijeenkomst van Wereldwinkels in Keulen [1987], IISH, LVvW, 191.
31. Franz VanderHoff Boersma, *Poverty Alleviation through Participation in Fair Trade Coffee Networks: The Case of UCIRI, Oaxaca, Mexico*, September 2002, http://cfat.colostate.edu/wp-content/uploads/2009/09/Case-Study-UCIRI-Oaxaca-Mexico.pdf (1 July 2016) 1.
32. SOS Wereldhandel aan de wereldwinkels, 7 December 1979, toelichting over Fedecocagua, IISH, LVVW, file Produktenwerkgroep Korrespondentie 10.12.
33. Quaas, *Fair Trade*, 245–48.
34. Fridell, *Fair Trade Coffee*, 185–86.
35. Quaas, *Fair Trade*, 250–51.
36. Fridell, *Fair Trade Coffee*, 185–86; Quaas, *Fair Trade*, 283–84.
37. 'Adventsactie bisschoppen voor Zuid-Amerika', *de Volkskrant*, 1 December 1967; 'Interkerkelijke actie voor Zuid-Amerika', *Leeuwarder Courant*, 15 October 1969.

38. 'Wie en wat is solidaridad?', *Wereldwinkel Bulletin* 6, no. 3. (1975): 4–5.
39. Paul van der Harst (Solidaridad) aan de wereldwinkels, Den Haag, [November 1979], KDC, Solidaridad, stukken betreffende acties, 1975–88, no. 134.
40. Paul van der Harst aan de bestellers van de Chili-kleedjes, Den Haag, mei 1980, KDC, Solidaridad, stukken betreffende acties, 1975–88, no. 135.
41. Samenvatting groepsgesprekken werkdag vechten voor voedsel, Amersfoort, oktober 1982, KDC, Solidaridad, stukken betreffende acties, 1975–88, no. 137; Verslag van de vergadering van het Aktiekomitee d.d. 20-3-1985 te Utrecht, KDC, Solidaridad, notulen van het Aktiekomitee Solidaridad, 1970–86, no. 73.
42. Raschke, *Fairer Handel*, 73–74; Sven Reichardt, *Authentizität und Gemeinschaft: linksalternatives Leben in den siebziger und frühen achtziger Jahren* (Berlin: Suhrkamp, 2014).
43. Solidaridad aan de redaktie, 8 December 1983, KDC, Solidaridad, stukken betreffende acties. 1975–88, no. 138; Solidaridad aan de Vaste Kamercommissie voor Financiën van de Tweede Kamer der Staten Generaal, 26 November 1984, KDC, Solidaridad, stukken betreffende acties, 1975–88, no. 139; Persbericht: Solidaridad vraagt aan kerkelijke basis steun voor IMF-Verzoekschrift. Ibid.
44. Peter van Dam, '"Onze rente, hun armoede": de fair trade-revolutie in de jaren tachtig heroverwogen', *Impressie*, no. 17 (2015): 8–11.
45. *Schuldkrant* (1984), KDC, Solidaridad, notulen van het Aktiekomitee Solidaridad, 1970–86, no. 72.
46. Actiewijzer Solidaridad-kampagne 1985, 'Onze rente, hun armoede', KDC, Solidaridad, stukken betreffende acties, 1975–88, no. 140.
47. Aan de betrokkenen bij de kampagne 'Zuivere koffie, een kwestie van smaak', KDC, Solidaridad, stukken betreffende acties, 1975–88, no. 141.
48. 'Kerken in gesprek met koffiebranders', *Leeuwarder Courant*, 13 January 1987, 5.
49. Gerlof van Rhenen aan geïnteresseerden voor het werk van Solidaridad, Den Haag, 19 August 1986, KDC, Solidaridad, stukken betreffende acties. 1975–88, no. 141; T.a.v. IKVOS Regiotaal: Nieuwe voedselaktie van Solidaridad. Ibid.; Interkerkelijk Overleg Wereldvoedselvraagstuk aan de Vereniging van Nederlandse Koffiebranders en Theepakkers, Max Havelaarlaan 317, 1183 LT Amstelveen, Zeist, 14 October 1986, KDC, Solidaridad, stukken betreffende acties, 1975–88, no. 141.
50. Verslag van het gesprek tussen de Vereniging van Nederlandse Koffiebranders en Theepakkers en het Interkerkelijk Overleg

Wereldvoedselvraagstuk d.d. 16 februari 1987 te Amersfoort, KDC, Solidaridad, stukken betreffende acties, 1975–88, no. 146; Verslag van het gesprek tussen de Vereniging van Nederlandse Koffiebranders en Theepakkers en het Interkerkelijk Overleg Wereldvoedselvraagstuk d.d. 23 maart 1987 te Amsterdam. Ibid.
51. Nico Roozen, 'Alleen goede argumenten helpen diskussie over "zuivere" koffie verder', KDC, Solidaridad, stukken betreffende acties, 1975–88, no. 143.
52. Interkerkelijk Overleg Wereldvoedselvraagstuk, 'Persbericht', Amsterdam, 29 June 1987, KDC, Solidaridad, stukken betreffende acties, 1975–88, no. 146.
53. Verslag van de vergadering van het Aktiekomitee van Solidaridad, dd. 13 mei 1987, KDC, Solidaridad, agenda's voor en verslagen van vergaderingen DB 1986–89, no. 238.
54. Mededeling aan de pers, 28 September 1987, KDC, Solidaridad, stukken betreffende acties, 1975–88, no. 143.
55. Franz VanderHoff Boersma, *Poverty Alleviation through Participation in Fair Trade Coffee Networks: The Case of UCIRI, Oaxaca, Mexico* (Fort Collins: Center for Fair & Alternative Trade): 7, 30, http://cfat.colostate.edu/wp-content/uploads/2009/09/Case-Study-UCIRI-Oaxaca-Mexico.pdf (25 February 2015).
56. VanderHoff Boersma, *Poverty Alleviation*, 30.
57. Nico Roozen, Notitie voor de evaluatie van de kampagne 'Zuivere koffie, een kwestie van smaak', najaar 1986 en een voorzichtige vooruitblik, January 1987, KDC, Solidaridad, notulen van het Aktiekomitee Solidaridad, 1970–86, no. 74.
58. Notitie haalbaarheid zuivere koffie, March 1987, KDC, Solidaridad. Stukken betreffende acties, 1975–88, no. 144.
59. Ibid.
60. Ibid.
61. Landelijke vereniging van wereldwinkels aan het bestuur van Solidaridad, 23 April 1987, KDC, Solidaridad. Agenda's voor en verslagen van vergaderingen DB 1986–89, no. 238; 'Nieuw elan voor derde wereldbeweging. Publieksmerk zuivere koffie', *Ontzet* 18, no. 9 (1987): 9; Voortgangsrapportage publieksmerk 'zuivere' koffie, 3 December 1987, KDC, Solidaridad. Agenda's voor en verslagen van vergaderingen van het algemeen bestuur (AB), met bijlagen, 1986–99, no. 297; 'Wereldwinkeldiskussie over plannen solidaridad', *Ontzet* 18, no 8. (1987): 6–7; 'Forse en speelse kritiek op publieksmerkplan', *Ontzet* 18, no. 10 (1987): 12–13; 'Kongres komt niet tot besluit over voorwaarden tot deelname aan publieksmerk', *Ontzet* 18, no. 11 (1987): 3–4; Vergadering van de stichting Max Havelaar op

7 februari 1988 te Utrecht, KDC, Solidaridad, agenda's voor en verslagen van vergaderingen van het algemeen bestuur (AB), met bijlagen, 1986–99, no. 298.

62. The board of the foundation was initially constituted by coffee producers (3 seats), Solidaridad (3 seats), SOS Wereldhandel (2 seats), Stichting Ideële Import (1 seat), Konsumenten Kontakt (1 seat), coffee roasters (1 seat), and Landelijke Vereniging van Wereldwinkels (1 seat as an observer), with a maximum of four seats reserved for potential representatives of other organizations, cf. Statuten van de Stichting Max Havelaar, gevestigd te 's-Gravenhage, KDC, Solidaridad, stukken betreffende acties, 1975–88, no. 144.

63. Voortgangsrapportage publieksmerk 'zuivere' koffie, 3 December 1987, KDC, Solidaridad, agenda's voor en verslagen van vergaderingen van het algemeen bestuur (AB), met bijlagen, 1986–99, no. 297.

64. Staf Solidaridad aan Algemeen Bestuur Solidaridad: Onderzoeksrapport haalbaarheid publieksmerk 'zuivere koffie', 27 August 1987, KDC, Solidaridad, agenda's voor en verslagen van vergaderingen van het algemeen bestuur (AB), met bijlagen, 1986–99, no. 297.

65. Vergadering van de stichting Max Havelaar op 4 mei 1988 te Utrecht, KDC, Solidaridad, agenda's voor en verslagen van vergaderingen van het algemeen bestuur (AB), met bijlagen, 1986–99, no. 298.

66. Magnus Boström and Mikael Klintman, *Eco-standards, Product Labelling and Green Consumerism* (Houndmills: Palgrave Macmillan, 2008): 2–18.

67. Nico Roozen, Voorstel Ahold t.a.v. keurmerk-constructie, June 1988, KDC, Solidaridad, agenda's voor en verslagen van vergaderingen DB 1986–89, no. 240.

68. Ibid.

69. Peter van Dam and Amber Striekwold, 'Small is Unsustainable: Alternative Food Movement in the Low Countries, 1969–1990', *BMGN/LCHR* 137, no. 4 (2022): 137–60.

70. 'Koffiekeurmerk', *Stichting Ideële Import Blad* 8, no. 4 (1988): 12–13; Aan de groepen die betrokken zijn bij de kampagne van Solidaridad, 26 September 1988, KDC, Solidaridad, stukken betreffende acties, 1975–88, no. 143.

71. Vgl. Van der Hoff and Roozen, *Fair Trade*, 118–30.

72. Solidaridad – Jaarverslag 1988, KDC, Solidaridad, jaarverslagen, 1986–98, no. 278.

73. 'Prins krijgt Max Havelaar-koffie', *De Telegraaf*, 16 November 1988.

74. 'Max Havelaar-koffie vliegt de schappen uit', *De Waarheid*, 26 November 1988, 1.
75. Persberichten Introduktie Max Havelaar Koffie 15 November 1988, KDC, Solidardidad, Agenda's voor en verslagen van vergaderingen van het algemeen bestuur (AB), met bijlagen, 1986–99, no. 298.
76. Solidaridad – Jaarverslag 1988, KDC, Solidaridad, jaarverslagen, 1986–98, no. 278.
77. Vgl. Jouke Turpijn, *80's dilemma: Nederland in de jaren tachtig* (Amsterdam: Bert Bakker, 2011).
78. Notulen DB 31-01-1991, IISH, Max Havelaar, file DB 1991; Notulen DB 15-09-1992, IISH, Max Havelaar, file DB 1991.
79. Stichting Max Havelaar – Jaarverslag 1991, KDC, Solidaridad, jaarverslagen, 1986–98, no. 278; 'Max Havelaar-koffie in de hele EG', *Het Vrije Volk*, 2 October 1990, 2.
80. In 2010, the international federations FLO, WFTO, and EFTA founded the *Fair Trade Advocacy Office* (FTAO) in Brussels. A precursor organization had been active since 2004 without a formal brief by these organizations.
81. ATO Meeting 8/9 December 1983 in Henndorf near Salzburg, Austria, Amsab, Oxfam-Wereldwinkels, 251/1126.
82. Agenda meeting small ATO group October 87: Managers, private archive Marlike Kocken, EFTA, file FLO 2005-
83. Minutes of the ATO-meeting in Salzburg, 20/21-11-1986, Amsab, Oxfam-Wereldwinkels, 251/1126.
84. The nine founders were Alternativ Handel (Norway), Artisans du Monde (France), EZA (Austria), Gepa (West Germany), Oxfam-Wereldwinkels (Belgium), Oxfam/Magasins du Monde (Belgium), OS3 (Switzerland), SOS Wereldhandel (the Netherlands) en Traidcraft (Great Britain). Proposal for set-up of federation, June 1987, private archive Marlike Kocken, EFTA: unfiled papers.
85. Meeting of the steering group of the ATO Federation, 8 January 1988, Amsab, OW, 251/1136.
86. Ton Tukker to EFTA-managers, 'Negotiations Fair Trade Mark International', 11 February 1992, Amsab, OW, 251/1146.
87. EFTA, Fair Trade Seal II, 2 February 1989, Amsab, OW, 251/1136.
88. Ton Tukker to EFTA-managers, 'Negotiations Fair Trade Mark International', 11 February 1992, Amsab, OW, 251/1146.
89. Ibid.
90. Ton Tukker to EFTA-managers, 7 May 1992, Amsab, OW, 251/1146.
91. Efta in times of labelling initiatives: what to do? 8 November 1993, private archive Marlike Kocken, EFTA: File Workplans Crisis Future 1991–2013.

92. Voornaamste punten en bedenkingen bij EFTA-Managers meeting Paris 3/4 juni 1994, Amsab, OW, 241/1141.
93. Provisional summary 'EFTA in the coming decade', 1 May 1995, private archive Marlike Kocken, EFTA: File Workplans Crisis Future 1991–2013.
94. Voornaamste punten en bedenkingen bij EFTA-Managers meeting Paris 3/4 juni 1994, Amsab, OW, 241/1141.
95. Anderson, *A History of Fair Trade*, 37–38, 117–23.
96. Ibid., 124–25.
97. Stichting Max Havelaar aan Transfair International, 16 July 1993, IISH, Max Havelaar, file DB 1993, 7-1 t/m 6-12-'93.
98. SOS Wereldhandel aan Stichting Max Havelaar, 21 March 1993, IISH, Max Havelaar, file DB 1993: 7-1 t/m 6-12-'93.
99. Notulen DB MH, 14 January 1993, IISH, Max Havelaar, file DB 1993: 7-1 t/m 6-12-'93.
100. Minutes of the TransMax meeting, 17 February 1994, Brussels, IISH, Max Havelaar, file DB 1994.
101. Elisabeth Bennett, 'A Short History of Fairtrade Certification Governance', in *The Processes and Practices of Fair Trade: Trust, Ethics, and Governance*, ed. Janet Dine en Brigitte Granville (London: Routledge, 2013), 53–78.
102. Jaarplan 1999, 2e versie, October 1998, IISH, Max Havelaar, file Bestuur 1998, 1999, 2000.
103. Breitinger, 'Ujamaa Revisited'; Konrad Kuhn, '"Entwicklung heisst Befreiung": Strategien und Protestformen der schweizerischen Dritte-Welt-Bewegung am Symposium der Solidarität 1981', *Mitteilungsblatt des Instituts für soziale Bewegungen* 38 (2007): 77–95; Ruben Quaas, 'Selling Coffee to Raise Awareness for Development Policy. The Emerging Fair Trade Market in Western Germany in the 1970s', *Historical Social Research* 36, no. 3 (2011): 164–81.
104. Ruerd Ruben, 'The Fair Trade Balance: New Challenges after 25 Years of Fair Trade', *FERDI Policy Brief*, no. 52 (2012): 1–7.
105. Sandra Bäthge, *Verändert der faire Handel die Gesellschaft?* (Saarbrücken: Ceval, 2017); Stolle and Micheletti, *Political Consumerism*, 211–43.
106. Paul Hoebink et al., *The Impact of Coffee Certification on Smallholder Farmers in Kenya, Uganda and Ethiopia* (Nijmegen: Centre for International Development Issues Nijmegen, 2014).
107. Notulen Bestuur MH, 6 January 1999, IISH, Max Havelaar, file Bestuur 1998, 1999, 2000; Stichting Max Havelaar ed., *Nieuwe oogst: Tien jaar Max Havelaar* (Leiden: Krikke, 1998).

108. Notulen Bestuur MH, 15 December 1998. IISH: Max Havelaar, doos Bestuur 1998, 1999, 2000.
109. Bäthge, *Verändert der faire Handel die Gesellschaft?*

5 Clothes

1. The placards can be found in IISH, C[lean] C[lothes] C[ampaign], 250A: Other campaigns NL.
2. Brief kort verslag kledingactie in Sittard, 23 May 1991, IISH, CCC, 250A: Other campaigns NL.
3. Ibid.
4. Landelijke C&A actiedag, IISH, CCC, 250A: Other campaigns NL. The modus operandi of the 'silent giant' C&A was analyzed in 1989 by researchers of a Dutch foundation engaging in critical business analysis, Stichting Onderzoek Multinationale Ondernemingen: Marijke Smit and Lorette Jongejans, *C&A, de stille gigant: Van kledingmultinational tot thuiswerkster* (Amsterdam: Stichting Onderzoek Multinationale Ondernemingen, 1989).
5. Letter 10 October 1990, IISH, CCC, 250A: Other campaigns NL; Landelijke C&A actiedag. Ibid.
6. John Trumpbour, 'Global Sweatshops: The History and Future of North-South Solidarity Campaigns in Bangladesh and Beyond', *Labor History* 62, no. 2. (2021): 109–14.
7. C&A-kleren zijn besmet! [8 March 1990], IISH, CCC, 250A: Other campaigns NL.
8. 'De vuile was van C&A hangt buiten', *Trouw*, 12 November 1990, 4.
9. 'C&A doelwit demonstratie, 2 *de Volkskrant*, 30 September 1988, 7.
10. Katharina Karcher, 'Violence for a Good Cause? The Role of Violent Tactics in West German Solidarity Campaigns for Better Working and Living Conditions in the Global South in the 1980s', *Contemporary European History* 28, no. 4 (2019): 566–80.
11. Edward P. Thompson, *The Making of the English Working Class* (London: Victor Gollancz, 1963).
12. Kish Sklar, 'The consumers' white label campaign'.
13. Harley L. Snyder (The Jute Works, Bangladesh) to Janet Yoder (MCC), 17 August 1974, MCC, box 230, folder 137/97.
14. Liesbeth Sluiter, *Clean Clothes: A Global Movement to End Sweatshops* (London, Pluto: 2009), 14–15.
15. Andreas Fickers and Pascal Griset, *Communicating Europe: Technologies, Information, Events* (London: Palgrave Macmillan, 2019), 283–329.

16. Anselm Doering-Manteuffel and Lutz Raphael, *Nach dem Boom: Perspektiven auf die Zeitgeschichte seit 1970* (Göttingen: Vandenhoeck & Ruprecht, 2010): 99; Manuel Castells, *The Rise of the Network Society* (Cambridge: Blackwell, 1996).
17. Mark Berger, 'After the Third World?', 27.
18. Relatie met licentiehouders, 9 August 1999, IISH, Max Havelaar, file Bestuur 1998, 1999, 2000.
19. Frederick Cooper, 'Writing the History of Development', *Journal of Modern European History* 8, no. 1 (2010): 17; Anderson, *A History of Fair Trade*, 133–35.
20. Sluiter, *Clean Clothes*, 14–15.
21. Bach, *Die Erfindung der Globalisierung*, 161–65.
22. George Ritzer, *The McDonaldization of Society: An Investigation into the Changing Character of Contemporary Social Life* (London: Pine Forge Press, 1992).
23. Castells, *The Rise of the Network Society*, 3.'
24. Martin Albrow, *The Global Age: State and Society Beyond Modernity* (Cambridge: Polity Press, 1996), 140–44.
25. Grant Jordan, *Shell, Greenpeace, and the Brent Spar* (Houndmills: Palgrave, 2001).
26. Donatella della Porta Della Porta et al., *Globalization from Below: Transnational Activists and Protest Networks* (Minneapolis: University of Minnesota Press, 2006), 10–14, 57–58.
27. 'De hobbezak voorbij', *IS – Internationale Samenwerking*, no. 3. (2006): 12–17. Cf. Sven Beckert, *Empire of Cotton: A Global History* (New York: Knopf, 2014).
28. ABAL Wereldwinkel Nieuwsbrief (1997) 1 [April], private archive Henk Morel.
29. Udo Sprang, '10 jaar Max Havelaar: We zijn geen hemelbestormers meer', *Handelskrant* 19, no. 4 (1998):6–8.
30. Cf. Ian Hussey and Joe Curnow, 'Fair Trade, Neocolonial Developmentalism, and Racialized Power Relations', *Interface* 5, no. 1 (2013): 40–68.
31. Sluiter, *Clean Clothes*, 23.
32. Barcelona Clean Clothes International Meeting, From Wednesday 7 March up to Sunday 11 March, IISH, CCC, 26: Barcelona 1997–2001.
33. Notulen sSKO-Internationaal, 21 April 1995, IISH, CCC, 31: Schone Kleren Overleg 1994–1995; Short and very incomplete overview of development in Europe relating to codes, IISH, CCC, 26: Barcelona 1997–2001.
34. Clean Clothes Campaign Discussion Paper, IISH, CCC, 26: Barcelona 1997–2001.

35. Frank den Hond, Sjoerd Stolwijk, and Jeroen Merk, 'A Strategic-Interaction Analysis of an Urgent Appeal System and its Outcomes for Garment Workers', *Mobilization* 19, no. 1 (2014): 83–111; Jeroen Merk and Sabrian Zajak, 'Workers' Participation and Transnational Social Movement Interventions at the Shop Floor: The Urgent Appeal System of the Clean Clothes Campaign' in *The Palgrave Handbook of Workers' Participation at Plant Level*, ed. Stefan Berger, Ludger Pries, and Manfred Wannöffel (New York: Palgrave Macmillan, 2019), 221–40.
36. Kelly Dent, Urgent Appeals Impact Study, IISH, CCC, 27: Impact study (2005).
37. Ibid.
38. Ibid.
39. Ibid.
40. Bangladesh People's Solidarity Center to CCC, 29 September 1998, IISH, CCC, 25: Saint Malo.
41. Clean Clothes Campaign Discussion Paper: Evaluating the CCC [c. 2001], IISH, CCC, 26: Barcelona.
42. Sluiter, *Clean Clothes*, 148–53.
43. Minutes of the meeting of the preparatory committee for the setting up of transfair international e.v., 4 April 1992, Amsterdam, Amsab, OW, 251/1146.
44. Voorstel tot hopheffing producentenzetels in Stichtingsraad Max Havelaar, October 1998, IISH, Max Havelaar, file Bestuur 1998, 1999, 2000.
45. Notulen Stichtingsraad MH 18-3-1997. IISH, Max Havelaar, file Bestuur 1996, 1997.
46. Elisabeth Bennett, *Stakeholder Inclusion and Power in INGOs: The Governance of Fairtrade International* (Providence: Brown University, 2014), 90–102.
47. Bennett, *Stakeholder Inclusion*, 106–8.
48. 1987 ATO Conference, Berlin-Spandau, Amsab, OW, 251/1128: Dossier betreffende de Alternative Trade Organization.
49. Sarah Lyon and Mark Moberg, 'What's Fair? The Paradox of Seeking Justice through Markets', in *Fair Trade and Global Justice: Global Ethnographies*, Sarah Lyon and Mark Moberg, eds., (New York: New York University Press, 2010): 1–23, see 5–6.
50. Report of the ATO conference, 8–12 May 1989, private archive Marlike Kocken, EFTA, file IFAT 81–02.
51. IFAT aan Oxfam Wereldwinkels, 22 October 1989, Amsab, OW, 251/1128: Dossier betreffende de Alternative Trade Organization.
52. IFAT: Report of the 1991 Word Conference, private archive Marlike Kocken, EFTA, file IFAT 81–02.

53. IFAT: Report of the second biennial conference, Manilla, Philippines, 27 April–1 May 1993, private archive Marlike Kocken, EFTA, file IFAT 81–02.
54. SS, OS3, 8150.1: file IFAT 1996–1997.
55. Minutes of the IFAT Europe AGM at the UNICEF in Rome, 25–27 September 2008, IISH, LVvW, unfiled papers concerning IFAT.
56. TMF – Subsidie Eerlijke Markttoegang, Eindverslag 2006–2011, IISH, LVvW, file TMF Proinvest EU subsidies.
57. World Commission on Environment and Development, *Our Common Future* (Oxford: Oxford University Press, 1987). Cf. Iris Borowy, *Defining Sustainable Development for Our Common Future: A History of the World Commission on Environment and Development (Brundtland Commission)* (London: Routledge, 2014); Stephen J. Macekura, *Of Limits and Growth: The Rise of Global Sustainable Development in the Twentieth Century* (Nex York: Cambridge University Press, 2015).
58. Franc, *Von der Makroökonomie zum Kleinbauern*.
59. Cf. Priyanka Parvathi, Ulrike Grote, and Hermann Waibel, eds., *Fair Trade and Organic Agriculture: A Winning Combination?* (Wallingford: CABI, 2018).
60. Gerd Nickoleit and Annette Bernd, Alternative Trading Organizations and IFOAM: What can we do together?, Augustus 1990, Amsab, OW, 251/1138; Annette Bernd, Three years as EFTA representative for bio questions – a summary, 1995, Amsab, OW, 251/1142.
61. Annette Bernd, Three years as EFTA representative for bio questions – a summary, 1995, Amsab, OW, 251/1142.
62. IFAT: Report of the second biennial conference, Manilla, Philippines, 27 April–1 May 1993, private archive Marlike Kocken, file IFAT 81–02.
63. Clean Clothes Campaign Discussion Paper: Clean Clothes Campaign Strategies [c. 2001], IISH, CCC, 26: Barcelona.
64. Clean Clothes Campaign Discussion Paper: Evaluating the CCC [c. 2001], IISH, CCC, 26: Barcelona.
65. Clean Clothes Campaign Discussion Paper: Clean Clothes Campaign Strategies [c. 2001], IISH, CCC, 26: Barcelona.
66. Ronan Le Velly, 'Fair Trade and Mainstreaming', in *Handbook of Research on Fair Trade*, eds. Laura Raynolds and Elizabeth Bennett (Cheltenham: Edward Elgar Publishing, 2015), 265–80.
67. Bowes, *The Fair Trade Revolution*; Van der Hoff and Roozen, *Fair Trade*; Lamb, *Fighting the Banana Wars*; Barratt Brown, *Fair Trade*; Fridell, *Fair Trade Coffee*; Daniel Jaffee, *Brewing Justice: Fair Trade Coffee, Sustainability, and Survival* (Berkeley: University of California Press, 2007).

68. Le Velly, 'Fair Trade and Mainstreaming', 266–67; Valerio Verrea, *The Fair Trade Innovation: Tensions Between Ethical Behavior and Profit* (Leipzig: University of Leipzig, 2014) 7–14.
69. Luc Fransen, 'Beyond Regulatory Governance? On the Evolutionary Trajectory of Transnational Private Sustainability Governance', *Ecological Economics* 146 (2018): 772–77.
70. Hans Beerends and Marc Broere, *De bewogen beweging: Een halve eeuw mondiale solidariteit* (Amsterdam: KIT Publishers 2004) 197–99; Beerends, *Tegen de draad in: Een beknopte geschiedenis van de (Derde)Wereldbeweging* (Amsterdam: KIT Publishers, 2013) 61–62.
71. Fair trade fair, 23 August 1999, SS, OS3, 8151.
72. IFAT update no. 19, 3 September 1999, SSZ, OS3, 8151.
73. IFAT Update 25/99, SS, OS3, 8151.
74. 1st daily Seattle Update from NEWS! – 28 November 1999, SS, OS3, 8151.
75. File on the Advocacy Lobby Group, private archive Marlike Kocken, EFTA.
76. Adam Rome, 'Beyond Compliance: The Origins of Corporate Interest in Sustainability', *Enterprise & Society* 22, no. 2 (2021): 409–37; Keetie Sluyterman, 'Corporate Social Responsibility of Dutch Entrepreneurs in the Twentieth Century', *Enterprise & Society* 13, no. 2 (2012): 313–49. Cf. Inga Nuhn, *Entwicklungslinien betrieblicher Nachhaltigkeit nach 1945: Ein deutsch-niederländischer Unternehmensvergleich* (Münster: Waxmann, 2013).
77. Discussion paper for the European CCC meeting (Saint Malo, October '98), IISH, CCC, 25: Saint Malo (1998).
78. Ibid.
79. Verslag interne SKO bijeenkomst over de inhoud van het EHH, 8 November 1994, SOMO offices, IISH, CCC, file 31: Schone Kleren Overleg 1994–1995.
80. Het Eerlijk Handels Handvest voor Kleding (December 1992), IISH, CCC, file 287: EHH 1992–1994.
81. Short and very incomplete overview of development in Europe relating to codes, IISH, CCC, 26: Barcelona 1997–2001.
82. Notulen SKO, 3 April 1995, IISH, CCC, file 31: Schone Kleren Overleg 1994–1995; Notulen 12 mei 1997, IISH, CCC, file 32: SKO 1996–1997; Notulen SKO Vergadering 8 februari 1999, IISH, CCC, file 33: SKO 1998–1999.
83. Notulen SKO Vergadering 8 februari 1999, IISH, CCC, file 33: SKO 1998–1999.
84. 'The Dutch Fair Wear Charter Foundation is Founded', *Clean Clothes Newsletter* (1999) 11, 20, IISH, CCC, 17: English newsletters.

85. 'Using Codes of Conduct: Some Backgrounds for the CCC Strategy Debate', *Clean Clothes Newsletter* (2000) 13, 18–23, IISH, CCC, 17: English newsletters.
86. 'Involving Workers in the Debate on Company Codes', *Clean Clothes Newsletter* (1999) 11, 4–6, IISH, CCC, 17: English newsletters.
87. 'Using Codes of Conduct: Some Backgrounds for the CCC Strategy Debate', *Clean Clothes Newsletter* (2000) 13, 18–23, IISH, CCC, 17: English newsletters.
88. Van der Hoff and Roozen, *Fair trade*, 214–17.
89. Ibid., 237–49.
90. Evert de Boer, Schone Kleren Kampagne, aan Solidaridad, 18 March 2003, IISH, CCC, 35: Notulen 2003.
91. Ibid.
92. Ibid.
93. Ibid.
94. 'Kuyichi International BV', www.fairwear.org/member/kuyichi-international-bv/ (10 February 2018).
95. 'Kuyichi', www.rankabrand.nl/duurzame-jeans-spijkerbroek/Kuyichi (10 February 2018).
96. Agenda EFTA/NEWS textile meeting, 12 September 1996, Amsab, OW, 251/1145.
97. Olaf Paulsen, FLO International, to Clean Clothes Campaign, 15 December [2003], IISH, CCC, 246: Fair trade.
98. Clean Clothes Campaign to Olaf Paulsen, 9 January, 004, IISH, CCC, 246: Fair trade.
99. Clean Clothes Campaign to Andreas Kratz, FLO International, 4 July 2005, IISH, CCC, 246: Fair trade.
100. Fenny Eshuis and Stephan Peijnenburg, Product Policy Max Havelaar Netherlands, June 2004, IISH, CCC, 246: Fair trade; Fenny Eshuis, Fairtrade Labelling en de textielketen, 19 September 2006, IISH, CCC, 246: Fair trade.
101. Dan Rees to Peter Williams, FLO and fairtrade factories, 15 September 2006, IISH, CCC, 246: Fair trade.
102. Jaffee, *Brewing Justice*, 218–20; Sasson, 'Milking the Third World'.
103. Cf. Lone Riisgaard, 'Fairtrade Certification, Conventions and Labor', in *Handbook of Research on Fair Trade*, 120–35.
104. 'Schone kleren vs. Made-By over arbeidsomstandigheden', *Communicatie* 13, no. 5 (2007): 45.
105. Excerpts from 'Fair Trade Garment Standards: Feasability Study', by Maureen Quigley and Charlotte Opal for TransFair USA, August 2006, IISH, CCC, 246: Fair Trade.
106. Hans Lévelt, 'Max Havelaar en de koffieproducent', 15 September 2003, private archive Hans Lévelt.

107. Ruerd Ruben and Simone Verkaart, 'Comparing fair and responsible coffee standards in East Africa', in *Value Chains, Social Inclusion and Economic Development: Contrasting Theories and Realities*, Bert Helmsing and Sietze Vellema ed. (London: Routledge, 2011), 65.
108. Anne Tallontire and Bill Vorley, *Achieving Fairness in Trading between Supermarkets and Their Agrifood Supply Chains* (UK Food Group 2005).
109. Een nieuwe doorbraak in de koffiecrisis: Utz Kapeh – doorbraak of schurkenstreek?, IISH, CCC, 224: Coffee.
110. Dara O'Rourke, 'Multi-Stakeholder Regulation: Privatizing or Socializing Global Labor Standards?', *World Development* no. 5 (2006): 899–918.
111. Jeroen Siebelink, *Het wereldschokkende en onweerstaanbaar lekkere verhaal van Tony's Chocolonely* (Amsterdam: Thomas Rap, 2018).
112. Sophie Derkzen, 'Hoe je een smartphone eerlijk maakt', *Vrij Nederland*, 22 February 2014; Katja Keuchenius, 'Eerlijk en duurzaam veel geld verdienen', *Trouw*, 1 November 2018.
113. Clean Clothes Communities, *Clean Clothes Newsletter* (1999) 11, 18–19, IISH, CCC, 17: English newsletters.
114. Notulen Platform vergadering Schone Kleren, 13 September 1999, Amsterdam, IISH, CCC, 33: Notulen 1998–1999.
115. Clean Clothes Communities, *Clean Clothes Newsletter* (1999) 11, 18–19, IISH, CCC, 17: English newsletters.
116. Notulen Platform Schone Kleren overleg, 12 September 2002, IISH, CCC, 34: Notulen 2001–2002.
117. 'Schone Kleren Gemeente (2002–2006)', https://schonekleren .nl/informatie/archief/schone-kleren-gemeente-2002-2006-1 (13 February 2018).
118. Kathryn Wheeler, *Fair Trade and the Citizen-Consumer: Shopping for Justice?* (Basingstoke: Palgrave Macmillan, 2012): 42–43.
119. Roberta Discetti, Matthew Anderson, and Adam Gardner, 'Campaign Spaces for Sustainable Development: A Power Analysis of the Fairtrade Town Campaign in the UK', *Food Chain* 9, no. 1 (2020): 8–28.
120. 'Keurmerken botsen in de rechtzaal', *Het Financiële Dagblad*, 17 March 2010.
121. Kengetallenonderzoek Cijfers 1998, IISHj, LVVW, unfiled papers.
122. Maatschappelijk Bedrijfsprofiel Wereldwinkels 2001, IISH, LVVW: unfiled papers.
123. Clean Clothes Campaign, *Four Years after Rana Plaza* (Amsterdam: Clean Clothes Campaign, 2017).

124. Cf. Peter Utting, 'Corporate Accountability, Fair Trade and Multi-Stakeholder Regulation' in: *Handbook of Research on Fair Trade*, 61–79.
125. Wheeler, *Fair Trade and the Citizen-Consumer*, 17.
126. Naomi Klein, *No Logo: No Space, No Choice, No Jobs* (London, Flamingo, 2000). Cf. Joseph Heath and Andrew Potter, *The Rebel Sell: How the Counterculture Became Consumer Culture* (Chichester: Capstone, 2006).

Conclusion

1. Samanth Subramanian, 'Is fair trade finished?', *The Guardian*, 23 July 2019, www.theguardian.com/business/2019/jul/23/fairtrade-ethical-certification-supermarkets-sainsburys (last accessed 22 February 2023).
2. Beerends, *Tegen de draad in*; Bowes, *Fair Trade Revolution*; Marco Coscione, *In Defense of Small Producers: The Story of CLAC* (Black Point: Fernwood, 2014); Caspar Dohmen, *Das Prinzip Fair Trade: Vom Weltladen in den Supermarkt* (Berlin: orange-press, 2017); Lamb, *Fighting the Banana Wars*; Gerd Nickoleit and Katharina Nickoleit, *Fair for Future: Ein gerechter Handel ist möglich* (Berlin: Ch. Links, 2021); Osman, *Traidcraft*.
3. Nickoleit, *Fair for Future*, 11.
4. Molly Doane, 'Relationship Coffees: Structure and Agency in the Fair Trade System', in *Fair Trade and Social Justice*, 275–306.
5. Jeronimo Pruijn, 'The Roots of Fair Trade and SPP: My Experiences Alongside Small Producers', in *The Fair Trade Handbook*, 86–87.
6. IFAT Europe Workplan 2009–2010, IISH, LVVW, unfiled papers concerning IFAT.
7. Carol Wills, 'History of WFTO', https://wfto.com/about-us/history-wfto (1 January 2018).
8. 'PRESS RELEASE: WFTO global product label launch at Ambiente in Frankfurt', https://wfto-europe.org/news/press-release-wfto-global-product-label-launch-at-ambiente-in-frankfurt/ (10 March 2023).
9. 'Living income', www.fairtrade.net/issue/living-income (10 March 2023); 'Living wage', www.fairtrade.net/issue/living-wage (10 March 2023).
10. Cf. Gavin Fridell and Kate Ervine, 'Demanding Justice: Can Trade Policy Be Fair?', in *The Fair Trade Handbook*, 192–201.

11. Quaas, *Fair Trade*, 35–47.
12. The subsuming of fair trade under the broader banner of sustainability reinforced this debate, as environmental considerations came to be seen as a primary marker of 'fair' products. Cf. Katrin Zander, Rosa Schleenbecker, and Ulrich Hamm, 'Consumer Behaviour in the Organic and Fair Trade Food Market in Europe', in *Fair Trade and Organic Agriculture*, 51–60.

BIBLIOGRAPHY

Archival and Unpublished Sources

Amsab-ISG, Ghent: Oxfam-Wereldwinkels
Beeld en geluid, Hilversum: Werkwinkel, 17 February 1974
Bodleian library, Oxford: Oxfam
Brethren Historical Library and Archive, Elgin: SERVV
International Institute of Social History, Amsterdam

- CCC
- LVvW
- X min Y
- Wereldwinkel Amstelveen
- Wereldwinkel Castricum
- Individual periodicals & brochures

KDC: Solidaridad
MCC: Self-help Crafts
RHC Wijk bij Duurstede: Sjaloom
Private archive Fair Trade Original
Private archive Hans Lévelt
Private archive Henk Morel

- ABAL
- Wereldwinkel Ceintuurbaan Amsterdam
- Wereldwinkel Amstelveen

Private archive Marlike Kocken: EFTA
Private archive Max Havelaar/Fair Trade Nederland (now transferred to International Institute of Social History, Amsterdam)
Private archive Paul van Tongeren: Cane sugar campaign
Schweizerisches Sozialarchiv, Zürich: Claro

Books and Articles

Ahmia, Mourad, ed. *The Collected Documents of the Group of 77. Volume IV: Environment and Sustainable Development*. New York: Oxford University Press, 2012.

Albrow, Martin. *The Global Age: State and Society beyond Modernity*. Cambridge: Polity Press, 1996.

Anderson, Matthew. *A History of Fair Trade in Contemporary Britain: From Civil Society Campaigns to Corporate Compliance*. Basingstoke: Palgrave Macmillan, 2015.

Anderson, Matthew. '"Cost of a Cup of Tea": Fair Trade and the British Co-operative Movement, c. 1960–2000'. In *Consumerism and the Co-Operative Movement in Modern British History: Taking Stock*, edited by Lawrence Black and Nicole Robertson, 240–59. Manchester: Manchester University Press, 2009.

Arnold, Paul. '"Went v'r jet dunt dan dunt v'r jot!" De geschiedenis van de Kerkraadse Stichting Steun Onderontwikkelde Streken, later S.O.S. Wereldhandel, 1959–1986'. *Studies over de Sociaal-Economische Geschiedenis van Limburg* 46 (2001): 2–43.

Bach, Olaf. *Die Erfindung der Globalisierung: Entstehung und Wandel eines zeitgeschichtlichen Grundbegriffs*. Frankfurt am Main: Campus, 2013.

Bahr, Hans-Eckehard, ed. *Politisiering des Alltags: Gesellschaftliche Bedingungen des Friedens*. Darmstadt: Luchterhand, 1972.

Barnett, Michael, and Janice Gross Stein. 'The Secularization and Sanctification of Humanitarianism'. In *Sacred Aid: Faith and Humanitarianism*, 3–36. Oxford: Oxford University Press, 2012.

Bäthge, Sandra. *Verändert der Faire Handel die Gesellschaft?* Saarbrücken: Ceval, 2017.

Beckert, Sven. *Empire of Cotton: A Global History*. New York: Knopf, 2014.

Beerends, Hans. *De derde wereldbeweging: Geschiedenis en toekomst*. Den Haag: Novib, 1992.

Beerends, Hans. *Tegen de draad in: een beknopte geschiedenis van de (derde)wereldbeweging*. Amsterdam: KIT Publishers, 2013.

Beerends, Hans, and Marc Broere. *De bewogen beweging: een halve eeuw mondiale solidariteit*. Amsterdam: KIT Publishers, 2004.

Beerends, Hans, and Ank Gerbrands, Willem van het Hekke, Rob Pannekoek, and Jan Rutges. *Anders nog iets?* Amersfoort: De Horstink, 1979.

Bennett, Elisabeth. 'A Short History of Fairtrade Certification Governance'. In *The Processes and Practices of Fair Trade: Trust, Ethics, and Governance*, edited by Janet Dine and Brigitte Granville, 53–78. London: Routledge, 2013.

Bennett, Elisabeth. *Stakeholder Inclusion and Power in INGOs: The Governance of Fairtrade International*. Providence: Brown University, 2014.

Berger, Mark. 'After the Third World? History, Destiny and the Fate of Third Worldism'. *Third World Quarterly* 25, no. 1 (2004): 9–39.

Berghoff, Hartmut, and Jakob Vogl. 'Wirtschaftsgeschichte Als Kulturgeschichte: Ansätze Zur Bergung Transdisziplinärer Synergiepotentiale'. In *Wirtschaftsgeschichte Als Kulturgeschichte: Dimensionen Eines Perspektivenwechsels*, edited by Hartmut Berghoff and Jakob Vogl, 9–41. Frankfurt am Main: Campus, 2004.

Bevir, Mark, and Frank Trentmann, eds. *Markets in Historical Contexts: Ideas and Politics in the Modern World*. Cambridge: Cambridge University Press, 2004.

Biersteker, Henk, and Huub Coppens. *Towards Internationalised Development Action. Report of the International Working-congress of Action-groups on International Development*. The Hague: Novib, 1970.

Black, Maggie. *A Cause for Our Times: Oxfam – the First 50 Years*. Oxford: Oxfam, 1992.

Borowy, Iris. *Defining Sustainable Development for Our Common Future: A History of the World Commission on Environment and Development (Brundtland Commission)*. London: Routledge, 2014.

Bos, Maarten van den, and Chris Dols. 'King Customer: Contested Conceptualizations of the Consumer and the Politics of Consumption in the Netherlands, 1920s–1980s'. *BMGN – Low Countries Historical Review* 132, no. 3 (2017): 94–114.

Bosma, Ulbe. *The Sugar Plantation in India and Indonesia: Industrial Production, 1770–2010*. New York: Cambridge University Press, 2013.

Bosma, Ulbe. *The World of Sugar: How the Sweet Stuff Transformed Our Politics, Health, and Environment over 2,000 Years*. Cambridge: Harvard University Press, 2023.

Boström, Magnus, and Mikael Klintman. *Eco-standards, Product Labelling and Green Consumerism*. Houndmills: Palgrave Macmillan, 2008.

Bowes, John, ed. *The Fair Trade Revolution*. London: Pluto Press, 2011.

Breitinger, Jan C. '"Ujamaa Revisited": zur entwicklungstheoretischen Verankerung und politischen Wahrnehmung eines spezifisch tansanischen Entwicklungsmodells'. *Comparativ* 23, no. 1 (2013): 89–111.

Brown, Michael Barratt. *Fair Trade. Reform and Realities in the International Trading System*. London: Zed Books, 1993.

Brown, Timothy Scott. *West Germany and the Global Sixties: The Antiauthoritarian Revolt, 1962–1978. New Studies in European History*. Cambridge: Cambridge University Press, 2015.

Buelens, Geert. *De jaren zestig: Een cultuurgeschiedenis*. Amsterdam: Balans, 2018.

Buettner, Elizabeth. *Europe after Empire: Decolonization, Society, and Culture*. Cambridge: Cambridge University Press, 2016.

Castells, Manuel. *The Rise of the Network Society*. Malden: Blackwell Publishers, 1996.

Christiaens, Kim. 'Between Diplomacy and Solidarity: Western European Support Networks for Sandinista Nicaragua'. *European Review of History: Revue Européenne d'histoire* 21, no. 4 (2014): 617–34.

Christiaens, Kim. 'Voorbij de 1968-Historiografie?' *Tijdschrift Voor Geschiedenis* 128, no. 3 (2015): 377–406.

Christiansen, Samantha, and Zachary A. Scarlett, eds. *The Third World in the Global 1960s*. New York: Berghahn Books, 2013.

Connely, Matthew. 'Future Shock: The End of the World As They Knew It'. In *The Shock of the Global: The 1970s in Perspective*, edited by Niall Ferguson, 337–50. Cambridge: Belknap, 2010.

Cooper, Frederick. 'Writing the History of Development'. *Journal of Modern European History* 8, no. 1 (2010): 5–23.

Coscione, Marco. *In Defense of Small Producers: The Story of CLAC*. Black Point: Fernwood, 2014.

Cox, Jeffrey. 'From the Empire of Christ to the Third World: Religion and the Experience of Empire in the Twentieth Century'. In *Britain's Experience of Empire in the Twentieth Century*, edited by Andrew Thompson, 76–122. Oxford: Oxford University Press, 2012.

Cox, Kevin R., ed. *Spaces of Globalization: Reasserting the Power of the Local. Perspectives on Economic Change*. New York: Guilford Press, 1997.

Dam, Peter van. *Religion und Zivilgesellschaft: Christliche Traditionen in der niederländischen und deutschen Arbeiterbewegung (1945–1980)*. Münster: Waxmann, 2010.

Dam, Peter van, and Wouter van Dis. 'Beyond the Merchant and the Clergyman: Assessing Moral Claims about Development Cooperation'. *Third World Quarterly* 35, no. 9 (2014): 1636–55.

Dam, Peter van. '"Onze rente, hun armoede": de fair trade-revolutie in de jaren tachtig heroverwogen'. *Impressie* 17 (2015): 8–11.

Dam, Peter van. 'Moralizing Postcolonial Consumer Society: Fair Trade in the Netherlands, 1964–1997'. *International Review of Social History* 61, no. 2 (2016): 223–50.

Dam, Peter van. 'In Search of the Citizen-Consumer: Fair Trade Activism in the Netherlands since the 1960s'. *BMGN – Low Countries Historical Review* 132, no. 3 (2017): 139–66.

Dam, Peter van. 'Challenging Global Inequality in Streets and Supermarkets: Fair Trade Activism since the 1960s'. In *Histories of Global Inequality*, edited by Christian Olaf Christiansen and Steven L. B. Jensen, 255–75. Cham: Palgrave MacMillan, 2019a.

Dam, Peter van. 'Goodbye to Grand Politics: The Cane Sugar Campaign and the Limits of Transnational Activism, 1968–1974'. *Contemporary European History* 28, no. 4 (2019b): 518–34.

Dam, Peter van. 'No Justice Without Charity: Humanitarianism After Empire'. *The International History Review* 44, no. 3 (2022a): 653–74.

Dam, Peter van, and Amber Striekwold. 'Small is Unsustainable: Alternative Food Movement in the Low Countries, 1969–1990'. *BMGN/LCHR* 137, no. 4 (2022b): 137–60.

Dietrich, Christopher R. W. 'Mossadegh Madness: Oil and Sovereignty in the Anticolonial Community'. *Humanity* 6, no. 1 (2015): 63–78.

Dinkel, Jürgen, Steffen Fiebrig, and Frank Reichherzer, eds. *Nord/Süd: Perspektiven auf eine globale Konstellation*. Berlin: De Gruyter, 2020.

Discetti, Roberta, Matthew Anderson, and Adam Gardner, 'Campaign Spaces for Sustainable Development: A Power Analysis of the Fairtrade Town Campaign in the UK'. *Food Chain* 9, no. 1 (2020): 8–28.

Doane, Molly. 'Relationship Coffees: Structure and Agency in the Fair Trade System'. In *Fair Trade and Social Justice: Global*

Ethnographies, edited by Sarah Lyon and Mark Moberg, 275–306. New York: New York University Press, 2010.

Doering-Manteuffel, Anselm, and Lutz Raphael. *Nach Dem Boom: Perspektiven Auf Die Zeitgeschichte Seit 1970*. Göttingen: Vandenhoeck & Ruprecht, 2010.

Dohmen, Caspar. *Das Prinzip Fair Trade: Vom Weltladen in den Supermarkt*. Berlin: orange-press, 2017.

Duyvendak, Jan Willem, Hein-Anton Heijden, Ruud Koopmans, and Luuk Wijmans, eds. *Tussen verbeelding en macht: 25 jaar nieuwe sociale bewegingen in Nederland*. Amsterdam: SUA, 1992.

Duyvendak, Jan Willem, and Menno Hurenkamp. *Kiezen voor de kudde: Lichte gemeenschappen en de nieuwe meerderheid*. Amsterdam: Van Gennep, 2004.

Eckel, Jan. 'Utopie der Moral, Kalkül der Macht: Menschenrechte in der globalen Politik seit 1945'. *Archiv für Sozialgeschichte* 49 (2009): 437–84.

Epple, Angelika. 'Lokalität und die Dimensionen des Globalen. Eine Frage der Relationen'. *Historische Anthropologie* 21, no. 1 (2013): 4–25.

Eshuis, J. J., F. C. de Jong, and G. J. de Gilde. *Suiker en de ontwikkelingslanden: bietsuiker-produktie een gezonde zaak*. Rotterdam: Ned. Suikerindustrie, 1968.

Ferguson, Niall. 'Crisis, What Crisis? The 1970s and the Shock of the Global'. In *The Shock of the Global: The 1970s in Perspective*, edited by Niall Ferguson, 1–21. Cambridge: Belknap, 2010a.

Ferguson, Niall, ed. *The Shock of the Global: The 1970s in Perspective*. Cambridge: Belknap, 2010b.

Fickers, Andreas, and Pascal Griset. *Communicating Europe: Technologies, Information, Events*. London: Palgrave Macmillan, 2019.

Fiebrig, Steffen. 'Unequal exchange? Post-koloniale Wirtschaftsordnung, Handelsliberalisierung und die UNCTAD'. In *Nord/Süd: Perspektiven auf eine globale Konstellation*, edited by Steffen Fiebrig, Jürgen Dinkel, and Frank Reichherzer, 135–70. Berlin: De Gruyter, 2020.

Fox, Nick J., and Pam Alldred. 'Social Structures, Power and Resistance in Monist Sociology: (New) Materialist Insights'. *Journal of Sociology* 54, no. 3 (2018): 315–30.

Franc, Andrea. *Von der Makroökonomie zum Kleinbauern: Die Wandlung der Idee eines gerechten Nord-Süd-Handels in der schweizerischen Dritte-Welt-Bewegung (1964–1984)*. Berlin: De Gruyter, 2020.

Franklin, Michael. *Joining the CAP: The Agricultural Negotiations for British Accession to the European Economic Community, 1961–1973*. Bern: Peter Lang, 2010.

Fransen, Luc. 'Beyond Regulatory Governance? On the Evolutionary Trajectory of Transnational Private Sustainability Governance'. *Ecological Economics* 146 (2018): 772–77.

Freeman, Dena. *Tearfund and the Quest for Faith-Based Development*. Abingdon: Routledge, 2019.

Fridell, Gavin. 'The Fair Trade Network in Historical Perspective'. *Canadian Journal of Development Studies* 25, no. 3 (2004): 411–28.

Fridell, Gavin. *Fair Trade Coffee: The Prospects and Pitfalls of Market-Driven Social Justice*. Toronto: University of Toronto Press, 2007.

Fridell, Gavin, and Kate Ervine. 'Demanding Justice: Can Trade Policy Be Fair?', in *The Fair Trade Handbook: Building a Better World, Together*, edited by Gavin Fridell, Zach Gross, and Sean McHugh, 192–201. Halifax: Fernwood Publishing, 2021.

Fridell, Gavin, Zach Gross, and Sean McHugh. 'Why Write a Book About Fair Trade?'. In *The Fair Trade Handbook: Building a Better World, Together*, edited by Gavin Fridell, Zach Gross, and Sean McHugh, 1–6. Halifax: Fernwood Publishing, 2021.

Frieden, Jeffry A. *Global Capitalism: Its Fall and Rise in the Twentieth Century*. New York: Norton, 2006.

Fukuyama, Francis. *The End of History and the Last Man*. New York: Free Press, 1992.

Garavini, Giuliano. *After Empires: European Integration, Decolonization, and the Challenge from the Global South, 1957–1985*. Oxford: Oxford University Press, 2012.

Gateau, Matthieu. 'Quelle(s) stratégie(s) de distribution pour les produits équitables ? Le cas Français ou la difficile alliance entre logique militante et logique commerciale'. *Économie et Solidarités* 37, no. 2 (2008): 109–22.

Getachew, Adom. *Worldmaking after Empire: The Rise and Fall of Self-Determination*. Princeton, NJ: Princeton University Press, 2019.

Gildea, Robert, James Mark, and Niek Pas. 'European Radicals and the "Third World": Imagined Solidarities and Radical Networks, 1958–73'. *Cultural and Social History* 8, no. 4 (2011): 449–71.

Glickman, Lawrence B. *Buying Power: A History of Consumer Activism in America*. Chicago: University of Chicago Press, 2009.

Goldsmith, Edward, and Robert Allen. *A Blueprint for Survival*. Harmondsworth: Penguin, 1972.

Goos, Mia, and Willem van het Hekke. *Wereldwinkels en produkten. Theorie & praktijk*. Utrecht: Landelijke Vereniging van Wereldwinkels, 1977.

Hajer, Maarten. *The Politics of Environmental Discourse: Ecological Modernization and the Policy Process*. Oxford: Oxford University Press, 1995.

Hansen, Peo, and Stefan Jonsson. *Eurafrica: The Untold History of European Integration and Colonialism*. London: Bloomsbury, 2014.

Hart, Gillian. 'Geography and Development: Development/s beyond Neoliberalism? Power, Culture, Political Economy'. *Progress in Human Geography* 25, no. 4 (2001): 649–58.

Heath, Joseph, and Andrew Potter. *The Rebel Sell: How the Counterculture Became Consumer Culture*. Chichester: Capstone, 2006.

Hellema, Duco. *Nederland en de jaren zeventig*. Amsterdam: Boom, 2012.

Hellema, Duco, and Margriet van Lith. *Dat hadden we nooit moeten doen: de PvdA en de neoliberale revolutie van de jaren negentig*. Amsterdam: Promotheus, 2020.

Hengel, Eduard van. *Suikerraffinement: Rietsuikeraktie 1968*. Amsterdam: Sekretariaat Rietsuikeraktie, 1968.

Hilton, Matthew. *Prosperity for All: Consumer Activism in an Era of Globalization*. Ithaca: Cornell University Press, 2009.

Hilton, Matthew, Emily Baughan, Eleanor Davey, Bronwen Everill, Kevin O'Sullivan, and Tehila Sasson. 'History and Humanitarianism: A Conversation'. *Past & Present* 241, no. 1 (2018): e1–38.

Hilton, Matthew, and Jean-François Mouhot, eds. *The Politics of Expertise: How NGOs Shaped Modern Britain*. Oxford: Oxford University Press, 2013.

Hoebink, Paul, Ruerd Ruben, Willem Elbers, and Bart van Rijsbergen. *The Impact of Coffee Certification on Smallholder*

Farmers in Kenya, Uganda and Ethiopia. Nijmegen: Centre for International Development Issues Nijmegen, 2014.
Hoff, Frans van der, and Nico Roozen. *Fair Trade: Het verhaal achter Max Havelaar-koffie, Oké-bananen en Kuyichi-jeans*. Amsterdam: Van Gennep, 2001.
Hoffmann, Stefan-Ludwig. 'Human Rights and History'. *Past & Present* 232, no. 1 (2016): 279–310.
Hoffmann, Stefan-Ludwig, ed. 'Introduction: Genealogies of Human Rights'. In *Human Rights in the Twentieth Century*, 1–26. Cambridge: Cambridge University Press, 2010.
Holcomb, Julie L. 'Blood-Stained Sugar: Gender, Commerce and the British Slave-Trade Debates'. *Slavery & Abolition* 35, no. 4 (2014): 611–28.
Hond, Frank den, Sjoerd Stolwijk, and Jeroen Merk, 'A Strategic-Interaction Analysis of an Urgent Appeal System and its Outcomes for Garment Workers'. *Mobilization* 19, no. 1 (2014): 83–111.
Hooghe, Marc. 'Een bewegend doelwit. De sociologische en historische studie van (nieuwe) sociale bewegingen in Vlaanderen'. *Belgisch Tijdschrift voor Nieuwste Geschiedenis* 34, no. 3 (2004): 331–57.
Horn, Gerd-Rainer. *The Spirit of '68: Rebellion in Western Europe and North America, 1956–1976*. Oxford: Oxford University Press, 2007.
Hudson, Mark, Ian Hudson, and Mara Fridell. *Fair Trade, Sustainability and Social Change*. Houndmills: Palgrave Macmillan, 2013.
Hunt, Lynn. *Inventing Human Rights: A History*. New York: Norton, 2007.
Hussey, Ian, and Joe Curnow. 'Fair Trade, Neocolonial Developmentalism, and Racialized Power Relations'. *Interface* 5, no. 1 (2013): 40–68.
Imig, Douglas R., and Sidney G. Tarrow. *Contentious Europeans: Protest and Politics in an Emerging Polity*. Lanham: Rowman & Littlefield, 2001.
Jacobs, Meg. *Pocketbook Politics: Economic Citizenship in Twentieth-Century America*. Princeton: Princeton University Press, 2005.
Jaffee, Daniel. *Brewing Justice: Fair Trade Coffee, Sustainability, and Survival*. Berkeley: University of California Press, 2007.

Jaffee, Daniel. 'Weak Coffee: Certification and Co-optation in the Fair Trade Movement'. *Social Problems* 59, no. 1 (2012): 94–116.

Jelsma, Simon. *Bezit en vrijheid: Een reeks pleinpreken*. Bussum: Brand, 1957.

Jensen, Steven L. B. *The Making of International Human Rights: The 1960s, Decolonization and the Reconstruction of Global Values*. New York: Cambridge University Press, 2017.

Jordan, Grant. *Shell, Greenpeace, and the Brent Spar*. Houndmills: Palgrave, 2001.

Kalter, Christoph. *The Discovery of the Third World: Decolonization and the Rise of the New Left in France, c.1950–1976*. Cambridge: Cambridge University Press, 2016.

Karcher, Katharina. 'Violence for a Good Cause? The Role of Violent Tactics in West German Solidarity Campaigns for Better Working and Living Conditions in the Global South in the 1980s'. *Contemporary European History* 28, no. 4 (2019): 566–80.

Keck, Margaret, and Kathryn Sikkink. *Activists beyond Borders: Advocacy Networks in International Politics*. Ithaca: Cornell University Press, 1998.

Kemnitzer, Konstanze. *Der ferne Nächste: zum Selbstverständnis der Aktion 'Brot für die Welt'*. Stuttgart: Kohlhammer, 2008.

Kish Sklar, Kathryn. 'The Consumers' White Label Campaign of the National Consumers' League, 1898–1918'. In *Getting and Spending: American and European Consumption in the Twentieth Century*, edited by Susan Strasser, Charles McGovern, and Matthias Judt, 17–35. New York: Cambridge University Press, 1998.

Klein, Naomi. *No Logo: No Space, No Choice, No Jobs*. London: Flamingo, 2000.

Krepp, Stella. 'Weder Norden noch Süden: Lateinamerika, Entwicklungsdebatten und die "Dekolonisierungskluft", 1948–1973'. In *Nord/Süd: Perspektiven auf eine globale Konstellation*, edited by Steffen Fiebrig, Jürgen Dinkel, and Frank Reichherzer, 109–34. Berlin: De Gruyter, 2020.

Kuchenbuch, David. '"Eine Welt": Globales Interdependenzbewusstsein und die Moralisierung des Alltags in den 1970er und 1980er Jahren'. *Geschichte und Gesellschaft* 38, no. 1 (2012): 158–84.

Kuhn, Konrad. '"Entwicklung heisst Befreiung". Strategien und Protestformen der schweizerischen Dritte-Welt-Bewegung am Symposium der Solidarität 1981'. *Mitteilungsblatt des Instituts für soziale Bewegungen* 38 (2007): 77–95.

Kuhn, Konrad. *Entwicklungspolitische Solidarität: die Dritte-Welt-Bewegung in der Schweiz zwischen Kritik und Politik (1975–1992)*. Zürich: Chronos, 2011.

Kuhn, Konrad. *Fairer Handel und Kalter Krieg: Selbstwahrnehmung und Positionierung der Fair-Trade-Bewegung in der Schweiz 1973–1990*. 1. Aufl. Bern: Ed. Soziothek, 2005.

Kuhn, Konrad. '"Handelsförderung ist notwendig und problematisch zugleich". Die Entstehung des fairen Handels als neue Handels- und Unternehmensform'. In *Dienstleistungen. Expansion und Transformation des 'Dritten Sektors' (15.–20. Jahrhundert)*, edited by Hans-Jörg Gilomen, 107–24. Zürich: Chronos, 2007.

Kuitenbrouwer, Maarten. 'Nederland Gidsland? De ontwikkelingssamenwerking van Nederland en gelijkgezinde landen, 1973–1985'. In *De geschiedenis van vijftig jaar ontwikkelingssamenwerking 1949–1999*, edited by Jan Nekkers, Peter Malcontent, and Peer Baneke, 183–200. Den Haag: Sdu Uitgevers, 1999.

Kunkel, Sönke. 'Zwischen Globalisierung, Internationalen Organisationen Und 'Global Governance'. Eine Kurze Geschichte Des Nord-Süd-Konflikts in Den 1960er Und 1970er Jahren'. *Vierteljahrshefte Für Zeitgeschichte* 60, no. 4 (2012): 555–77.

Kunkel, Sönke. 'Contesting Globalization: The United Nations Conference on Trade and Development and the Transnationalization of Sovereignty'. In *International Organizations and Development, 1945–1990*, edited by Marc Frey, Sönke Kunkel, and Corinna R. Unger, 240–58. Houndmills: Palgrave Macmillan, 2014.

Lamb, Harriet. *Fighting the Banana Wars and Other Fairtrade Battles: How We Took on the Corporate Giants to Change the World*. London: Rider, 2008.

Lange, H. M. de. *Rijke en arme landen: een verantwoordelijke maatschappij in mondiaal perspectief. Anatomie van de toekomst*. Baarn: Wereldvenster, 1967.

LeCain, Timothy J. *The Matter of History: How Things Create the Past*. Cambridge: Cambridge University Press, 2017.

Le Velly, Ronan. 'Fair Trade and Mainstreaming'. In *Handbook of Research on Fair Trade*, ed. Laura Raynolds and Elizabeth Bennett, 265–80. Cheltenham: Edward Elgar Publishing, 2015.

Lyon, Sarah, and Mark Moberg, eds. *Fair Trade and Social Justice: Global Ethnographies*. New York: New York University Press, 2010.

MacAdam, Doug, Sidney Tarrow, and Charles Tilly. *Dynamics of Contention. Cambridge Studies in Contentious Politics*. Cambridge: Cambridge University Press, 2001.

Macekura, Stephen J. *Of Limits and Growth: The Rise of Global Sustainable Development in the Twentieth Century*. New York: Cambridge University Press, 2015.

Maul, Daniel. *The Politics of Service: US-amerikanische Quäker und internationale humanitäre Hilfe 1917–1945*. Berlin: De Gruyter, 2021.

May, Alex. 'The Commonwealth and Britain's Turn to Europe, 1945–73'. *The Round Table* 102, no. 1 (2013): 29–39.

Meadows, Donella H., Dennis L. Meadows, Jorgen Randers, and William W. Behrens III. *The Limits to Growth; a Report for the Club of Rome's Project on the Predicament of Mankind*. Potomac Associates Books. New York: Universe Books, 1972.

Meijs, Paul. *Ontwikkelingsstrategie van S.O.S. Derde Wereldhandel voor de periode 1970–1980*. Kerkrade: Stichting Ontwikkelings-Samenwerking Wereldhandel, 1971.

Mellink, Bram, and Merijn Oudenampsen. *Neoliberalisme: Een Nederlandse geschiedenis*. Amsterdam: Boom, 2022.

Mensink, Wouter. *Kun je een betere wereld kopen? De consument en het fairtrade-complex*. Amsterdam: Boom, 2015.

Merk, Jeroen, and Sabrian Zajak. 'Workers' Participation and Transnational Social Movement Interventions at the Shop Floor: The Urgent Appeal System of the Clean Clothes Campaign'. In *The Palgrave Handbook of Workers' Participation at Plant Level*, edited by Stefan Berger, Ludger Pries and Manfred Wannöffel, 221–40. New York: Palgrave Macmillan, 2019.

Mintz, Sidney W. *Sweetness and Power: The Place of Sugar in Modern History*. New York: Viking, 1985.

Möckel, Benjamin. 'The Material Culture of Human Rights: Consumer Products, Boycotts and the Transformation of Human Rights Activism in the 1970s and 1980s'. *International*

Journal for History, Culture And Modernity 6, no. 1 (2018): 76–104.

Möckel, Benjamin. 'Consuming Anti-Consumerism: The German Fairtrade Movement and the Ambivalent Legacy of "1968"'. *Contemporary European History* 28, no. 4 (2019): 550–65.

Moyn, Samuel. *The Last Utopia: Human Rights in History*. Cambridge: Belknap, 2010.

Nickoleit, Gerd, and Katharina Nickoleit. *Fair for Future: Ein gerechter Handel ist möglich*. Berlin: Ch. Links, 2021.

Nuhn, Inga. *Entwicklungslinien betrieblicher Nachhaltigkeit nach 1945: Ein deutsch-niederländischer Unternehmensvergleich*. Münster: Waxmann, 2013.

Nye, Joseph S., and Robert O. Keohane. 'Transnational Relations and World Politics: An Introduction'. *International Organization* 25, no. 3 (1971): 329–49.

Offe, Claus. 'New Social Movements: Challenging the Boundaries of Institutional Politics'. *Social Research* 52, no. 4 (1985): 817–68.

Oldenziel, Ruth, and Liesbeth Bervoets. 'Speaking for Consumers, Standing up as Citizens: The Politics of Dutch Women's Organization and the Shaping of Technology, 1880–1980'. In *Manufacturing Technology, Manufacturing Consumers: The Making of Dutch Consumer Society*, edited by Adri Albert de la Bruhèze, 41–71. Amsterdam: Aksant, 2009.

Oldenziel, Ruth, and Mikael Hård. *Consumers, Tinkerers, Rebels: The People Who Shaped Europe*. Houndmills: Palgrave Macmillan, 2013.

Olejniczak, Claudia. *Die Dritte-Welt-Bewegung in Deutschland: konzeptionelle und organisatorische Strukturmerkmale einer neuen sozialen Bewegung*. Wiesbaden: DUV, 1999.

Olejniczak, Claudia. 'Dritte-Welt-Bewegung'. In *Die Sozialen Bewegungen in Deutschland seit 1945: Ein Handbuch*, edited by Roland Roth and Dieter Rucht, 319–45. Frankfurt am Main: Campus, 2008.

O'Rourke, Dara. 'Multi-Stakeholder Regulation: Privatizing or Socializing Global Labor Standards?' *World Development*, Part Special Issue (pp. 868–932). *Making Global Corporate Self-Regulation Effective in Developing Countries* 34, no. 5 (2006): 899–918.

Osman, Joe. *Traidcraft: Inspiring a Fair Trade Revolution*. Oxford: Lion Hudson, 2020.

Osterhammel, Jürgen. *Die Verwandlung der Welt: eine Geschichte des 19. Jahrhunderts*. München: Beck, 2009.

O'Sullivan, Kevin. 'The Search for Justice: NGOs in Britain and Ireland and the New International Economic Order, 1968–82'. *Humanity* 6, no. 1 (2015): 173–87.

O'Sullivan, Kevin. *The NGO Moment: The Globalisation of Compassion from Biafra to Live Aid. Human Rights in History*. Cambridge: Cambridge University Press, 2021.

O'Sullivan, Kevin, Matthew Hilton, and Juliano Fiori. 'Humanitarianisms in Context'. *European Review of History: Revue Européenne d'histoire* 23, no. 1–2 (2016): 1–15.

Parvathi, Priyanka, Ulrike Grote, and Hermann Waibel, eds., *Fair Trade and Organic Agriculture: A Winning Combination?* Wallingford: CABI, 2018.

Pasture, Patrick. *Christian Trade Unionism in Europe since 1968. Tensions between Identity and Practice*. Aldershot: Brookfield, 1994.

Patel, Kiran Klaus. 'Widening and Deepening? Recent Advances in European Integration History'. *Neue Politische Literatur* 64, no. 2 (2019): 327–57.

Paulmann, Johannes. 'Conjunctures in the History of International Humanitarian Aid during the Twentieth Century'. *Humanity: An International Journal of Human Rights, Humanitarianism, and Development* 4, no. 2 (2013): 215–38.

Poel, Jan van de. '35 jaar Oxfam-Wereldwinkels: Over groei en organisatorische vernieuwing'. *Brood & Rozen* 11, no. 4 (2006): 7–25.

Poel, Jan van de. 'Solidarity without Borders? The Transnational Integration of the Flemish Solidarity Movement'. *Belgisch Tijdschrift voor Filologie en Geschiedenis/Revue Belge de Philologie et d'Histoire* 89, no. 3–4 (2011): 1381–404.

Porta, Donatella della Porta Della, Massimillano Andretta, Lorenzo Mosca, and Herbert Reiter. *Globalization from Below: Transnational Activists and Protest Networks*. Minneapolis: University of Minnesota Press, 2006.

Prashad, Vijay. *The Darker Nations. A People's History of the Third World*. New York: New Press, 2007.

Quaas, Ruben. 'Selling Coffee to Raise Awareness for Development Policy. The Emerging Fair Trade Market in Western Germany in the 1970s'. *Historical Social Research* 36, no. 3 (2011): 164–81.

Quaas, Ruben. *Fair Trade: eine global-lokale Geschichte am Beispiel des Kaffees*. Köln: Böhlau Verlag, 2015.

Raschke, Markus. *Fairer Handel: Engagement für eine gerechte Weltwirtschaft*. Ostfildern: Matthias-Grünewald-Verlag, 2009.

Raynolds, Laura, and Elisabeth Bennett, 'Introduction to Research on Fair Trade'. In *Handbook of Research on Fair Trade*, edited by Laura Raynolds and Elizabeth Benett. 3–23. Cheltenham: Edward Elgar Publishing, 2015.

Raynolds, Laura, Douglas Murray, and John Wilkinson, eds. *Fair Trade: The Challenges of Transforming Globalization*. Abingdon: Routledge, 2007.

Reckman, Piet. *Je geld of je leven: Naar een nieuwe wereldhandel en -wandel*. Baarn: In den Toren, 1968.

Reckman, Piet. *Riet: Het verhaal van de suiker*. Baarn: Anthos, 1969.

Reckman, Piet. *Rohr: Die Geschichte des Zuckers*. Nürnberg: Laetare Verlag, 1970.

Reckman, Piet. *De Multinationale*. Odijk: Sjaloom, 1976.

Reichardt, Sven. *Authentizität und Gemeinschaft: linksalternatives Leben in den siebziger und frühen achtziger Jahren*. Berlin: Suhrkamp, 2014.

Riisgaard, Lone. 'Fairtrade certification, conventions and labor'. In *Handbook of Research on Fair Trade*, edited by Laura Raynolds and Elizabeth Bennett, 120–35. Cheltenham: Edward Elgar Publishing, 2015.

Ritzer, George. *The McDonaldization of Society: An Investigation into the Changing Character of Contemporary Social Life*. London: Pine Forge Press, 1992.

Robertson, Robbie. *The Three Waves of Globalization: A History of a Developing Global Consciousness*. London: Zed Books, 2003.

Robertson, Roland, and David Inglis. 'The Global "Animus": In the Tracks of World Consciousness'. *Globalizations*, no. 1 (2004): 38–49.

Rome, Adam. 'Beyond Compliance: The Origins of Corporate Interest in Sustainability'. *Enterprise & Society* 22, no. 2 (2021): 409–37.

Ruben, Ruerd. 'The Fair Trade Balance: New Challenges after 25 Years of Fair Trade'. *FERDI Policy Brief* 52 (2012): 1–7.

Ruben, Ruerd, and Simone Verkaart. 'Comparing Fair and Responsible Coffee Standards in East Africa'. In *Value Chains, Social Inclusion and Economic Development: Contrasting Theories and Realities*, edited by Bert Helmsing and Sietze Vellema, 61–81. London: Routledge, 2011.

Rucht, Dieter. 'The Transnationalization of Social Movements: Trends, Causes, Problems'. In *Social Movements in a Globalizing World*, edited by Donatella Della Porta, Dieter Rucht, and Hanspeter Kriesi, 206–22. Houndmills: Macmillan, 1999.

Sassen, Saskia. 'The Many Scales of the Global: Implications for Theory and for Politics'. In *The Postcolonial and the Global*, edited by Revathi Krishnaswamy and John C. Hawley, 82–93. Minneapolis: University of Minnesota Press, 2008.

Sasson, Tehila. 'Milking the Third World? Humanitarianism, Capitalism, and the Moral Economy of the Nestlé Boycott'. *The American Historical Review* 121, no. 4 (2016): 1196–224.

Sauvant, Karl P. *The Group of 77. Evolution, Structure, Organization*. New York: Oceana Publications, 1981.

Schmied, Ernst. *Wandel Durch Handel. Die Aktion Dritte Welt Handel, Ein Entwicklungspolitisches Lernmodell*. Stuttgart: AEJ, 1978.

Schultz, Hans Jürgen, ed. *Von Gandhi bis Câmara. Beispiele gewaltfreier Politik*. Stuttgart: Kreuz, 1971.

Schwarz, Bill. 'Actually Existing Postcolonialism'. *Radical Philosophy* 104 (2000): 16–24.

Siebelink, Jeroen. *Het wereldschokkende en onweerstaanbaar lekkere verhaal van Tony's Chocolonely*. Amsterdam: Thomas Rap, 2018.

Siegenthaler, Hansjörg. 'Geschichte Und Ökonomie Nach Der Kulturalistischen Wende'. *Geschichte Und Gesellschaft* 25, no. 2 (1999): 276–301.

Skotnicki, Tad. *The Sympathetic Consumer: Moral Critique in Capitalist Culture*. Stanford: Stanford University Press, 2021.

Slobodian, Quinn. *Foreign Front: Third World Politics in Sixties Germany*. Durham: Duke University Press, 2012.

Slobodian, Quinn. *Globalists: The End of Empire and the Birth of Neoliberalism*. Cambridge: Harvard University Press, 2018.

Sluiter, Liesbeth. *Clean Clothes: A Global Movement to End Sweatshops*. London: Pluto Press, 2009.

Sluyterman, Keetie. 'Corporate Social Responsibility of Dutch Entrepreneurs in the Twentieth Century'. *Enterprise & Society* 13, no. 2 (2012): 313–49.

Smit, Marijke, and Lorette Jongejans. *C&A, de stille gigant: van kledingmultinational tot thuiswerkster*. Amsterdam: Stichting Onderzoek Multinationale Ondernemingen, 1989.

Stamatov, Peter. *The Origins of Global Humanitarianism: Religion, Empires, and Advocacy*. New York: Cambridge University Press, 2013.

Stichting, Max Havelaar, ed. *Nieuwe oogst: tien jaar Max Havelaar*. Leiden: Krikke, 1998.

Stolle, Dietlind, and Michele Micheletti. *Political Consumerism: Global Responsibility in Action*. New York: Cambridge University Press, 2013.

Swyngedouw, Erik. 'Neither Global nor Local: "Glocalization" and the Politics of Scale'. In *Spaces of Globalization: Reasserting the Power of the Local.*, edited by Kevin R. Cox, 137–64. New York: Guilford Press, 1997.

Tallontire, Anne, and Bill Vorley. *Achieving Fairness in Trading between Supermarkets and Their Agrifood Supply Chains*. London: UK Food Group, 2005.

Tängerstad, Erik. '"The Third World" as an Element in the Collective Construction of a Post-Colonial European Identity'. In *Europe and the Other and Europe as the Other*, edited by Bo Stråth, 157–93. Brussel: Peter Lang, 2000.

Tarrow, Sidney G. *Power in Movement: Social Movements and Contentious Politics*. Cambridge: Cambridge University Press, 2011.

Taylor, Ian, and Karen Smith. *United Nations Conference on Trade and Development (UNCTAD)*. London: Routledge, 2007.

Teichmann, Ulf, and Christian Wicke. '"Alte" und "Neue soziale Bewegungen": Einleitende Bemerkungen'. *Arbeit – Bewegung – Geschichte: Zeitschrift für historische Forschung* 17, no. 3 (2018), 11–19.

Thompson, Edward P. *The Making of the English Working Class*. London: Gollancz, 1963.

Tongeren, Paul van, and Ben ter Veer. *28 Mondiale Aktiegroepen in Nederland. Prisma. Dokumentatie; IKV-Brosjures/Interkerkelijk Vredesberaad; Nr 2; Act-If 6*. Voorburg: IKV-dokumentatie, 1971.

Toye, John. 'Assessing the G77: 50 Years after Unctad and 40 Years after the NIEO'. *Third World Quarterly* 35, no. 10 (2014): 1759–74.

Trentmann, Frank. 'Before "Fair Trade": Empire, Free Trade, and the Moral Economies of Food in the Modern World'. *Environment and Planning D: Society and Space* 25, no. 6 (2007a): 1079–102.

Trentmann, Frank. 'Citizenship and Consumption'. *Journal of Consumer Culture* 7, no. 2 (2007b): 147–58.

Trentmann, Frank. *Free Trade Nation: Commerce, Consumption, and Civil Society in Modern Britain*. Oxford: Oxford University Press, 2008.

Trumpbour, John. 'Global Sweatshops: The History and Future of North-South Solidarity Campaigns in Bangladesh and Beyond'. *Labor History* 62, no 2. (2021): 109–14.

Turpijn, Jouke. *80's Dilemma: Nederland in de Jaren Tachtig*. Amsterdam: Bakker, 2011.

Utting, Peter. 'Corporate Accountability, Fair Trade and Multi-Stakeholder Regulation'. In *Handbook of Research on Fair Trade*, edited by Laura Raynolds and Elizabeth Bennett, 61–79. Cheltenham: Edward Elgar Publishing, 2015.

VanderHoff Boersma, Franz. 'Poverty Alleviation through Participation in Fair Trade Coffee Networks: The Case of UCIRI, Oaxaca, Mexico'. Fort Collins: Center for Fair & Alternative Trade. https://cfat.colostate.edu/wp-content/uploads/sites/63/2009/09/Case-Study-UCIRI-Oaxaca-Mexico.pdf. Accessed February 25, 2015.

Verrea, Valerio. *The Fair Trade Innovation: Tensions between Ethical Behavior and Profit*. Leipzig: University of Leipzig, 2014.

Visser, Jelle. 'Learning to Play: The Europeanisation of Trade Unions'. In *Working-class Internationalism and the Appeal of National Identity. Historical Debates and Current Perspectives on Western Europe*, edited by Patrick Pasture and Johan Verberckmoes, 231–57. Oxford: Berg, 1998.

Warmerdam, Gien van. 'En het begon in Breukelen: De geschiedenis van Wereldwinkel Breukelen 1969–2009'. *Tijdschrift Historische Kring Breukelen* 24, no. 2 (2009): 48–57.

Westad, Odd Arne. *The Global Cold War: Third World Interventions and the Making of Our Times*. Cambridge: Cambridge University Press, 2005.

Wheeler, Kathryn. *Fair Trade and the Citizen-Consumer: Shopping for Justice?* Basingstoke: Palgrave Macmillan, 2012.

Wieters, Heike. *The NGO CARE and food aid from America, 1945–1980*. Manchester: Manchester University Press, 2017.

Wijmans, Luuk. 'De solidariteitsbeweging. Onverklaard maakt onbekend'. In *Tussen verbeelding en macht. 25 jaar nieuwe sociale bewegingen in Nederland*, edited by Jan Willem Duyvendak, Hein-Anton Heijden, Ruud Koopmans, and Luuk Wijmans, 121–40. Amsterdam: SUA, 1992.

Wilkinson, John. 'Fair Trade: Dynamic and Dilemmas of a Market Oriented Global Social Movement'. *Journal of Consumer Policy* 30 (2007): 219–39.

Willems, Ulrich. *Entwicklung, Interesse und Moral: die Entwicklungspolitik der Evangelischen Kirche in Deutschland*. Opladen: Leske Budrich, 1998.

World Commission on Environment and Development. *Our Common Future*. Oxford: Oxford University Press, 1987.

Young, Alasdair R. 'European Consumer Groups. Multiple Levels of Governance and Multiple Logics of Collective Action'. In *Collective Action in the European Union. Interests and the New Politics of Associability*, edited by Justin Greenwood and Mark Aspinwall, 149–75. London: Routledge, 1998.

Zander, Katrin, Rosa Schleenbecker, and Ulrich Hamm. 'Consumer Behaviour in the Organic and Fair Trade Food Market in Europe'. *Fair Trade and Organic Agriculture*, 51–60.

Zimmer, Magali. 'Des échances économiques au service d'un changement global: Le context d'émergence d'Artisans du monde'. *Le sociographe* 5 (2015): 97–113.

INDEX

Aachen, 33
Aarhus, 66, 70, 99
Abbé Pierre, 32–33
Adams, Richard, 151
Adler, 138
Ahold, 123–24
Akron (Pennsylvania), 24
Aktion Dritte-Welt-Handel, 62, 78
Aktion Selbstbesteuerung, 60, 63
Albert Heijn, 88–90
Albrow, Martin, 143
Algeria, 99, 102–3, 140, 187
Antoine, Allard, 82
Allende, Salvador, 73, 86
Almelo, 124
Amnesty International, 117, 170
Amstelveen, 65
Amsterdam, 1, 49–50, 75, 96, 144, 167
Angola, 9, 66, 68, 85, 87–88, 90, 102, 110
Angola-comité, 87–88, 90
Antwerp, 82
Appalachia, 26, 186
Arbeitsgemeinschaft Kleinbauernkaffee, 129, 180
Argentina, 55
Aristotle, 19
Ariyaratne, 101
Australia, 97
Austria, 33–34, 54, 94, 100, 127–28

Bangladesh, 32, 96, 139, 146, 151, 159, 173, 182
Bangladesh People's Solidarity Center, 149
Barbados, 58
Beatles, the, 6
Beatrix of the Netherlands, 124
Beekman, Bert, 131
Beerends, Hans, 39
Belgium, 33–34, 54, 60, 69, 71, 82, 94, 99–100, 114, 126, 128–31, 147
Bergen op Zoom, 99
Berlin, 134, 150–51
Bernd, Annette, 154
Beveridge, William, 39
Bhagalpur, 29
Black, Maggie, 39
Blair, Tony, 107
Block, Leo de, 44
Boer, Evert de, 161
Bolscher, Hans, 146
Bonn, 132
Bontemps, Marc, 130
Boskoop, 88
Brent Spar, 143
Breukelen, 74–75, 85
Bridge, 93–94, 97
Broek, Loek uit het, 115
Broere, Marc, 40
Brot für die Welt, 20
Brundtland, Gro Harlem, 153
Brussels, 66, 69, 127, 131, 182
Bundestag, 62
Byler, Edna, 23–24, 26, 35–36, 42, 91, 186

Cafédirect, 130
Canada, 24, 36, 69, 175

C&A, 136–38
Candappa, Eileen, 83–84
Cane Sugar Campaign, 16, 39, 43–44, 46, 49–53, 55–57, 59–67, 69–71, 75, 77, 80–81, 103, 109, 126–27
Cape Verde, 102, 151
CARE, 6
Castells, Manuel, 140, 142
Catholic Fund for Overseas Development, 130
Charity Commission, 30–31
Chile, 9, 73, 90, 117
China, 16, 29
Chiquita, 164
Christian Aid, 130
Christian Organization for Relief and Rehabilitation, 139
Church of the Brethren, 26
Church World Service, 26
Clean Clothes Campaign, 1–2, 12, 17, 136–39, 141–42, 146–49, 155, 159–64, 167–68, 173–75, 181–82, 184–85
Clinton, Bill, 107, 141
Club of Rome, 72
Cologne, 114
Columbia, 109
Committee on Society, Development and Peace, 54
Commonwealth Sugar Exporters, 58–59
Confederación latinoamerica de sindacalistos cristianos, 55
Conrad of Marburg, 19
Consumers White Label, 19
Crabbé, Carole, 163
Cuba, 9, 84

della Porta, Donatella, 143
Denmark, 54, 60, 99–100
Derks, Joan, 74
Divine Chocolate, 131
Doesburg, 87
Dongen, 99
Douwe Egberts, 88, 90, 170
Duyvendak, Jan Willem, 73
Dworp, 66, 69–71, 77

Ecuador, 96
Egmond aan Zee, 59, 65, 71
Egypt, 46
Eindhoven, 79
Elizabeth of Thuringia, 19
Emmaüs, 32–33
Encafé, 112–13
Eppler, Erhard, 63
Equal Exchange, 130
Erklärung von Bern, 20
European Commission, 57, 66, 127
European Economic Community, 43, 47–48, 52, 56–61, 64, 66, 70, 75, 179
European Fair Trade Association, 128–31, 151, 154, 158, 173, 182
European Parliament, 127
European Union, 153, 158, 182

Fair Trade Advocacy Office, 158, 182
Fair Trade International, 182, 184
Fair Trade Towns, 168, 173
Fair Trade USA, 164
Fair Wear Foundation, 160, 162, 168
Fairphone, 167
Fairtrade Foundation, 130, 164, 180
Fairtrade International, 150, 181, 185
Fairtrade Labelling Organizations International, 132, 150, 158, 163–64, 166, 170–71
Famine Relief Committee, 28
Fedecocagua, 112, 115
Federal Ministry of Economic Cooperation (West Germany), 62
Fiji, 58
FLO, 150
Fokkinga, Jan, 124
Ford Foundation, 132
France, 31–33, 54, 60, 99–100, 126, 128–29, 131, 147
Frankfurt am Main, 140
Frauenfeld, 78
Friedrich Ebert Foundation, 129
Friesen, Dorothy, 91

Gebert, Werner, 60, 62
Geneva, 56
Germany, 29, 32, 40, 107, 126, 129, 131, 147, 150
    West, 21, 24, 33–34, 40, 54, 60–62, 77, 94–95, 99–100, 102, 111–12, 115, 127–28, 138–39, 186
Gesellschaft zur Förderung der Partnerschaft mit der Dritten Welt, 95, 112, 115–16, 126, 129–30, 143, 154
Ghana, 46
Giesbrecht, Anne, 24–25
Glickman, Lawrence, 12
Global Exchange, 158
Grasveld, Carl, 150
Greece, 24, 28–29
Green & Black, 131
Greenpeace, 143, 156
Guatemala, 80, 112, 115, 151
Guinee Bissau, 102

Haarlem, 75
Haas, Harry, 83–84
Hagenaars, Wout, 99
The Hague, 43–44, 53
Haig, Ian, 70
Haiti, 21, 151
Harst, Paul van der, 117
Hartmann, Dieter, 150–51
Haslemere Group, 38
Heath, Edward, 58
Helping by Selling, 30, 93, 95
Hensman, Dick, 69
Hernández Contreras, Alfredo, 112
Hissel, Jan, 115–16, 126
Hoff, Frans van der, 115, 121, 126, 166
Hong Kong, 24, 29, 140, 159, 186

Imig, Douglas, 45
Indermuehle, Stefan, 163
India, 24, 46, 96, 146, 151, 159
    Bihar, 29
Indonesia, 46, 148
International Coalition for Development Action, 109

International Coffee Agreement, 120
International Federation for Alternative Trade, 151–53, 155, 158
International Labour Organization, 148
International Monetary Fund, 106, 118
Ireland, 152
Italy, 54, 60, 100, 131

Jackson-Cole, Cecil, 28–29
Jakarta, 148
Jamaica, 55, 58
Japan, 140
Jaydee, Vincent, 97
Jordan, 24
Jute statt Plastik, 32
Jute Works, 97, 139

Katholieke Volkspartij, 34
Kensington, 57
Kenya, 29, 151
Kerkrade, 33
Kilkenny, 152
Klein, Naomi, 175
Kok, Wim, 107
Koopmans, Ruud, 73
Kuapa Kokoo, 131
Kuhn, Konrad, 41
Kuyichi, 161–63
Kyle, Ray, 26–27

Lévelt, Hans, 115, 126, 154, 165
Longley, Clifford, 58
Lutheran World Federation Department of World Services, 29
Luxembourg, 57, 100, 131

Maastricht, 158
Magasins du Monde, 33
Malawi, 33
Manila, 152
Manitoba, 24
Máspero, Emilio, 55
Mauritius, 58, 151
Max Havelaar, 12, 17, 122, 124–26, 128–34, 138, 146, 150, 159, 161, 163, 165–66, 177

McDonalds, 142
Meijs, Paul, 23, 33–36, 42, 74, 75, 81, 92–96, 127
Mennonite Central Committee, 24–26, 28, 86, 91, 97, 139
Mexico, 6, 29, 114–15, 120, 131, 149, 151, 166
Misereor, 33–34, 112
Mitty, Joe, 30
Moscow, 142
Mozambique, 85, 102
Mumby, Philip, 131
Myrdal, Gunnar, 50

Napoleon Bonaparte, 49
Nasser, Gamal Abdel, 46
National Consumers' League, 139
Naturland, 116
Nehru, Jawaharlal, 46
Nestlé, 68, 164
Netherlands, the, 28, 31, 33, 39, 43, 47, 50, 52–54, 57–59, 60, 62–63, 71, 74–75, 77–78, 85, 87, 90, 92, 94, 97–100, 102, 107, 110–13, 116–21, 126–29, 131, 133, 136, 138, 147, 152, 160–61, 168, 170
Neuteboom, 124
New Consumer, 130
New Delhi, 38–39, 47
New International Economic Order, 68
New Windsor (Maryland), 26
New Zealand, 59
NEWS!, 153, 158
Nicaragua, 9, 68, 102, 112–13, 115, 121, 140, 183
Nickoleit, Gerd, 115, 126, 154, 178
Nkrumah, Kwame, 46
Noordwijk aan Zee, 152
Noordwijkerhout, 96, 144
North Atlantic Treaty Organization, 84, 89
Norway, 57, 100, 128, 153
Nyce, William P., 97
Nyerere, Julius, 78, 112

Olejniczak, Claudia, 40
Oomen, Ellen, 158
OS$_3$, 112
Otter, Henk, 88
Outspan, 90
Oxfam, 6, 20, 23, 28–31, 36, 38–39, 57–58, 74, 77, 81, 86, 93–94, 130, 141, 185
Oxfam-Wereldwinkels, 82, 114, 130
Oxford, 28, 30

Palestine, 16, 21, 186
Paris, 32–33, 99
Paulsen, Olaf, 163
Peijnenburg, Stephan, 166
Peru, 54, 69
Philippines, 69, 159
Pinochet, Augusto, 90
Portugal, 85, 87, 89, 102, 110
Puerto Rico, 24
Putten, Maartje van, 127
Pye, Edith, 28

Rainforest Alliance, 180
Reagan, Ronald, 107
Reckman, Piet, 38, 47–48, 92, 109
Ritgen, Gerd, 63
Ritzer, George, 142
Roozen, Nico, 118, 120, 126, 161, 165–66
Rote Zora, 138
Rotterdam, 75
Russia, 142

Sales Exchange for Refugee Rehabilitation Vocations, 26–28, 36, 38, 74, 95, 97, 151
Santiago de Chile, 66, 72–73
Sargent, Margaret, 57
Sarvodaya Shramadana, 101
Save the Children, 6
Scherpenzeel, Dick, 47
Schröder, Gerhard, 107
Scott, Roy, 93–94
Seattle, 156

Self-Help Crafts, 23, 28, 32, 36, 38, 74, 91, 95, 143, 151
Shell, 87, 143
Simon Lévelt, 111, 118
Singapore, 140
Sittard, 136, 142
Sjaloom, 13, 38–39, 47–48, 54, 81, 92
Snyder, William T., 24–25
Society of Friends, 28
Solidaridad, 116–18, 120–26, 134, 138, 141, 145, 161, 166, 180
South Africa, 9, 66, 85, 87, 90
South Korea, 24, 138, 140
Soviet Union, 4, 27, 107
Spain, 100
Sri Lanka, 69, 83, 101, 146
Stadskanaal, 88
Stichting Eerlijk Handels Handvest. *See* Fair Wear Foundation
Stichting Ideële Import, 102, 113, 118, 150, 152
Stichting Ontwikkelings-Samenwerking, 23, 28, 33–38, 74–75, 77–78, 87, 91–95, 97, 112, 116, 118, 126–27, 130, 143
Stockholm, 72
Stoltzfus, Gene, 91
Stumpf, Ludwig, 29
Subramanian, Samanth, 177
Sukarno, 46
Suriname, 55, 63, 79, 85–86
Sweden, 54
Switzerland, 33–34, 41, 54, 78, 84, 94–95, 99–100, 110–11, 114, 126–28

Taiwan, 24, 140
Tanerang, 148–49
Tanzania, 78, 96, 110–12, 115, 183
Tarrow, Sidney, 45
Tate & Lyle, 60
Tearfund, 32
Ten Thousand Villages. *See* Self-Help Crafts
Thailand, 96
Thatcher, Margaret, 107

Third World Centre, 56
Tinbergen, Jan, 50
Tindemans, Leo, 127
Tokyo, 140
Tongeren, Paul van, 70, 75
Tony's Chocolonely, 167
Trade Action, 97
Traidcraft, 130
Transfair, 129–32, 150
Tuxtla, 181
Twin Trading, 130

Uganda, 74
U-Gruppen, 66, 70, 99
Ukraine, 24
Unión de Comunidades Indígenas del Región del Istmo, 115–16, 120–21, 165–66
United Kingdom, 28–30, 36, 38, 54, 57–60, 62, 64, 78, 81, 99–101, 107, 130–31, 138, 147, 164
United Nations, 3, 36, 46, 48, 68, 73, 153
  Development Decade, 36, 73
  Conference for Trade and Development, 10
  Conference on the Human Environment, 72
  Conference on Trade and Development, 16, 38–39, 47, 52–54, 65–67, 72–73, 95–96, 109–10, 134, 179
United States, 4, 19, 22, 24, 27, 32, 36, 42, 74, 81, 87, 97, 107, 113, 132, 134, 139, 141, 168, 186
Uster, 78
Utz Kapeh, 166, 180–81, 184

Valdez, Juan, 109–11
Van Nelle, 89
Vienna, 97, 144
Vietnam, 140, 183, 187
von Amsberg, Claus, 124
Vredeling, Henk, 52
Vrije Universiteit Amsterdam, 101

Wageningen, 64
War on Want, 6, 101
Webb, Robert J., 97
Wheeler, Kathryn, 175
Wijmans, Luuk, 41
Wolak, Enny, 33
Wöldecke, Klaus, 158
Working Congress of Action Groups on International Development, 54
World Bank, 106–7
World Council of Churches, 54
World Development Movement, 57–60, 66, 70, 130
World Fair Trade Organization, 2, 151, 153, 181–82, 184–85
World Student Christian Federation, 56
World Trade Organization, 157–58

X min Y, 54, 56

Yugoslavia, 54

Zeldenrust, Ineke, 141, 146, 163–64

Printed in the United States
by Baker & Taylor Publisher Services